I0814383

The Life Compass

The Life Compass

Rules for Navigating Personal Growth

SAMER ABDO

This publication is designed to provide accurate and authoritative information in regard to the subject matter covered. It is sold with the understanding that the publisher and author are not engaged in rendering legal, accounting, or other professional services. Nothing herein shall create an attorney-client relationship, and nothing herein shall constitute legal advice or a solicitation to offer legal advice. If legal advice or other expert assistance is required, the services of a competent professional should be sought.

Published by Greenleaf Book Group Press
Austin, Texas
www.gbgpress.com

Copyright © 2025 Samer Abdo

All rights reserved.

Thank you for purchasing an authorized edition of this book and for complying with copyright law. No part of this book may be reproduced, stored in a retrieval system, or transmitted by any means, electronic, mechanical, photocopying, recording, or otherwise, without written permission from the copyright holder.

Distributed by Greenleaf Book Group

For ordering information or special discounts for bulk purchases, please contact Greenleaf Book Group at PO Box 91869, Austin, TX 78709, 512.891.6100.

Design and composition by Greenleaf Book Group
Cover design by Greenleaf Book Group

Publisher's Cataloging-in-Publication data is available.

Print ISBN: 979-8-88645-358-4

eBook ISBN: 979-8-88645-359-1

To offset the number of trees consumed in the printing of our books, Greenleaf donates a portion of the proceeds from each printing to the Arbor Day Foundation. Greenleaf Book Group has replaced over 50,000 trees since 2007.

Printed in the United States of America on acid-free paper

25 26 27 28 29 30 31 32 10 9 8 7 6 5 4 3 2 1

First Edition

This world is a guest house, and we are guests:
Each morning brings a new arrival.
A joy, a sorrow, a meanness,
A fleeting thought or sudden insight—
All unexpected visitors.

Welcome them all!
Even if they bring sorrow and sweep your house bare,
Still, treat each as an honored guest.
For they may be clearing the way
For some new delight to enter in.

—Rumi, "The Guest House,"
translated by Edward Henry Whinfield

To you, dear reader, and to myself,

Inspired by Rumi's timeless wisdom in "The Guest House," I dedicate this book to us as a guide for navigating life's ever-changing experiences. Rumi reminds us that every emotion—whether joy, sadness, or sorrow—is an unexpected visitor at our door, each carrying its own lesson and purpose. By welcoming them with openness and gratitude, we allow them to shape and guide us toward growth.

Contents

Introduction

"The journey of a thousand li commenced with a single step."

—Lao Tzu, *Tao Te Ching*

Throughout life, we often face challenges that lead us to seek wisdom and direction. My own quest for guidance led me to explore countless books filled with insights. Yet, many of these books share common shortcomings: They often fail to help us retain knowledge, connect insights to practical applications, or provide meaningful cultural and educational enrichment. Most importantly, they struggle to address the complexities of our fast-paced modern lives.

A common issue with self-help books is the short-lived impact of their insights. Lessons often fade as our initial motivation wanes and daily routines take over. *The Life Compass* tackles this challenge with a structured framework for daily, weekly, and monthly engagement. Its end-of-book questionnaire ensures these lessons remain fresh and fosters deeper integration into our daily lives for lasting impact.

Many self-help books also present lofty ideals without actionable steps, leaving us inspired but unsure of how to implement what we've learned. *The Life Compass* bridges this gap by offering clear, practical examples that demonstrate the benefits of applying its lessons and the consequences of neglect.

Unlike narrowly focused self-help books, *The Life Compass* blends historical wisdom with modern examples, enriching our experience. This fusion not only promotes personal growth but also enhances cultural and historical understanding, adding an educational dimension that sets the book apart in a crowded market. In today's fast-paced world, we need accessible resources we can return to repeatedly. *The Life Compass* provides a comprehensive yet digestible guide to help us navigate life's complexities without feeling overwhelmed.

The Life Compass is divided into two parts, reflecting the dual journey of life: an inward voyage of self-exploration and an outward voyage of engaging with the world.

Part One: Inner Voyage

This introspective section consists of seven chapters, each addressing a key aspect of personal growth:

- Inner peace
- Worry
- Authenticity
- Personal growth
- Dreams and aspirations
- Life's challenges
- Forgiveness

Part Two: Outer Voyage

This section focuses on outward interactions and relationships, exploring four key areas:

- Interpersonal relationships
- Social dynamics
- Conflict
- When to speak, pause, and listen

Each chapter includes specific rules and real-life examples, highlighting the positive outcomes of applying these lessons and the consequences of neglecting them. These narratives offer practical, real-world context for the book's principles.

How to Use This Book

The Life Compass is designed to transform knowledge into daily practice. Here's how to make the most of it:

- **Systematic exploration for full understanding:** Begin at the start and progress chapter by chapter to gain a thorough understanding and feel inspired to implement its ideas.
- **Focused engagement for immediate needs:** When facing a specific challenge, turn directly to the relevant chapter for actionable insights.
- **Daily practice and reflection:**
    - » **Reflect daily:** At the end of each day, evaluate your actions and interactions, considering how well you adhered to the book's principles.
    - » **Apply rules daily:** Focus on one rule or chapter

each day, using your experiences and mistakes as lessons.

  - » **Read thoughtfully daily:** Choose a challenging rule or chapter and reflect deeply on its relevance to your life.
- **Regular self-evaluation for deeper assimilation:** Use the end-of-book questionnaire weekly or monthly to assess your progress. These self-checks highlight areas for improvement and track your growth.
- **Collective discussion and insight-sharing:** Share your reflections with friends, family, or groups. Discussions foster diverse perspectives and deepen understanding.

The Life Compass is more than a collection of rules—it is a guide for lifelong growth, helping us navigate life's challenges with wisdom and clarity. Each day offers an opportunity to apply its lessons, unlocking our potential and guiding us toward balance and fulfillment. As an everyday companion, *The Life Compass* empowers us to embrace life's journey with purpose and resilience.

The Life Compass is a compilation of principles and insights drawn from diverse sources. While the interpretations and examples are my own, they aim to clarify and contextualize this collective wisdom. Please note that the illustrative examples and their interpretations provided within this book are not definitive or factual events; their purpose is to offer relatable context for the principles discussed.

PART ONE

Inner Voyage

"Mastering others is strength; mastering yourself is true power."

—**Lao Tzu,** *Tao Te Ching*

Here, we embark on a transformative journey toward self-mastery. This exploration delves deep into our psyche and soul, fostering introspection, reflection, and empowerment. It sets the stage for mastering our internal experiences, unlocking our potential, building resilience, and nurturing personal fulfillment.

The opening chapter explores the art of maintaining inner peace amid life's turbulence. It focuses on cultivating calm and equilibrium—essential tools for navigating everyday challenges. Next, we address the common struggles of worry and anxiety. Practical strategies are offered to help us manage these feelings and foster a more serene, proactive mindset. From there, we turn to authenticity. This chapter encourages us to shed external expectations, embrace our genuine selves, and understand how living authentically can reshape our experiences.

The journey then continues with personal development, emphasizing continuous evolution. By honing our skills, perspectives, and habits, we enrich our lives and open the door to growth. We then explore dreams and aspirations. This chapter invites us to identify our deepest desires, dream boldly, and set meaningful goals, offering guidance to transform our aspirations into reality. Next, we confront life's challenges. Here, we'll find tools to build resilience and strength, learning how to turn obstacles into opportunities for growth. Finally, we delve into the power of forgiveness. This chapter guides us in releasing past burdens and grievances, empowering us to embrace a future of freedom, lightness, and peace.

Part 1 lays a robust foundation of inner strength and wisdom. It equips us to confidently navigate life's journey, fostering profound self-awareness and personal evolution. This section isn't just about transforming our thoughts—it's about reshaping our entire approach to living.

CHAPTER 1

Navigating Inner Peace

"Peace comes from within. Do not seek it without."

—commonly attributed to Buddha

Rule One: Realize True Happiness Within

"The mind is its own place, and in itself can make a heaven of hell, a hell of heaven."

—John Milton, *Paradise Lost*

In our pursuit of happiness, we often look outward—toward possessions, achievements, or relationships—believing they hold the key to contentment. While these may bring moments of joy, true happiness is a deeper, enduring state of peace that arises from within, independent of external circumstances.

True happiness is like a well-built house resting on a solid foundation. Just as a sturdy home withstands life's storms, inner happiness is anchored in strong pillars: self-awareness, gratitude, and resilience. Life's challenges may shake this structure, but they cannot dismantle a foundation built with care and intention.

To nurture this foundation, we can practice gratitude by finding beauty in everyday moments, cultivate self-love by celebrating our strengths and accepting our imperfections, and embrace mindfulness by grounding ourselves in the present. These deliberate actions equip us to face uncertainty with grace and discover joy even in life's smallest blessings.

Rule One reminds us that happiness is not granted by external circumstances but cultivated within. By investing in our inner foundation, we gain the freedom to fully engage with life's richness and the strength to navigate its storms. True happiness is a gift we give ourselves—through intention, care, and a commitment to nurturing inner peace.

EXAMPLE 1: SIDDHARTHA GAUTAMA, THE BUDDHA (C. 563–C. 483 BC)

Born in the Shakya kingdom of ancient Nepal, Siddhartha Gautama, later known as the Buddha, was born into a life of privilege, shielded from the realities of the outside world. Despite his luxurious surroundings, Siddhartha felt a profound restlessness, sensing that material wealth and indulgence could not provide lasting fulfillment.

This restlessness deepened when he ventured beyond the palace walls and encountered the inescapable truths of human existence: impermanence and suffering. These experiences awakened him to life's fragility and inspired him to renounce his royal life at twenty-nine. Determined to understand the nature of suffering and uncover the path to inner peace, Siddhartha embarked on a transformative journey.

Initially, he pursued extreme asceticism, depriving himself of basic needs in his quest for enlightenment. However, Siddhartha soon realized that neither indulgence nor deprivation led to true happiness. This insight gave rise to the Middle Way—a balanced path between extremes. Through profound meditation under the Bodhi Tree in Bodh Gaya, he attained enlightenment, discovering that true happiness resides within. His teachings emphasized mindfulness, self-awareness, and the acceptance of life's impermanence as the foundation for lasting contentment.

Siddhartha Gautama's journey perfectly exemplifies Rule One. By rejecting material wealth and external comforts, he discovered that true happiness cannot be found in possessions, status, or achievements. Similarly, he realized that extreme deprivation offers no peace. Instead, lasting happiness is cultivated within, through mindfulness, balance, and self-awareness. Siddhartha's life reminds us that inner peace is not something external to pursue—it is a state of being that arises from nurturing our inner foundation with intentionality and care.

EXAMPLE 2: MATTHIEU RICARD (1946–)

Born in Aix-les-Bains, France, Matthieu Ricard began his career as a promising molecular biologist, earning recognition for his research and achievements. Despite his professional success, Ricard felt a profound emptiness—a void that his accolades and accomplishments could not fill. He realized that external achievements, no matter how impressive, could not bring the lasting happiness he sought.

Driven by a desire to understand true happiness, Ricard traveled to India in the 1970s and immersed himself in Tibetan Buddhism. There, he discovered that happiness is not dependent on external success but is cultivated within through mindfulness, compassion, and self-awareness. Inspired by this understanding, Ricard transitioned from his scientific career to a monastic life in the Himalayas, dedicating himself to spiritual growth and the service of others.

Ricard's spiritual transformation, however, did not mean abandoning his connection to science. Instead, he became a bridge between science and spirituality, collaborating with neuroscientists to explore the effects of mindfulness on the brain. His research demonstrated how meditation fosters positive emotions and inner peace. In a study at the University of Wisconsin, Ricard's brain scans revealed extraordinarily high levels of positive emotions during meditation, earning him the title of "the happiest man in the world."

Matthieu Ricard's journey vividly illustrates Rule One. By recognizing the limitations of external validation and focusing on cultivating his inner foundation, Ricard achieved enduring happiness. His life reminds us that true happiness is not found in accolades or material success but in nurturing mindfulness, compassion, and self-awareness. Ricard's story inspires us to prioritize inner peace, showing that fulfillment arises from within, regardless of external circumstances.

Rule Two: Live in the Present Moment

"Seize the day, put very little trust in tomorrow."
—Horace, *Odes*

Living in the present moment, a timeless principle rooted in traditions like Stoicism and Buddhism, invites us to fully immerse ourselves in the "now." By embracing the present, we uncover life's beauty and richness, often obscured by regrets about the past or anxieties about the future.

This practice enhances mental and emotional well-being by reducing stress, sharpening focus, and fostering resilience. Living in the present empowers us to face challenges with clarity and balance, creating harmony within ourselves and in our relationships. At the heart of this practice is mindfulness. Simple acts—focusing on our breath, noticing the colors of a sunset, or savoring the taste of a meal—anchor us in the present. When thoughts drift to past mistakes or future uncertainties, gently guiding our attention back to the "now" helps us rediscover the richness of life as it unfolds.

Living in the present does not mean ignoring the past or future. It means learning from the past without dwelling on regret, preparing for the future without being consumed by worry, and fully experiencing life as it happens. Whether listening intently to a friend, laughing with loved ones, or pausing to feel the warmth of sunlight, mindfulness transforms the ordinary into the extraordinary.

Rule Two reminds us that the present moment is where life truly happens. By reflecting on the past, preparing for the future, and fully embracing the "now," we cultivate deeper growth, connection, and joy. Each moment becomes an opportunity to foster clarity, balance, and a profound appreciation for life's journey.

EXAMPLE 1: MARCUS AURELIUS (121–180)

Born in Rome, Marcus Aurelius, a Roman emperor and Stoic philosopher, ruled during one of the most turbulent periods in Roman history. Amid relentless military conflicts and the devastating Antonine Plague, which claimed millions of lives, Aurelius anchored himself in the present moment to navigate these crises with clarity and composure.

During the Antonine Plague, fear and uncertainty spread rapidly across the empire. Instead of lamenting the past or worrying about an unpredictable future, Aurelius focused entirely on what could be done in the moment. He organized relief efforts, stabilized the economy, and inspired hope among his people. His ability to concentrate on immediate actions enabled him to meet the empire's urgent needs while maintaining his own mental and emotional balance.

Aurelius's reflections, captured in his timeless work *Meditations*, reveal his commitment to living in the "now." "Forget everything else," he wrote, "and focus every bit of yourself on the task at hand, as if it were your last." This philosophy of present-moment awareness allowed him to remain calm and decisive amid chaos, turning his focus toward what truly mattered in each moment.

Marcus Aurelius's leadership exemplifies Rule Two. By releasing distractions from the past and anxieties about the future, he demonstrated how living in the present allows us to face challenges with resilience and wisdom. His life reminds us that clarity, peace, and purpose are found when we fully engage with the "now," regardless of life's uncertainties.

EXAMPLE 2: DAN HARRIS (1971–)

Born in Newton, Massachusetts, Dan Harris, a prominent broadcaster and coanchor of ABC's *Nightline*, faced a life-altering moment in 2004 when he suffered a panic attack live on air. This public and deeply personal incident forced Harris to confront the overwhelming stress and anxiety that consumed his life, fueled by the relentless demands of his career and unresolved personal insecurities.

Determined to regain control, Harris began exploring mindfulness and meditation, initially approaching them with skepticism. Over time, he embraced these practices, learning to anchor himself in the present moment. By focusing on the "now," Harris discovered how to calm his racing thoughts, reduce anxiety, and approach life's challenges with clarity and focus. This shift not only improved his emotional well-being but also allowed him to navigate his demanding career with newfound balance and resilience.

Harris chronicled his transformation in his bestselling book *10% Happier*, where he shared how mindfulness reshaped his perspective. He emphasized that living in the present moment freed him from dwelling on past mistakes or obsessing over future outcomes, enabling him to fully engage with life as it unfolded. This practice of staying present became a powerful tool for managing stress and fostering inner peace, even amid the chaos of his high-pressure profession.

Dan Harris's journey exemplifies Rule Two. By grounding himself in the present moment, Harris overcame the anxieties of his past and fears about the future, finding clarity and balance. His story reminds us that living in the "now" enables us to manage stress, connect more deeply with ourselves and others, and navigate life's complexities with confidence and composure.

Rule Three: Control Your Thoughts to Control Your Life

"Very little indeed is necessary for living a happy life; but what lies within yourself, in your own way of thinking, makes all the difference."
—Marcus Aurelius, *Meditations*

Our thoughts shape the reality we experience. What we focus on, how we interpret events, and where we direct our mental energy determine not only our happiness but also our ability to overcome challenges and build a fulfilling life.

Rule Three reminds us that the mind is not a passive observer but a powerful tool. By mastering our thoughts, we can transform negativity into resilience, doubt into optimism, and obstacles into opportunities. This doesn't mean ignoring difficulties; it's about consciously choosing how we respond to them and directing our energy toward solutions and growth.

Mastering our thoughts begins with mindfulness—becoming aware of the patterns that shape our perceptions. Gratitude shifts our focus from what's lacking to what's abundant, revealing opportunities even in adversity. Purposeful focus, directed toward meaningful goals, fuels progress and creates a sense of fulfillment. By maintaining perspective during challenges and affirming positive thoughts, we build resilience and clarity, enabling us to navigate life's uncertainties with confidence.

Rule Three teaches us that mastering our thoughts is the key to mastering our lives. Life will always present challenges, but by cultivating clarity, confidence, and resilience, we can create a meaningful reality. The power to overcome adversity and find fulfillment lies within us—starting with how we think.

EXAMPLE 1: MAYA ANGELOU (1928–2014)

Born in St. Louis, Missouri, Maya Angelou, a poet, an author, and an activist, endured profound hardships throughout her life. Growing up in the segregated South, Angelou faced systemic racism, poverty, and the trauma of childhood abuse. At just eight years old, these experiences left her voiceless for nearly five years, consumed by fear and self-doubt.

During this silence, Angelou turned inward, immersing herself in books and the world of her imagination. Through the written word, she began to reshape her inner narrative, finding solace in stories of resilience and hope. As she grew older, Angelou actively reframed her thoughts, transforming her pain into strength and her silence into purpose.

Her decision to write *I Know Why the Caged Bird Sings* marked a turning point in her journey. By confronting her trauma and channeling it into self-expression, Angelou reclaimed her voice, demonstrating that mastering our thoughts allows us to transcend even the most difficult circumstances. Her work celebrated dignity, resilience, and human potential, inspiring millions to overcome their own challenges.

Maya Angelou's life exemplifies Rule Three. By recognizing the power of her thoughts, Angelou replaced despair with empowerment and fear with self-belief. Her journey reminds us that while we cannot control our circumstances, we can control how we think about them. Angelou's mastery of thought not only helped her overcome personal adversity but also enabled her to create a meaningful, impactful life. Her story teaches us that true transformation begins within, where clarity, resilience, and hope can rewrite even the darkest chapters of our lives.

EXAMPLE 2: ADAM NEUMANN (1979–) AND WEWORK

Born in Beersheba, Israel, Adam Neumann, cofounder of WeWork, set out to revolutionize the concept of shared workspaces. His vision of fostering collaboration and innovation propelled the company's meteoric rise, achieving a valuation of $47 billion at its peak. However, Neumann's inability to control his thoughts—particularly his overconfidence and unchecked ambition—ultimately led to his downfall.

As WeWork expanded rapidly, Neumann became enamored with his own success. His growing belief in his invincibility caused him to dismiss warnings from advisors and ignore sound business practices. Instead of balancing ambition with strategic planning, he pursued risky investments and grandiose ideas, such as attempting to "elevate the world's consciousness" through his company's mission.

By 2019, cracks in the company's foundation became evident. The failed IPO exposed inflated valuations, financial mismanagement, and a lack of strategic focus. Neumann's impulsive decisions, rooted in overconfidence and a lack of disciplined thinking, left WeWork in turmoil. The company's valuation plummeted, Neumann was forced to resign, and thousands of employees faced layoffs as WeWork struggled to recover.

Adam Neumann's story vividly illustrates the dangers of failing to master one's thoughts. His inability to balance ambition with mindfulness led to impulsive decisions that jeopardized his vision and the company's future. Neumann's experience serves as a cautionary tale, reminding us that thought mastery requires humility, clarity, and alignment with long-term goals. Without these, even the most promising vision can unravel, leaving behind a legacy of missed opportunities and unmet potential.

Rule Four: Avoid the "If-Then" Model for Happiness

"Happiness is like a butterfly; the more you chase it, the more it will elude you, but if you turn your attention to other things, it will come and sit softly on your shoulder."
—Unknown

Many of us fall into the trap of believing that happiness depends on external achievements or possessions—the "if-then" model of happiness. This mindset convinces us that achieving a certain goal or acquiring something will finally bring joy. For example, we might tie happiness to securing a promotion, buying a dream home, or gaining social recognition. While these milestones may bring fleeting satisfaction, they often leave us chasing the next goal, perpetuating an endless cycle of pursuit.

True happiness, however, is cultivated within. It is not tethered to external conditions but rooted in our ability to find contentment in the present moment and align our lives with our core values. The "if-then" mindset traps us in a state of dependence on circumstances, making us vulnerable to disappointment when outcomes fail to meet expectations or when the joy they bring quickly fades.

Breaking free from this mindset begins with shifting our focus inward. Practicing gratitude reveals the abundance in our lives and highlights the beauty of small, everyday moments. Engaging in activities that bring genuine fulfillment, such as nurturing relationships, pursuing hobbies, or embracing mindfulness, fosters lasting joy. Setting meaningful goals, aligned with our values, encourages us to find joy in the journey rather than tying our happiness to distant outcomes.

Rule Four reminds us that happiness is not something to be chased—it is something we cultivate within. By letting go of the "if-then" mindset, we liberate ourselves to experience life more fully, finding joy in the present while building a foundation for enduring contentment. This shift allows us to embrace the richness of life as it unfolds, unlocking deeper fulfillment and peace.

EXAMPLE 1: ALEXANDER THE GREAT'S PURSUIT OF WORLD DOMINATION (356–323 BC)

Born in Pella, Macedonia, Alexander the Great, tutored by the philosopher Aristotle, became king at just twenty years old. With extraordinary ambition and military genius, he launched a series of conquests that unified Greece and toppled the Persian Empire, extending his rule from Egypt to India. Yet, Alexander's insatiable hunger for conquest defined not only his victories but also his undoing.

Despite achieving what no ruler had before, Alexander remained perpetually dissatisfied, believing fulfillment lay in his next triumph. His relentless pursuit of more—more land, more power, more glory—strained his relationships with allies and soldiers, many of whom grew disillusioned with his endless campaigns. He overlooked opportunities for peace, neglected the well-being of his men, and failed to appreciate his unprecedented achievements.

Ultimately, Alexander's failure to practice gratitude left him restless and isolated, chasing goals that brought no lasting satisfaction. By tying his happiness solely to external accomplishments, he undermined the inner peace that could have allowed him to truly enjoy his legacy.

Alexander's life reveals a profound truth central to Rule Four: Fulfillment cannot be found in what lies ahead but rather in the ability to appreciate the present moment. Even with the world at his feet, Alexander's restless heart reminds us that true greatness is not measured by the empires we build but by the peace we cultivate within. His story challenges us to reflect on our own pursuits, urging us to anchor our happiness in gratitude and to find a balance between ambition and contentment.

EXAMPLE 2: KING HENRY VIII'S QUEST FOR A MALE HEIR (1491–1547)

Born into the Tudor dynasty, Henry VIII became king of England in 1509, beginning his reign with great promise and potential. Initially celebrated for his intelligence and leadership, his rule was later overshadowed by an obsessive focus on having a male heir to secure his family's legacy.

His first marriage to Catherine of Aragon produced a daughter, Mary, but no surviving sons. Convinced that a male heir was essential for his happiness and the stability of his kingdom, Henry VIII divorced Catherine, defied the Pope, and broke away from the Catholic Church to marry Anne Boleyn. Yet Anne, too, failed to provide a son and was executed. While his third wife, Jane Seymour, gave him a son, Edward, her death during childbirth left Henry VIII grieving and alone. His later marriages brought neither the stability nor the happiness he desperately sought, leaving his life filled with turmoil.

By obsessing over a single goal—the birth of a male heir—Henry VIII ignored the blessings already in his life: his thriving kingdom, capable daughters, and personal achievements. His belief in "if-then" happiness caused emotional and political chaos, showing the dangers of neglecting gratitude and inner balance.

Henry VIII's life vividly illustrates the central lesson of Rule Four. True fulfillment does not come from endlessly chasing external goals but from appreciating what we already have. Without gratitude, even the most powerful individuals can feel empty and unfulfilled. Henry VIII's story reminds us to seek joy in the present, to value the people and opportunities around us, and to understand that peace is created by how we think about our lives—not by what we think is missing.

Rule Five: Avoid Engaging in Negative Self-Talk

"Talk to yourself like you would to someone you love."
—**Brené Brown,** *The Gifts of Imperfection*

Setbacks and mistakes are inevitable parts of life. These moments often give rise to negative self-talk—statements like "I'm worthless" or "I can't do anything right." This internal dialogue, though subtle, profoundly impacts our mental, emotional, and physical well-being. Left unchecked, it drains confidence, saps resilience, and traps us in cycles of self-doubt.

The connection between our thoughts and well-being cannot be overstated. Negative self-talk fosters emotional distress, heightens stress responses, and increases the risk of anxiety and depression. Conversely, cultivating positive self-affirmations transforms our inner dialogue into a source of strength. Words of kindness and encouragement foster emotional balance, mental clarity, and resilience, laying the foundation for healthier relationships with ourselves and others.

This rule advocates for balance. While acknowledging and taking responsibility for mistakes is essential, harsh self-judgment neither rectifies the past nor supports growth. Instead, viewing errors as natural parts of the learning process fosters self-forgiveness and enables us to focus on the lessons within our experiences. By replacing criticism with compassion, we create space for growth and inner peace.

Rule Five reminds us that the words we speak to ourselves carry immense power. Transforming self-criticism into self-compassion builds resilience, fosters emotional stability, and equips us to navigate life's challenges with grace. By embracing kindness in our inner dialogue, we unlock the strength to accept imperfections, grow wiser, and live more balanced, fulfilling lives.

EXAMPLE 1: TONI MORRISON (1931–2019)

Born in Lorain, Ohio, during the 1930s, Toni Morrison grew up in a nation deeply divided by racial segregation. Her childhood was steeped in stories of hardship, resilience, and the unyielding strength of her Black community. Despite these cultural roots, she often faced a world that undervalued her identity as a woman of color. Early in her academic and professional career, Morrison encountered systemic barriers that reinforced societal narratives of inadequacy and exclusion, fueling moments of self-doubt.

Yet, Morrison refused to let these challenges define her sense of self. She deliberately confronted the negative narratives imposed upon her and chose to transform her internal dialogue into one of empowerment. This shift became the cornerstone of her literary career. Morrison's debut novel, *The Bluest Eye*, boldly addressed the themes of racial identity, internalized self-hatred, and the longing for validation. Drawing from her own experiences and those of others, Morrison illuminated the profound psychological toll of societal prejudice, while simultaneously celebrating the resilience of marginalized voices.

As Morrison's career flourished, her mastery of her inner voice became a catalyst for her creative and cultural impact. Works like *Beloved* epitomized her ability to transform personal and collective struggles into powerful narratives of healing and strength. By reframing adversity and embracing self-compassion, Morrison's journey became a testament to the resilience born from mastering one's inner dialogue.

Toni Morrison's life exemplifies Rule Five, illustrating the transformative power of self-compassion and the deliberate choice to replace negative self-talk with empowerment. Her story reminds us that mastering our internal dialogue is not just a personal victory—it is a profound act of reclamation that can inspire and uplift others. Through her life and work, Morrison shows us that cultivating a kinder inner voice is essential to building a legacy of strength, purpose, and hope.

EXAMPLE 2: VIRGINIA WOOLF (1882–1941)

Born in London, England, Virginia Woolf emerged as one of the most celebrated modernist authors of the twentieth century, with groundbreaking works such as *Mrs. Dalloway* and *To the Lighthouse*. Beneath her literary brilliance, however, lay a life marked by profound personal struggles. Woolf battled what is believed to have been bipolar disorder, a condition exacerbated by personal traumas, including the loss of loved ones and societal pressures. Her private writings—letters and diaries—reveal a recurring cycle of negative self-talk, where doubts about her worth and abilities magnified her inner turmoil.

Despite her literary achievements, Woolf often questioned her contributions and identity. Her self-criticism became a powerful force, undermining her resilience and amplifying her emotional fragility. The unrelenting weight of her inner struggles overshadowed her ability to fully embrace her successes. In 1941, overwhelmed by despair, Woolf filled her pockets with stones and walked into the River Ouse, leaving behind a poignant farewell letter that reflected her pain.

Virginia Woolf's life is a powerful testament to Rule Five, illustrating the critical importance of mastering our inner dialogue. Without a compassionate inner voice to counter her destructive thoughts, her emotional resilience eroded, leaving her vulnerable to life's challenges. Woolf's story reminds us that nurturing self-compassion is not just a means of personal growth but a vital practice for safeguarding our mental well-being. By transforming our internal dialogue, we create space for resilience, balance, and the ability to navigate even the most profound adversities with strength and grace.

Rule Six: Practice Nonattachment

"Attachment leads to suffering."
—paraphrased from the Buddha, *Dhammapada*

In our search for happiness, we often become entangled in attachments—to possessions, relationships, and even our own thoughts and emotions. These attachments, rooted in insecurity and fear of loss, create a cycle of suffering as we cling to what is impermanent. They distort our perspective, increase stress, and prevent us from fully appreciating life's beauty and richness.

Nonattachment is not about disengaging from life or suppressing emotions; it is about living fully while maintaining inner balance. It allows us to love unconditionally, free from possessiveness or fear, and to pursue goals without tying our self-worth to outcomes. In relationships, nonattachment nurtures trust and mutual growth. In careers, it fosters focus and resilience, enabling us to navigate successes and setbacks with clarity. By practicing nonattachment, we approach life's experiences with steadiness and composure, finding freedom amid inevitable changes.

Cultivating nonattachment requires mindfulness and self-awareness. This can be practiced by observing emotions without letting them control us, releasing frustrations, and letting go of limiting thoughts. For example, accepting the loss of an opportunity as a stepping stone rather than a setback or cherishing a fleeting moment with loved ones highlights how impermanence makes life precious. By embracing the transient nature of possessions and experiences, we learn to savor each moment before moving forward.

Rule Six reminds us that nonattachment leads to freedom and inner peace. It empowers us to live without fear or expectation, to savor life's beauty, and to embrace each moment with gratitude. By letting go of clinging, we free ourselves to discover lasting contentment and engage with life fully as it unfolds.

EXAMPLE 1: CHUCK FEENEY (1931–)

Born in Elizabeth, New Jersey, Charles "Chuck" Feeney built a global business empire as the cofounder of Duty-Free Shoppers (DFS) in the 1960s, generating billions of dollars in revenue. Despite his immense wealth, Feeney embraced a life of simplicity, guided by a belief that wealth held its greatest value when used to improve the lives of others. His extraordinary ability to detach from material possessions and focus on meaningful contributions exemplifies nonattachment.

Guided by this philosophy, Feeney transferred nearly his entire fortune—amounting to over $8 billion—into Atlantic Philanthropies, a foundation dedicated to global initiatives in health, education, and human rights. By 2020, the foundation had spent its entire endowment, funding transformative projects such as public health campaigns in Vietnam, brain health research, and scholarships for underprivileged students. Feeney's contributions to institutions like Cornell University and the University of Limerick left a legacy of lasting impact, improving countless lives and inspiring future generations.

Chuck Feeney's life perfectly demonstrates Rule Six. By letting go of material and ego-driven attachments, he found freedom and fulfillment in serving others. His philosophy of using wealth as a tool for creating meaningful change, rather than a symbol of status, reflects the essence of nonattachment. Feeney reminds us that true happiness lies not in what we accumulate but in the positive impact we leave behind, showing that detachment from possessions and recognition fosters a deeper sense of purpose and contentment.

EXAMPLE 2: MARCUS LICINIUS CRASSUS (115–53 BC)

Born in Rome in 115 BC, Marcus Licinius Crassus rose to immense wealth through real estate speculation, silver mining, and controversial practices that prioritized personal gain over ethics. One of his most infamous ventures was organizing Rome's first fire brigade, which would only act if property owners sold their burning buildings at a fraction of their value. Crassus's fortune secured him political influence, but his relentless ambition for greater power and glory consumed him.

Determined to rival the military achievements of his contemporaries, Julius Caesar and Pompey, Crassus launched an ill-fated campaign against the Parthian Empire. The campaign, driven more by a desire for prestige than strategic necessity, ignored significant risks. In 53 BC, at the Battle of Carrhae, Crassus suffered a devastating defeat that cost him his life and dealt catastrophic losses to the Roman army. His attachment to wealth and personal recognition ultimately led to his downfall.

Marcus Licinius Crassus's life perfectly demonstrates the dangers of failing to practice Rule Six. His relentless pursuit of wealth and glory blinded him to risks, clouded his judgment, and disrupted his inner balance. Anchoring his self-worth to external achievements not only undermined his legacy but also brought unnecessary harm to others. Crassus's story serves as a cautionary tale, reminding us that clinging to material possessions and ego-driven desires leads to suffering, while letting go fosters clarity, balance, and freedom.

CHAPTER 2

Navigating Worry

"Worry is the interest paid by those who borrow trouble."

—commonly attributed to George Washington

Rule One: Realize That Worries Are Created by Your Imagination, Not by Reality

"Our anxiety does not come from thinking about the future, but from wanting to control it."

—commonly attributed to Kahlil Gibran

Worries often affect our lives more than we realize. They rarely arise from present circumstances but are instead created by imagined scenarios that may never come to pass. Our minds, while powerful, can exaggerate uncertainties, convincing us of outcomes that exist only in our imagination. These imagined worries carry little basis in reality, yet they influence our emotions, decisions, and well-being, creating unnecessary stress and fear.

Worries are internal creations, not direct reflections of external events. Recognizing this distinction allows us to approach our worries with greater objectivity and rationality. By practicing mindfulness and introspection, we can identify when our thoughts are generating unnecessary fear. This awareness empowers us to shift our focus from imagined fears to addressing real-life challenges with clarity and purpose.

This rule does not dismiss the importance of worries entirely. Instead, it encourages understanding and management. By distinguishing between imagination and reality, we reduce the impact of worries on our mental health and channel our energy toward constructive solutions.

Rule One reminds us that by recognizing the origins of our worries, we prevent them from dominating our lives. Understanding that worries often stem from imagination enables us to reclaim our mental space and focus on the present. Through mindfulness and self-awareness, we cultivate clarity, resilience, and inner peace, enriching our lives with purpose and joy.

EXAMPLE 1: FYODOR DOSTOEVSKY (1821–1881)

Born in Moscow, Russia, Fyodor Dostoevsky is celebrated as one of the greatest literary minds in history. Yet, his life was marked by persistent emotional turmoil and existential anxiety. Orphaned at a young age, imprisoned for political dissent, and burdened by financial instability, Dostoevsky faced significant external challenges. However, many of his struggles were exacerbated by irrational fears born entirely of his imagination. Among these, his haunting phobia of being buried alive consumed his thoughts and intensified his inner torment.

During Dostoevsky's time, sensationalized reports of premature burial fueled widespread paranoia, despite the phenomenon being exceedingly rare. For Dostoevsky, this fear became an obsession, dominating his mind and adding to the emotional strain of his already difficult life. His preoccupation with exaggerated fears disrupted his ability to find peace, creating a worldview deeply rooted in dread. While his literary works, such as *The Double* and *Notes from Underground*, reflect these themes, they also illustrate how unchecked imagination can magnify anxieties and overshadow reality.

Dostoevsky's life vividly illustrates Rule One. His irrational fear, disconnected from any real threat, disrupted his emotional well-being and limited his ability to fully enjoy life. Instead of focusing on tangible realities, Dostoevsky's imagination fed anxieties that shaped his worldview and constrained his peace of mind. His story reminds us of the profound impact of unchecked worries, emphasizing the importance of challenging imagined fears to reclaim clarity, balance, and emotional freedom.

EXAMPLE 2: HOWARD HUGHES (1905–1976)

Born in Houston, Texas, Howard Hughes became one of the most famous aviators, filmmakers, and business magnates of the twentieth century. Renowned for his daring innovations and larger-than-life persona, Hughes's brilliance was overshadowed by a deep-seated fear of germs and contamination. This irrational worry, rooted entirely in his imagination, came to dominate his life and decisions, leading to severe consequences for his well-being.

Hughes's obsession with cleanliness manifested in extreme

behaviors. He avoided physical contact, insisted on sterilizing his environment, and even wore tissue boxes as makeshift shoes to prevent contamination. These fears were disconnected from reality, as there was no immediate threat of infection to justify such actions. Yet, Hughes's vivid imagination magnified these worries, isolating him from others and causing significant strain on his personal and professional relationships.

As his fears worsened, Hughes withdrew entirely from public life, living in seclusion for decades. His imagined worries not only disrupted his emotional balance but also prevented him from fully engaging with the world. Despite his immense wealth and achievements, Hughes's inability to distinguish between reality and imagination led to a life dominated by anxiety and regret.

Howard Hughes's life vividly illustrates Rule One. His irrational fears, fueled by imagination rather than tangible reality, disrupted his mental clarity, strained his relationships, and undermined his ability to live fully. His story serves as a cautionary tale, reminding us that unchecked worries can consume our thoughts and limit our potential. By recognizing and addressing fears born of imagination, we reclaim clarity, freedom, and emotional well-being.

Rule Two: Recognize That Most of Your Worries Never Materialize

"My life has been filled with terrible misfortune; most of which never happened."
—commonly attributed to Michel de Montaigne

As we navigate life's uncertainties, we often carry the weight of worries about the future. These worries, though they feel real, are often illusions—products of our imagination that rarely turn into actual problems. Paradoxically, life's true challenges often arise from unforeseen events, not the scenarios we anxiously anticipate. Recognizing this tendency helps us manage worries more effectively and avoid the stress caused by fears that never materialize. Left unchecked, imagined worries can cloud judgment, drain energy, and undermine mental health.

To manage worries with clarity, we can evaluate them by asking three structured questions:

1. **Is this worry happening now, likely to happen soon, or purely imagined?** If it is happening now or likely to happen soon, it is a challenge, not a worry, and can be addressed with actionable steps. If it is purely imagined, we can let it go and refocus on the present through mindfulness or grounding exercises.
2. **If this worry were to come true, how likely is it to significantly impact my life?** If the impact is minimal, we can release the worry—it is unlikely to matter in the long-term. If the impact could be significant, we move to the next question.
3. **Can I take any actionable steps right now to address this worry?** If yes, creating a plan and taking proactive

steps provide clarity and control. If no, we can practice acceptance and redirect our energy toward what is within our control.

By answering these questions, we prevent baseless fears from dominating our thoughts, allowing us to shift from anxiety to constructive action. This structured approach encourages mindfulness and helps us focus on what truly matters.

Rule Two reminds us that most worries never come to pass, and questioning their validity empowers us to reclaim clarity and peace of mind. By thoughtfully evaluating fears, practicing mindfulness, and acting with purpose, we cultivate resilience and strength. This process frees us from unnecessary stress, allowing us to manage our worries with confidence and calm.

EXAMPLE 1: THE 2012 MAYAN APOCALYPSE PREDICTION

Born from a misinterpretation of the ancient Maya Long Count calendar, the 2012 Mayan Apocalypse prediction led to widespread fear. The calendar marked the end of a 5,125-year cycle, but the Maya intended it as a moment of renewal, not destruction. Despite clarifications from scholars, sensationalist media and apocalyptic films amplified global anxieties, sparking fear that the world would end on December 21, 2012.

Across the globe, people prepared for imagined disasters. In France, groups gathered on a mountain rumored to offer protection from catastrophe, while in Russia, officials urged calm as fear spread. Communities stockpiled supplies, built bunkers, and braced for calamities that never came. When December 21 passed uneventfully, it became clear that these fears had no basis in reality. The imagined catastrophe, fueled by misinformation, consumed thoughts and actions but had no tangible impact.

The reaction to the 2012 Mayan Apocalypse vividly demonstrates Rule Two. It shows how unfounded worries, born of imagination and amplified by speculation, can dominate our thoughts and lead to irrational behavior. This event reminds us of the importance of critically evaluating our fears, distinguishing between imagined and real threats, and grounding our actions in evidence. By recognizing that most worries never materialize, we free ourselves from unnecessary stress and reclaim clarity and peace of mind.

EXAMPLE 2: THE 2009 SWINE FLU (H1N1) PANDEMIC

Born from memories of the deadly 1918 flu pandemic, the emergence of H1N1 in 2009 sparked widespread alarm. Early reports described a highly contagious virus with no vaccine, fueling predictions of global devastation. Governments enacted emergency measures, and fear spread rapidly as people braced for the worst, anticipating overwhelmed healthcare systems and catastrophic loss of life.

As the pandemic unfolded, the gap between initial fears and reality became clear. While the virus was highly contagious, its lethality was far lower than anticipated. Healthcare systems managed the outbreak effectively in most regions, and mortality rates were significantly lower than early projections. Though the pandemic presented real challenges, it fell far short of the catastrophic scenarios many had imagined.

The response to H1N1 illustrates Rule Two by revealing how exaggerated fears can overshadow evidence and lead to unnecessary stress. While vigilance and preparation were crucial, this case reminds us of the importance of grounding our worries in reality and distinguishing between speculation and actionable risks. By critically evaluating fears, we free ourselves from undue anxiety and approach life's uncertainties with clarity, resilience, and calm.

Rule Three: Worries Are Transient—Don't Jump to Conclusions or Act on Them

"Don't believe everything you think. Thoughts are just that—thoughts."
—Allan Lokos, *Pocket Peace*

Worries often arise unexpectedly, intruding on our thoughts and emotions. They can feel overwhelming, pushing us to imagine worst-case scenarios that amplify stress and anxiety. However, dwelling on these imagined outcomes magnifies their emotional impact, making worries seem larger and more significant than they truly are.

Worries are fleeting thoughts, shaped by imagination rather than reality. Recognizing their impermanence allows us to observe them calmly, resist the urge to jump to conclusions, and avoid letting them dictate our actions. Fixating on potential outcomes only intensifies stress and regret, whereas pausing to acknowledge these thoughts without judgment helps us maintain clarity and perspective.

Mindfulness is key to managing transient worries. Techniques such as deep breathing, journaling, or simply observing thoughts as they arise enable us to stay grounded and redirect our focus to the present moment. This practice not only prevents worries from consuming our decisions but also empowers us to respond thoughtfully to life's uncertainties.

Rule Three reminds us that worries are like passing clouds—temporary and ever-changing. By observing them with patience and grounding our actions in reality, we free ourselves from unnecessary stress and regain clarity. Embracing this principle fosters resilience, balance, and inner peace, equipping us to approach life's uncertainties with calm and confidence.

EXAMPLE 1: NICHOLAS II OF RUSSIA (1868–1918)

Born into the Romanov dynasty, Nicholas II ruled during one of Russia's most turbulent periods. Confronted with widespread social and political unrest, he clung tightly to autocratic traditions, driven by a fear of losing control over the monarchy. This transient worry about preserving power overshadowed broader, long-term considerations for the stability of his empire.

Rather than addressing the root causes of public dissatisfaction, Nicholas II responded to protests and calls for reform with resistance and repression. The Bloody Sunday massacre in 1905, when peaceful demonstrators were shot by the Imperial Guard, further alienated the public. His fear of conceding power led to missed opportunities for modernization and compromise, deepening the divide between the monarchy and the people. By prioritizing short-term control over long-term stability, Nicholas II's decisions accelerated the revolutionary fervor that would culminate in the Russian Revolution of 1917. The collapse of the Romanov dynasty and his eventual execution marked the tragic end of his rule.

Nicholas II's story vividly illustrates the dangers of acting on transient fears. By allowing his worries to dictate decisions, he failed to pause, reflect, and ground his actions in rational thought. Rule Three reminds us that fleeting concerns, when left unchecked, can magnify immediate problems and undermine broader goals. Nicholas II's inability to see past his transient worries serves as a stark reminder of the importance of acting with clarity and perspective to avoid lasting consequences.

EXAMPLE 2: RICHARD NIXON (1913–1994)

As the thirty-seventh president of the United States, Richard Nixon faced one of the most defining moments of his career during the Watergate scandal. In 1972, driven by fears of losing re-election, members of Nixon's re-election campaign orchestrated a break-in at the Democratic National Committee headquarters in the Watergate office complex. The operation was intended to gather information and undermine his political opponents. Nixon, though not directly involved in planning the break-in, approved efforts to protect his campaign once the crime was exposed.

Initially, Nixon dismissed the break-in as a minor issue, but as investigations began to uncover links to his campaign, his transient fears about political vulnerability escalated. Worried about losing public trust and control over his presidency, Nixon approved covert actions to obstruct justice, including paying hush money to the burglars and using government resources to interfere with investigations. These actions, rather than resolving the crisis, deepened it. The release of incriminating White House tapes ultimately revealed Nixon's role in the cover-up. By 1974, bipartisan support had collapsed, and Nixon became the first US president to resign, leaving a permanent stain on his legacy.

Richard Nixon's story illustrates the profound consequences of acting on fleeting fears. His inability to pause and address the situation with transparency turned a manageable issue into a career-ending scandal. Rule Three reminds us that transient worries, if left unchecked, can drive decisions that lead to irreversible damage. Nixon's presidency demonstrated the importance of stepping back, recognizing worries as temporary, and choosing actions grounded in clarity and integrity to effectively navigate challenges.

Rule Four: Practice "Worry Time" Allocation

"Don't stew about the future. Just live each day until bedtime."
—Dale Carnegie, *How to Stop Worrying and Start Living*

In today's fast-paced world, worries often intrude on our thoughts, disrupting focus and reducing productivity. Left unchecked, this constant state of anxiety can weigh heavily on our mental well-being. Setting aside a designated "worry time" each day offers a structured way to manage concerns without letting them take over our lives. By assigning a specific time—such as 6 p.m.—to reflect on worries, we create boundaries that help us remain present and productive throughout the day.

When a worry arises outside of this allocated time, we can acknowledge it, remind ourselves it will be addressed later, and redirect our attention to the task at hand. This simple practice prevents us from fixating on concerns in the moment. During the designated worry time, we systematically review our thoughts. Often, many worries resolve themselves or lose their urgency. For unresolved concerns, we evaluate their importance, assess their validity, and brainstorm actionable solutions.

The practice of worry time allocation fosters focus, reduces mental clutter, and enables us to distinguish between minor anxieties and genuine challenges. Over time, it cultivates greater emotional resilience, helping us approach life's uncertainties with clarity and calmness.

Rule Four reminds us that while worries are natural, they do not have to dominate our lives. By organizing our thoughts and dedicating specific time to address concerns, we free our minds for more meaningful experiences. This structured approach enhances focus, reduces anxiety, and empowers us to live with balance, productivity, and peace.

EXAMPLE 1: BILL GATES (1955–) AND THINK WEEKS

Born in Seattle, Washington, Bill Gates is celebrated as the cofounder of Microsoft and one of the world's leading philanthropists. With responsibilities spanning global business and charitable initiatives, Gates often found himself overwhelmed by the constant demands of leadership. To manage these challenges and maintain clarity, he developed a unique practice called Think Weeks.

Each year, Gates retreats to a secluded cabin for two weeks, disconnecting from daily distractions. During this time, he dedicates himself to reviewing proposals, exploring innovative ideas, and reflecting on long-term strategies for his business and philanthropic efforts. Think Weeks are not merely a retreat but a structured period of deep focus, allowing Gates to compartmentalize his concerns and address them systematically. By confining his reflection and strategic thinking to these designated periods, Gates prevents worries from intruding on his daily life, freeing his mind to focus on present priorities.

Bill Gates's Think Weeks vividly demonstrate the essence of Rule Four. By setting aside dedicated time to address concerns and plan strategically, he prevents worries from dominating his thoughts and workflow. This structured approach fosters clarity, innovation, and emotional balance, enabling him to navigate complex responsibilities with confidence. Gates's practice reminds us that allocating specific time for reflection can transform how we manage concerns, helping us achieve greater focus and peace of mind.

EXAMPLE 2: TIM FERRISS (1977–) AND THE FEAR-SETTING EXERCISE

Born in East Hampton, New York, Tim Ferriss is a bestselling author, entrepreneur, and podcaster who has inspired millions with his practical strategies for personal growth. Early in his career, Ferriss often found himself paralyzed by vague anxieties about potential failures and risks. Recognizing that unresolved fears were hindering his progress, he developed a structured method called the fear-setting exercise.

Ferriss dedicates specific time to confront his worries systematically. During this exercise, he writes down his fears, evaluates their potential outcomes, and outlines actionable steps to mitigate risks. By breaking his concerns into manageable components, Ferriss transforms abstract anxieties into clear, structured plans. This practice has proven transformative, helping him make confident decisions in moments of uncertainty, whether navigating career changes or personal challenges.

Tim Ferriss's fear-setting exercise exemplifies Rule Four. By dedicating deliberate time to evaluate his concerns, he prevents worries from lingering and overwhelming his thoughts. This structured process not only reduces the emotional weight of fears but also fosters mental clarity and proactive decision-making. Ferriss's story highlights the power of addressing worries constructively, freeing us to focus on growth, opportunity, and purposeful action.

Rule Five: Be Aware That Worries Are Counterproductive and Harmful

"Your worst enemy cannot harm you as much as your own unguarded thoughts."
—paraphrased from the Buddha, Dhammapada

Worries rob us of the present, creating a false sense of control over the future while draining our energy and joy. Left unchecked, they lead to mental health challenges such as stress, anxiety, and depression, as well as physical issues like insomnia, high blood pressure, and a weakened immune system. Constant worry traps us in a cycle of "what-ifs," limiting our ability to think clearly and act effectively, while distracting us from meaningful actions that could improve our circumstances.

Recognizing the futility and harm of worry motivates us to manage it constructively. Practices such as deep breathing, grounding exercises, or mindfulness help us refocus on the present and regain a sense of calm. These techniques allow us to observe our thoughts without judgment and redirect our energy toward actionable solutions rather than dwelling on imagined fears. Over time, this approach transforms worry into a tool for clarity and purposeful action, enabling us to approach challenges with renewed confidence.

Rule Five reminds us that unchecked worries are not only harmful but also counterproductive. By shifting our focus from unproductive anxieties to intentional solutions, we restore clarity, resilience, and inner peace. This principle empowers us to reclaim our mental energy and focus, paving the way for a calmer, more purposeful life.

EXAMPLE 1: SERGEI RACHMANINOFF (1873–1943)

Born in Staraya Russa, Russia, Sergei Rachmaninoff is remembered as one of the most celebrated composers and pianists of the Romantic era. However, his career nearly ended before it began. In 1897, the premiere of his First Symphony was met with scathing criticism. Dismissed as chaotic and uninspired, the failure left Rachmaninoff consumed by self-doubt and unproductive worries about his talent and future.

For years, these worries dominated his thoughts, trapping him in a cycle of fear and self-recrimination. Sleepless nights and physical exhaustion compounded his struggles, and he became creatively paralyzed, unable to compose. His fixation on the past magnified his anxiety, robbing him of joy and clarity. Rachmaninoff's inability to manage his worries turned a single setback into a prolonged crisis, jeopardizing his career and well-being.

It was only through the intervention of Dr. Nikolai Dahl, a physician who used therapeutic techniques akin to modern mindfulness and self-affirmation, that Rachmaninoff began to heal. Under Dr. Dahl's guidance, he learned to reframe his thoughts, let go of unproductive worries, and focus on constructive action. This breakthrough culminated in the composition of *Piano Concerto No. 2*, a masterpiece that marked his triumphant return to the world of music.

Rachmaninoff's story vividly illustrates Rule Five. His unaddressed worries nearly derailed his career, showing the destructive power of unchecked anxieties. Yet, his deliberate efforts to manage his fears transformed his life, reminding us that addressing worries with purpose fosters resilience, clarity, and the ability to unlock our potential.

EXAMPLE 2: ERNEST HEMINGWAY (1899–1961)

Born in Oak Park, Illinois, Ernest Hemingway became one of the most celebrated authors of the twentieth century, earning the Nobel Prize for *The Old Man and the Sea*. Behind his literary fame, however, Hemingway struggled with relentless worries that shaped his life and decisions. Plagued by fears of irrelevance, declining health, and fractured relationships, he often found himself caught in a spiral of self-doubt and anxiety.

In the later years of his life, Hemingway's worries became increasingly destructive. Haunted by his inability to replicate his earlier successes, he obsessively revised his manuscripts, fearing they would fail to meet his exacting standards. These worries robbed him of the joy of writing, turning his craft into a source of stress rather than fulfillment. His declining physical health, including injuries from two plane crashes in 1954, further fueled his anxieties. Hemingway began fixating on worst-case scenarios, imagining his creative decline as inevitable and irreversible.

Unable to manage these fears, Hemingway turned to alcohol

as a coping mechanism, deepening his struggles with depression and alienating those closest to him. His unchecked worries distorted his perception of reality, eroding his confidence and mental clarity. Despite his immense achievements, he became consumed by imagined failures and unresolved fears, ultimately leading to his tragic suicide in 1961.

Hemingway's life vividly illustrates the dangers of allowing worries to dominate our thoughts, as cautioned by Rule Five. His inability to address these anxieties constructively not only overshadowed his accomplishments but also led to profound suffering. Hemingway's story reminds us of the critical importance of managing worries with awareness and purpose. By recognizing their harm and focusing on the present, we can safeguard our mental health and reclaim clarity, enabling us to face challenges with resilience and peace.

Rule Six: Don't Worry About Things You Didn't Arrive with and Can't Depart With

"You came empty-handed, and you will leave empty-handed.
What is yours today belonged to someone else yesterday,
and will belong to someone else tomorrow."
—Hindu proverb

We often worry about material possessions and social status, forgetting that when we are born, we arrive without them, and when we leave, we take none of them with us. This reality challenges us to rethink our attachment to things that are ultimately fleeting. While material wealth and status can bring comfort and opportunity, they are impermanent and cannot define our true worth.

Societal pressures often lead us to equate self-worth with what we own or achieve, creating unnecessary stress and obscuring life's deeper treasures. Instead of worrying excessively about transient things, we can focus on what truly matters: meaningful relationships, love, personal growth, and contributing positively to the world. These are the enduring sources of fulfillment and joy.

This rule does not discourage us from enjoying material comforts or pursuing success but reminds us to maintain perspective. By appreciating what we have without becoming overly attached to it, we free ourselves from the burden of possession. This balance allows us to strive for more without letting worries about wealth or status dominate our lives.

Rule Six reminds us that material wealth and social status are fleeting, but the values we cultivate and the impact we leave behind endure. By valuing material comforts without clinging to them, we can live a richer, more balanced life rooted in clarity, peace, and purpose.

EXAMPLE 1: SULTAN SULEIMAN THE MAGNIFICENT (1494–1566)

Born in Trabzon, Turkey, Sultan Suleiman the Magnificent was one of the Ottoman Empire's greatest rulers, known for his military conquests, cultural achievements, and groundbreaking legal reforms. Yet, in his later years, Suleiman's attachment to power and his legacy clouded his judgment. Consumed by fears of rebellion and instability, he prioritized control over trust, compassion, and justice—values that had once defined his reign.

One of the most devastating consequences of this attachment was the execution of his eldest son and heir, Mustafa.

Admired for his competence and loved by the people, Mustafa was seen as a symbol of hope for the empire's future. However, Suleiman, influenced by court intrigues and his own insecurities, feared that Mustafa might rise against him. Acting on these transient fears, Suleiman ordered his son's execution in 1553. This decision shattered public morale, fractured his family, and left an indelible stain on his legacy.

Suleiman's story vividly demonstrates the dangers of clinging to transient concerns like power and control. His inability to embrace the impermanence of his rule led him to prioritize fleeting worries over enduring values. Rule Six reminds us that true fulfillment lies in cultivating principles like trust and compassion, rather than clinging to achievements or possessions that we cannot take with us. Suleiman's choices serve as a cautionary tale about the lasting consequences of prioritizing control over humanity.

EXAMPLE 2: JEAN PAUL GETTY (1892–1976)

Born in Minneapolis, Minnesota, Jean Paul Getty became one of the wealthiest men of the twentieth century, building a vast fortune through his success with Getty Oil. Yet, his attachment to wealth often overshadowed his ability to prioritize deeper values like love and family. This fixation became tragically evident during a high-profile family crisis that shocked the world.

In 1973, Getty's grandson, John Paul Getty III, was kidnapped in Italy. The captors demanded a $17 million ransom, but Getty hesitated, fearing that paying would encourage further extortion attempts. Even after receiving proof of his grandson's suffering—a severed ear mailed by the kidnappers—Getty delayed payment, negotiating the ransom down to $2.9 million.

He agreed to pay only the amount his accountants deemed tax-deductible. Shockingly, Getty required his son—John Paul Getty Jr., the kidnapped boy's father, who was struggling financially—to repay the ransom money with interest.

Getty's decision, driven by his attachment to wealth and control, horrified the public and strained his family relationships. The delay not only prolonged his grandson's suffering but also left lasting emotional scars within the family. Despite his immense resources, Getty's inability to prioritize compassion over material concerns marked his legacy with criticism and estrangement.

Jean Paul Getty's story vividly demonstrates the dangers of clinging to transient concerns like wealth and control, as cautioned by Rule Six. His actions serve as a stark reminder that possessions we neither arrive with nor depart with cannot provide true fulfillment. Rule Six inspires us to focus on meaningful relationships and enduring values, reminding us that what truly matters transcends material wealth.

Rule Seven: Don't Worry Too Much About the Future, As It May Not Include You

"Life exists in the present; the past is history, the future is a mystery, but today is a gift. That's why it's called the present."
—ancient proverb

Worries about the future often distract us from the richness of the present. No matter how much we plan or worry, the future remains uncertain, and our presence in it is not guaranteed. This truth challenges us to reconsider how much energy we devote to what lies ahead and inspires us to focus instead on fully living today.

Excessive worry about the future creates a false sense of control, filling our minds with imagined scenarios that may never come to pass. This fixation robs us of joy, clarity, and the opportunities available to us now. Instead of fearing what the future might bring—a future that is not promised—we can embrace the present, finding fulfillment in the people, experiences, and beauty that surround us.

This rule does not dismiss the importance of thoughtful preparation for the future but reminds us to balance it with gratitude for the present. By planning with intention while living fully in the now, we free ourselves from unnecessary anxieties and cultivate resilience for life's uncertainties.

Rule Seven reminds us that life's impermanence is not a reason to fear but an invitation to live with purpose. By cherishing today while preparing thoughtfully for tomorrow, we create a life of clarity, balance, and peace.

EXAMPLE 1: ANNE BOLEYN (C. 1501–1536)

Anne Boleyn's rise to power as the second wife of King Henry VIII placed her at the center of England's most volatile court. Her intelligence and ambition helped her ascend to the throne, but her time as queen was overshadowed by relentless fear about her future. Central to her anxieties was the pressure to produce a male heir, which she believed was essential to securing her position and influence in a court rife with betrayal and intrigue.

In 1533, Anne gave birth to a daughter, Elizabeth, a child destined for greatness but not the son Anne believed would protect her from falling out of favor. Her worries about the future pushed her into divisive actions. She alienated powerful figures in court, including Queen Catherine of Aragon's supporters, and fueled political tensions. Driven by desperation, Anne also supported the downfall of her former ally, Thomas Cromwell, a misstep that further isolated her and emboldened her enemies.

By 1536, Anne's fears culminated in her arrest on fabricated charges of treason, adultery, and incest. Within months, she was tried and executed, her tragic end marking the culmination of a life consumed by future-focused anxieties. Ironically, the future Anne fought so desperately to secure—a stable position in court—was one she never lived to see.

Anne Boleyn's story vividly demonstrates the dangers of being consumed by fears of an uncertain future. Her relentless fixation on what lay ahead blinded her to the risks of her present actions, leading to her downfall. Rule Seven reminds us that while the future is uncertain, the present is where we hold influence. By acting with clarity and intention, we avoid the tragic consequences of letting future-focused anxieties dominate our lives.

EXAMPLE 2: KING LOUIS XVI OF FRANCE (1754–1793)

King Louis XVI of France ascended the throne at a time of profound social and financial turmoil. Faced with a mounting financial crisis and widespread public dissatisfaction, Louis XVI became consumed by worries about preserving the monarchy's future. His fears of destabilizing the institution led to hesitation and inaction, as he sought to maintain control through avoidance rather than decisive reform.

One of his most critical failures was his reluctance to convene the Estates General—a step necessary to address France's financial collapse. Instead, Louis XVI delayed, hoping the crisis would resolve itself. This hesitation fueled public frustration and protests, which escalated into riots. Even as revolution loomed, Louis XVI focused more on preserving the monarchy's image than addressing the immediate needs of his people. His anxieties about the monarchy's long-term survival blinded him to the urgent problems of inequality, hunger, and fiscal instability that demanded immediate attention.

By the time Louis XVI acted, it was too late. His delayed decisions deepened the public's mistrust, and the French Revolution erupted in full force. In 1793, Louis XVI was deposed and executed, his throne and legacy dismantled. Tragically, the future he had worked so hard to protect became one he did not live to see.

King Louis XVI's story vividly illustrates the dangers of excessive worry about the future. His fixation on preserving the monarchy's legacy distracted him from addressing the present moment, where meaningful action was possible. Rule Seven reminds us that while the future is uncertain, the present is where we have the power to make a difference. By focusing on thoughtful actions today, we can create a better future without being paralyzed by fears of what lies ahead.

Rule Eight: Consider Worries from Your Deathbed Perspective

"Therefore do not worry about tomorrow, for tomorrow will worry about itself. Each day has enough trouble of its own."
—The Bible, Matthew 6:34 (KJV)

Worries often feel overwhelming in the moment, paralyzing us with their intensity. This rule invites us to evaluate these concerns from the perspective of our older selves or our final moments. By imagining today's worries from our "deathbed" perspective, we gain clarity about what truly matters, helping us navigate life with purpose and focus.

This mental exercise allows us to filter fleeting anxieties from those aligned with our deepest values and goals. Many worries fade into insignificance when viewed through this lens, freeing us from unnecessary burdens. For the few concerns that remain meaningful, this perspective prompts us to take purposeful action, ensuring our energy is devoted to what truly matters. By focusing on enduring values, we shift our efforts away from trivial distractions and toward the pursuits that bring lasting fulfillment.

Rule Eight offers a transformative way to prioritize life's challenges. By filtering our worries through the lens of our final moments, we focus on the people, values, and goals that endure beyond fleeting concerns. This rule reminds us that living with clarity and authenticity begins with devoting ourselves to what truly matters.

EXAMPLE 1: STEVE JOBS (1955–2011) AND HIS 2005 STANFORD COMMENCEMENT SPEECH

Born in San Francisco, California, Steve Jobs was a visionary entrepreneur and the cofounder of Apple. His life was marked by extraordinary innovation but also profound challenges. In 2004, Jobs was diagnosed with terminal pancreatic cancer, forcing him to confront his mortality. This moment reshaped his outlook on life, inspiring him to filter out trivial concerns and focus only on what truly mattered.

In 2005, Jobs shared this life-altering realization in his Stanford Commencement Speech, where he famously said, "If today were the last day of my life, would I want to do what I am about to do today?" Reflecting on this question daily, Jobs explained, helped him prioritize meaningful pursuits and release fleeting anxieties. Guided by this perspective, Jobs focused his energy on innovating at Apple, nurturing relationships, and leaving behind a legacy aligned with his deepest values.

Steve Jobs's story vividly illustrates Rule Eight. By embracing the deathbed perspective, he gained clarity about what deserved his time and attention, enabling him to live authentically and purposefully. His ability to act with intention, free from the distractions of fleeting worries, allowed him to create lasting contributions that continue to inspire. Jobs's reflections remind us that viewing life through the lens of impermanence can free us to focus on what truly matters, guiding us to live with clarity, purpose, and authenticity.

EXAMPLE 2: NAPOLEON BONAPARTE'S EXILE AND REFLECTIONS (1769–1821)

Born in Corsica, France, Napoleon Bonaparte rose to become one of Europe's most powerful rulers, celebrated for his military genius and political vision. Yet, his reign was marked by an unrelenting worry about his empire's future. Obsessed with securing his dominance, Napoleon became consumed by concerns over maintaining control and expanding his territory, often at the expense of practical realities.

This worry drove him to launch risky campaigns, including the ill-fated invasion of Russia in 1812. Ignoring warnings and logistical challenges, Napoleon's obsession with immediate victories blinded him to the long-term consequences of his decisions. The catastrophic failure of the Russian campaign weakened his empire, leaving it vulnerable to his enemies. Despite these setbacks, Napoleon's anxieties about his legacy pushed him into further conflicts, culminating in his defeat at the Battle of Waterloo in 1815.

Exiled to the remote island of Saint Helena, Napoleon spent his final years reflecting on his life and choices. Stripped of power, he realized that many of the worries that consumed him—territorial gains, fleeting victories, and the approval of others—had little significance in the face of mortality. His preoccupation with these concerns had cost him the opportunity to focus on enduring values like peace, relationships, and the well-being of his people.

Napoleon's story vividly illustrates Rule Eight. His obsessive worries about control and conquest blinded him to what truly mattered. Reflecting from the perspective of life's impermanence, Napoleon came to understand the futility of prioritizing transient concerns. Rule Eight reminds us to focus on meaningful actions today and devote our energy to pursuits that bring fulfillment and lasting impact, rather than being consumed by fleeting anxieties.

CHAPTER 3

Navigating Authenticity

"Always be a first-rate version of yourself, instead of a second-rate version of somebody else."

—**Judy Garland,** as quoted in *Business Etiquette for the Nineties*

Rule One: Be Aware of the Illusion of Sudden Success

"Beware of false knowledge; it is more dangerous than ignorance."

—**George Bernard Shaw,** *Man and Superman*

Life occasionally presents moments of sudden success or unexpected gains. While these experiences can feel exhilarating, they often distort our understanding of genuine achievement. True success is frequently the result of years of unseen effort, while fleeting gains often arise from luck or timing. The danger lies in mistaking unearned, effortless success for lasting achievement, fostering overconfidence and the false belief that meaningful success requires little effort or planning.

Economic bubbles provide a vivid illustration of this phenomenon. Rapid asset growth creates a sense of invincibility, leading people to believe their gains are sustainable. History, however, shows that unsustainable growth inevitably collapses, leaving significant financial and emotional consequences. Similarly, personal success without a strong foundation can lead to complacency, blinding us to the persistence, resilience, and strategy required for enduring growth.

This rule does not dismiss the value of success, even when it comes suddenly, but urges us to approach it thoughtfully. Success grounded in effort and dedication deserves celebration, while fleeting gains call for caution and reflection. By remaining grounded and valuing consistent effort, growth, and resilience, we ensure that our achievements are meaningful and lasting. To navigate the deceptive allure of sudden success, we must do the following:

- Maintain skepticism about rapid success, understanding that lasting achievement often requires time and effort.
- Recognize the temporary nature of sudden gains and question their sustainability.
- Value consistent effort and skill development as the building blocks of meaningful success.
- Seek guidance and ongoing learning, particularly from experienced mentors who can provide clarity and direction.

Rule One reminds us that true success requires time, resilience, and a strong foundation. By recognizing the illusion of sudden success, we free ourselves from its traps and embrace the journey of sustainable achievement.

EXAMPLE 1: MARK ZUCKERBERG (1984–) AND FACEBOOK (NOW META)

Born in White Plains, New York, Mark Zuckerberg is the cofounder of Facebook, one of the most influential companies in the digital age. In 2004, while studying at Harvard University, Zuckerberg launched Facebook as a college networking platform. Within two years, its meteoric rise caught the attention of Yahoo, which offered $1 billion to acquire the company.

For a twenty-two-year-old entrepreneur, the offer seemed like a once-in-a-lifetime opportunity. Many advised Zuckerberg to accept, highlighting the immediate financial security it promised. However, Zuckerberg saw Facebook's potential to revolutionize global communication and believed this vision required long-term growth and control. Accepting Yahoo's offer would have meant sacrificing the chance to build a platform aligned with his deeper mission. Despite immense pressure and the risks involved, he declined the offer, choosing instead to focus on sustainable growth and innovation. His decision proved transformative—Facebook (now Meta) grew to connect billions of users worldwide and is valued today at over $800 billion.

Mark Zuckerberg's story vividly illustrates Rule One. By rejecting the illusion of sudden success, he demonstrated the importance of prioritizing sustainable growth and long-term vision. His journey highlights that true success requires persistence, resilience, and the ability to resist short-term gains in favor of meaningful, enduring achievements. Zuckerberg's decision serves as a powerful reminder that lasting success is built on clarity, patience, and unwavering commitment to one's goals.

EXAMPLE 2: NICK LEESON (1967–)

Born in Watford, England, Nick Leeson joined Barings Bank, one of Britain's oldest and most prestigious financial institutions, as a clerk in 1989. His talent for identifying trading opportunities and delivering results quickly earned him a promotion to Barings Bank's Singapore office. There, he was tasked with managing the bank's derivatives trading, a highly lucrative but risky market. By the early 1990s, Leeson was hailed as a star trader, generating significant profits that bolstered the bank's reputation. His meteoric rise created the appearance of effortless success, earning him the trust of his superiors and unchecked control over his operations.

However, Leeson's early victories planted the seeds of overconfidence. Determined to maintain his winning streak, he began taking increasingly risky bets. When trades started going wrong, Leeson concealed his losses and doubled down on high-risk strategies, convinced he could recover and restore his reputation. As the pressure mounted, he created a secret account to hide mounting losses, believing he could outmaneuver the market. Over time, the hidden losses grew to $1.4 billion. In 1995, a series of devastating trades on the Japanese stock market led to the collapse of Barings Bank—a shocking downfall for an institution that had stood for over 230 years.

Nick Leeson's story vividly illustrates Rule One. His initial successes created an illusion of invincibility, blinding him to the importance of humility, sustainable practices, and risk management. By chasing short-term wins and neglecting the foundations of lasting success, Leeson succumbed to the illusion of sudden success. His story serves as a cautionary tale, reminding us that true success requires accountability, persistence, and the ability to remain grounded amid early achievements.

Rule Two: Always Stay Humble in Success and Patient in Adversity

"Life is made up of two days: One that is for you and one that is against you. When it is for you, do not become arrogant; and when it is against you, be patient, for both shall pass."

—commonly attributed to Ali ibn Abi Talib

Life's duality ensures we all encounter moments of success and adversity. Recognizing this reality helps us navigate life's unpredictable path with wisdom and balance, embracing both the highs and lows as opportunities for reflection and growth.

Success, while rewarding, is fleeting. It is easy to fall into arrogance or overconfidence, particularly with sudden success, as discussed in Rule One. Practicing humility during success reminds us to stay grounded, recognizing the roles of hard work, support, and opportunity in our achievements. By embracing humility, we cultivate gratitude for our blessings and remain aware of the impermanence of success. This mindset keeps us connected to others, fosters personal growth, and prepares us for life's inevitable challenges.

Adversity, like success, is transient. Embracing patience during challenging times builds resilience, fosters hope, and helps us approach difficulties with grace. Patience enables us to focus on solutions rather than despair, reinforcing our confidence that brighter days will come. Through patience, we emerge stronger, turning hardships into opportunities for growth.

Rule Two reminds us that humility and patience are the cornerstones of a balanced and fulfilling life. By staying grounded in success and hopeful in adversity, we cultivate resilience, gratitude, and inner peace, empowering us to navigate life's ups and downs with wisdom and grace.

EXAMPLE 1: MALALA YOUSAFZAI (1997–)

Born in Mingora, Pakistan, Malala Yousafzai grew up in a region where the Taliban systematically suppressed women's rights, particularly access to education. From a young age, Malala defied these oppressive norms, becoming a fearless advocate for girls' education. On October 9, 2012, her activism nearly cost her life when a Taliban gunman shot her in the head while she was riding her school bus.

Malala's recovery was long and challenging, but she used this time to reflect and deepen her commitment to her cause. Refusing to let adversity silence her, she emerged even stronger, addressing the United Nations, founding the Malala Fund, and publishing her memoir, *I Am Malala*. At just seventeen, she became the youngest-ever Nobel Peace Prize laureate, recognized for her unwavering dedication to education and women's rights.

Despite her global acclaim, Malala remained deeply humble. She consistently shifted the focus away from her personal achievements to highlight the millions of girls worldwide still deprived of education. Even amid fame, she expressed gratitude for her opportunities and used her platform to amplify the voices of those less fortunate.

Malala Yousafzai's life vividly illustrates Rule Two. Her patience in adversity allowed her to transform personal tragedy into global advocacy, while her humility in success ensured her message remained focused on others. Malala's story reminds us that humility and patience not only strengthen character but also amplify one's ability to create meaningful change.

EXAMPLE 2: LEONA HELMSLEY (1920–2007)

Born in Marbletown, New York, Leona Helmsley rose to prominence as a shrewd businesswoman, building a vast real estate empire that included the iconic Helmsley Palace Hotel. Her ambition and sharp instincts made her one of the wealthiest women in America, but her success also revealed a darker side. Known as the "Queen of Mean," Helmsley became infamous for her arrogance, imperious behavior, and disdainful treatment of employees.

Her hubris reached its peak during her 1989 tax evasion trial, where she was famously quoted saying, "Only the little people pay taxes." This remark, coupled with her lavish lifestyle and dismissive attitude toward the law, ignited widespread public outrage. Her confrontational demeanor during the trial alienated allies and undermined her defense. Convicted of tax evasion, she served nineteen months in prison. By the time of her release, Helmsley's once-formidable reputation was irreparably damaged, and her legacy was forever associated with arrogance and excess.

Leona Helmsley's life vividly demonstrates nonadherence to Rule Two. Her arrogance in success blinded her to the importance of humility, and her lack of patience in adversity alienated those around her. Helmsley's fall from grace underscores the dangers of unchecked ego and entitlement. Her story serves as a cautionary tale, reminding us that humility preserves respect and relationships, while hubris can overshadow even the greatest achievements.

Rule Three: Avoid the Lust for Power

"Nearly all men can stand adversity, but if you want to test a man's character, give him power."

—commonly attributed to Abraham Lincoln

Power is often considered the ultimate goal in our pursuit of success, offering control, influence, and authority. However, unchecked power can significantly affect our psyche, leading to self-deception, overconfidence, and a dangerous detachment from our core values.

The intoxicating effects of power often create a false sense of superiority and invincibility, clouding judgment and diminishing the ability to act ethically. History is filled with examples of leaders—from ancient emperors to modern politicians—whose relentless pursuit of power led to unethical actions and eventual downfall. These stories serve as cautionary reminders of the dangers of unchecked ambition and the importance of humility.

To handle power responsibly, we must balance it with humility, empathy, and self-reflection. True power lies not in possessing authority but in using it to uplift and positively impact others. Regular accountability ensures we prevent the misuse of power, keeping us aligned with our values and mindful of the consequences of our actions.

Rule Three warns us about the seductive nature of power and its potential to corrupt. By using power responsibly and focusing on the greater good, we safeguard our integrity and ensure that our actions leave a meaningful, lasting impact on society.

EXAMPLE 1: OMAR IBN AL-KHATTAB (584–644)

Born in Mecca, Omar ibn al-Khattab rose to power as the second caliph of the Islamic state during a period of rapid territorial expansion and societal transformation. Despite overseeing a vast empire, Omar remained committed to humility and justice, rejecting the privileges that often accompany power. He lived in a modest home, wore simple clothing, and often said, "I am but a servant of the people," believing leadership was a responsibility, not a privilege.

Omar's humility was reflected in his personal engagement with his people. On one occasion, disguised as a commoner, he encountered a mother boiling stones to give her starving children the illusion of food. Deeply moved, Omar personally carried sacks of flour to her home, declaring, "I fear that God will hold me accountable for their hunger." This hands-on approach to governance ensured he remained empathetic and connected to the struggles of his people.

As a ruler, Omar institutionalized the Bayt al-Mal (House of Wealth), a financial system aimed at redistributing resources and reducing inequality. He also held himself accountable under the same laws as his people, famously stating, "If a camel were to trip in Iraq, I would be responsible before God for not paving the way for it." His humility and accountability earned him the unwavering trust of his subjects.

Omar ibn al-Khattab's leadership vividly demonstrates Rule Three. By rejecting the trappings of power and using his authority to serve others, Omar exemplified humility and empathy in leadership. His story reminds us that true power lies not in dominance but in service, and that humility is the key to wielding power responsibly and ethically.

EXAMPLE 2: JOSEPH STALIN AND THE GREAT PURGE (1936–1938)

Born in Gori, Georgia, Joseph Stalin rose to power in the Soviet Union after Vladimir Lenin's death, consolidating his authority as general secretary of the Communist Party. Determined to eliminate any perceived threats to his rule, Stalin initiated the Great Purge, a campaign of political repression marked by mass arrests, forced confessions, and public trials. His paranoia and unchecked lust for power created a reign of terror that profoundly scarred Soviet society.

Under Stalin's orders, the NKVD, his secret police, targeted party elites, military officers, and ordinary citizens alike. Innocent individuals were falsely accused of treason, subjected to brutal interrogations, and often executed. Families were torn apart as millions were deported to gulags—labor camps notorious for their inhumane conditions and high mortality rates. Stalin's obsession with consolidating power blinded him to the suffering of his people, prioritizing control over their welfare.

The consequences were devastating. The Great Purge left a legacy of fear, trauma, and societal stagnation. Stalin's unchecked ambition and refusal to embrace accountability eroded trust within the Soviet Union, dismantling societal cohesion and weakening the nation.

Joseph Stalin's life vividly demonstrates nonadherence to Rule Three. His unchecked ambition and misuse of power highlight the dangers of authority wielded without empathy or accountability. Stalin's actions serve as a stark reminder that power, when divorced from moral restraint, becomes a destructive force, harming both the leader and the society they govern. His story underscores the importance of humility, self-restraint, and a focus on the greater good in positions of power.

Rule Four: Trust Your Inner Voice

"Don't let the noise of others' opinions drown out your own inner voice."
—Steve Jobs, 2005 Stanford Commencement Speech

In today's hyperconnected world, we are constantly surrounded by external opinions, data-driven predictions, and societal expectations. Amid this noise, trusting our inner voice—a quiet guide reflecting our deepest truths, emotions, and aspirations—is essential. This inner wisdom is uniquely ours, offering insights shaped by our values and lived experiences that no algorithm or external opinion can replicate.

While data and expert advice can inform our choices, relying on them blindly can detach us from our authentic selves, leading to decisions that conflict with our values and passions. True fulfillment comes when external input complements the clarity of our inner voice, creating harmony between informed analysis and personal truth.

Trusting our inner voice doesn't mean dismissing outside perspectives. Instead, it requires reflection and intentionality. Practices like mindfulness, meditation, and journaling help us tune out distractions, strengthen our self-awareness, and distinguish between external noise and genuine desires.

Rule Four is a call to reclaim our agency in a world dominated by external influences. By integrating external wisdom with the guidance of our inner voice, we make decisions that are not only informed but also deeply authentic. This alignment empowers us to live courageously, guided by our unique values, dreams, and passions.

EXAMPLE 1: J. K. ROWLING (1965–) AND THE CHARACTER OF HARRY POTTER

Born in Yate, England, J. K. Rowling displayed a passion for storytelling from a young age, often creating imaginative tales to entertain her family. However, her journey to literary success was anything but easy. As a single mother living on welfare, Rowling faced intense societal pressure to abandon her dreams of writing and focus on finding a stable job. Many dismissed her aspirations as impractical, but her inner voice—the unwavering belief in her story—compelled her to persevere.

In 1990, during a delayed train journey, Rowling vividly envisioned the character of Harry Potter and the magical world of Hogwarts. Trusting her intuition, she began writing, often working late into the night after caring for her young daughter. Each word she wrote was guided by her inner voice, reminding her of the story's potential even as she faced financial hardship and self-doubt.

When her manuscript was complete, Rowling encountered another obstacle: finding a publisher. Over the course of a year, twelve publishers rejected her manuscript. Each rejection tested her resolve, but her inner voice encouraged her to persist. Her determination paid off when Bloomsbury agreed to publish *Harry Potter and the Philosopher's Stone*. The series became a global phenomenon, selling over six hundred million copies, spawning a blockbuster film franchise, and transforming Rowling into one of the world's most successful authors.

J. K. Rowling's story vividly illustrates Rule Four. By trusting her inner voice and refusing to let external doubts deter her, she turned adversity into a legacy that continues to inspire millions. Her journey reminds us that intuition, when paired with persistence, can guide us to extraordinary achievements and a life aligned with our deepest passions.

EXAMPLE 2: RICHARD FULD (1946–) AND SUBPRIME MORTGAGES

Born in New York City in 1946, Richard Fuld joined Lehman Brothers in 1969 and rose to become its CEO in 1994. Under his leadership, Lehman grew into one of Wall Street's most prominent firms, achieving remarkable success and profitability. However, the immense pressure to sustain this dominance drove the company to take increasingly risky bets, particularly in the subprime mortgage market.

By the mid-2000s, as cracks in the housing market began to emerge, concerns about Lehman's overexposure to risky assets grew within the firm. Even Fuld reportedly questioned the sustainability of their strategy, as mounting risks became apparent. Yet, fearing a loss of confidence from shareholders and competitors, he ignored his instincts and chose to stay the course. His reluctance to challenge external pressures or trust his inner voice ultimately set Lehman on a perilous path.

In 2008, the housing market collapse revealed Lehman's vulnerability, leading to its bankruptcy—the largest in US history—and sparking a global financial crisis. In his testimony before Congress, Fuld admitted he had doubts about the firm's strategy but failed to act on them. His decision to prioritize external validation over his intuition not only led to the collapse of Lehman Brothers but also triggered widespread economic fallout, costing millions their jobs and savings.

Richard Fuld's story vividly illustrates nonadherence to Rule

Four. Overwhelmed by external pressures, he silenced his inner voice and ignored his instincts, prioritizing external validation over sound judgment. His failure to trust his intuition serves as a cautionary tale, highlighting the catastrophic consequences of neglecting one's inner guidance. Fuld's downfall reminds us that intuition, when ignored, can lead to decisions that harm not only individuals but entire industries and societies.

Rule Five: Align Your Inner Self with Your External Image

"Be yourself; everyone else is already taken."
—commonly attributed to Oscar Wilde

As we navigate societal expectations, we often face the challenge of aligning our authentic inner self with the external image we present to the world. This alignment is crucial for psychological well-being and personal growth. When our inner identity—shaped by our values, aspirations, and experiences—misaligns with a constructed public image aimed at admiration or validation, it can lead to emotional disconnection, superficial relationships, and mental exhaustion.

Achieving alignment requires introspection, self-acceptance, and courage. Living authentically means shedding societal pressures and embracing both our strengths and vulnerabilities. This fosters self-respect, personal growth, and deeper, more meaningful connections. True belonging is achieved not by projecting a facade, but by presenting our genuine self, allowing others to connect with us on a foundation of mutual understanding and respect.

Rule Five emphasizes the transformative power of living authentically. By aligning our internal identity with our external image, we cultivate emotional well-being, build fulfilling relationships, and lead lives rooted in purpose and integrity. Embracing our true selves enables us to celebrate our uniqueness, make meaningful contributions to society, and foster authentic connections that enrich both ourselves and those around us.

EXAMPLE 1: HATIM AL-TA'I (SIXTH CENTURY)

Born in Hail, Arabia, during the sixth century, Hatim al-Ta'i became a legendary figure known for his extraordinary generosity and selflessness. Raised in a culture that prized hospitality, Hatim embraced these values wholeheartedly, aligning his actions with his deeply held principles of empathy and compassion.

One of the most famous stories about Hatim occurred during a time of severe scarcity. A weary traveler arrived at his home seeking refuge. Despite his family's poverty and limited resources, Hatim sacrificed his only camel to provide a feast for the traveler, ensuring his guest felt welcomed and cared for. When questioned about his decision, Hatim replied, "True wealth lies in giving, not in keeping." This act of selflessness reflected not only Hatim's unwavering commitment to hospitality but also his belief that true generosity stems from living in harmony with one's core values.

Hatim's generosity was not performative; it was an authentic expression of his character. His consistent alignment of values and actions earned him respect and admiration, creating a legacy that endures as a symbol of altruism and hospitality. By staying true to his principles, Hatim fostered trust and meaningful relationships, demonstrating the transformative power of authenticity.

Hatim al-Ta'i's life vividly illustrates Rule Five. His generosity was a genuine reflection of his inner values, reminding us that aligning our external actions with our inner beliefs fosters trust, respect, and integrity. Hatim's story inspires us to live authentically, ensuring our outward image reflects our true selves and builds meaningful connections rooted in mutual respect.

EXAMPLE 2: BERNIE MADOFF (1938–2021)

Born in New York City in 1938, Bernie Madoff built a reputation as a respected figure in the financial world. In 1960, he founded his investment firm, which quickly gained the trust of individuals, organizations, and charities alike. By the 1990s, Madoff reached the pinnacle of his career, serving as chairman of the NASDAQ stock exchange. To the public, he embodied trust and success, projecting an image of reliability and integrity.

However, behind this carefully curated persona lay a massive Ponzi scheme. For decades, Madoff orchestrated a fraudulent operation, using funds from new investors to pay returns to earlier ones. This deception allowed him to sustain the illusion of stability and success while concealing unethical practices. By 2008, the financial crisis exposed the fragility of his scheme. The collapse revealed the staggering scale of his $65 billion fraud, leading to his arrest and the collapse of his firm.

The consequences were devastating. Thousands of investors lost their life savings, and charities were forced to close, unable to recover their funds. Madoff's betrayal eroded trust across the financial industry, leaving a legacy of distrust and disillusionment. Personally, he lost everything—his wealth, reputation, and freedom—ultimately dying in prison in 2021. The emotional toll of his deceit reverberated through his family, with his son Mark taking his own life in 2010.

Bernie Madoff's story vividly illustrates the dangers of ignoring Rule Five. His failure to align his public image with ethical actions led to catastrophic consequences, destroying lives and trust on a massive scale. Madoff's life serves as a cautionary tale, reminding us that authenticity and integrity are essential for building trust and achieving lasting success.

Rule Six: Never Crave Someone Else's Life

"The reason we struggle with insecurity is because we compare our behind-the-scenes with everyone else's highlight reel."
—Steven Furtick, *Crash the Chatterbox*

In today's era of social media and constant digital connectivity, we are often captivated by curated images of success, fame, and wealth. These portrayals highlight triumphs while concealing struggles, creating an illusion of idealized lives. Comparing our reality to these carefully crafted "highlight reels" can lead to insecurity, dissatisfaction, and a distorted view of our own worth.

It is crucial to remember that everyone, no matter how fortunate they appear, faces their own hardships. Wishing for someone else's life means desiring not only their successes but also their unseen struggles—battles that may be far more overwhelming than they seem. Instead of longing for someone else's path, we can draw inspiration from their admirable qualities, such as resilience, creativity, or determination, and apply these lessons to our own journey.

Equally important is recognizing the uniqueness of our own life. Each of us is shaped by a blend of triumphs and challenges that contribute to our growth and individuality. By focusing on our path and nurturing our talents, we cultivate a fulfilling life that reflects our authentic selves. This mindset frees us from the trap of comparison and helps us appreciate the richness of our experiences.

Rule Six reminds us to celebrate our unique journey while learning from others' qualities. By valuing our individuality and focusing on authentic growth, we create a life of fulfillment and self-acceptance, free from the burden of comparison.

EXAMPLE 1: PRINCESS DIANA (1961–1997)

Born into British aristocracy, Diana Spencer became Lady Diana Spencer in 1975 when her father inherited the title of Earl of Spencer. Her 1981 marriage to Prince Charles captivated the world, with millions watching as she transformed into the Princess of Wales. Known for her elegance, compassion, and dedication to charitable causes, Diana raised awareness about HIV/AIDS, homelessness, and landmine eradication, earning her the title "the People's Princess."

Behind the glamorous public image, however, Diana faced profound personal struggles. Her marriage to Prince Charles was fraught with challenges, including infidelity and intense media scrutiny. Despite the pressures of royal life, Diana broke tradition by speaking openly about her battles with bulimia, depression, and feelings of isolation—issues that were rarely discussed publicly at the time. Her decision to share these vulnerabilities inspired millions, showing that even those who appear to "have it all" face hidden challenges.

Diana's tragic death in 1997 shocked the world, leaving behind a complex legacy of compassion and authenticity. Her ability to connect deeply with people, coupled with her courage to address personal struggles openly, highlighted the importance of embracing one's humanity and valuing one's unique journey.

Princess Diana's life vividly illustrates Rule Six. While her public image seemed perfect, her private struggles revealed the hidden complexities behind outward appearances. Diana's story reminds us to resist idealizing others' lives, value our own path, and embrace authenticity, recognizing that every life carries unseen challenges.

EXAMPLE 2: ROBIN WILLIAMS (1951–2014)

Robin Williams, born in Chicago, Illinois, rose to global fame as one of Hollywood's most beloved actors and comedians. Known for his quick wit, improvisational brilliance, and iconic roles in *Dead Poets Society*, *Aladdin*, and *Good Will Hunting* (for which he won an Academy Award), Williams brought joy and laughter to millions. His vibrant public persona made him a global icon of humor and creativity, admired for his ability to brighten lives with his boundless energy.

However, behind the scenes, Williams battled deep personal struggles. He faced lifelong challenges with depression and anxiety, which he openly discussed in interviews, as well as a history of substance abuse earlier in his career. The pressure to maintain his public image as a cheerful and inspiring figure often masked the depth of his inner turmoil. In 2014, Williams's battle with mental health culminated in his tragic suicide, later attributed to an undiagnosed neurodegenerative disorder called Lewy body dementia.

The aftermath of his death shocked the world, sparking conversations about mental health and the hidden struggles behind public personas. While Williams's public image embodied humor and brilliance, his story reminds us that outward appearances often conceal unseen challenges. His journey highlights the dangers of comparing our lives to others and underscores the importance of valuing our own unique path, with all its complexities and imperfections.

Robin Williams's life poignantly illustrates Rule Six. His public persona masked personal struggles that remind us to resist idealizing others' lives. Williams's story teaches us to embrace our own journey, recognize the hidden complexities in every life, and draw strength from our unique experiences rather than comparing ourselves to others.

Rule Seven: Avoid Being Limited by Your Identity

"There is only one evil in the world, and that is limited identity."
—**Sadhguru,** 2020 interview with Lewis Howes,
School of Greatness podcast

Our identities, shaped by beliefs, culture, and associations, offer a sense of belonging and purpose. However, when narrowly defined by labels such as nationality, ideology, or religion, they can limit how we see ourselves and others. These restrictions foster bias, rigidity, and division, preventing us from embracing broader perspectives and deeper connections.

The consequences of limited identity are profound. At a personal level, it confines our potential, stifling growth and adaptability. At a societal level, it fuels division, prejudice, and conflict, often with lasting repercussions. History is filled with examples of individuals and groups clinging to exclusive identities, prioritizing separation over unity. Even in technology, AI systems trained on limited data sets develop biases, highlighting the risks of restrictive perspectives.

Breaking free from these limitations begins with self-awareness. By recognizing how identity shapes our beliefs and actions, we can question biases, embrace diverse viewpoints, and foster inclusivity. Engaging with different cultures and expanding our understanding of others enriches our worldview and fosters empathy. Realizing our connection to a global community empowers us to transcend labels and strengthen mutual respect.

Rule Seven reminds us that transcending narrow identities opens the door to growth, empathy, and unity. By embracing the diversity of human experience, we enrich our lives, build meaningful connections, and contribute to a more inclusive and harmonious world.

EXAMPLE 1: OSKAR SCHINDLER (1908–1974)

Born in Austria-Hungary, Oskar Schindler grew up in a German Catholic family and initially embraced the opportunities offered by the Nazi regime in Germany. As a member of the Nazi Party and an industrialist in Krakow, Poland, he benefited from the system by employing Jewish workers who were marginalized and persecuted under Nazi policies.

However, Schindler's perspective changed as he witnessed the brutal realities of the Holocaust. Through his daily interactions with his employees, he came to see their humanity beyond the labels imposed by the regime. This awakening marked a turning point in his life. At great personal risk, Schindler used his position and resources to shield his workers from deportation to concentration camps. By bribing officials, falsifying documents, and leveraging his connections, he compiled "Schindler's List," saving over one thousand Jewish lives.

Schindler's decision came at a high cost. He sacrificed his fortune, faced constant danger, and ultimately fled Germany as a fugitive. Yet, his actions left an indelible legacy, demonstrating the transformative power of breaking free from restrictive labels. Schindler chose to prioritize humanity over profit and ideology, transcending the identity of a Nazi industrialist to become a symbol of compassion and moral courage.

Oskar Schindler's story vividly illustrates Rule Seven. By rejecting narrow identities and embracing universal human values, he showed that true identity lies in our actions and choices. Schindler's life reminds us that breaking free from restrictive labels empowers us to uphold empathy, integrity, and the shared humanity that connects us all.

EXAMPLE 2: POL POT (1925–1998)

Born Saloth Sâr in Cambodia, Pol Pot transitioned from a Paris-educated Marxist to the leader of the Khmer Rouge, where his rigid ideological identity came to define his rule. When his regime came to power in 1975, Pol Pot sought to transform Cambodia into a self-sufficient agrarian utopia. Driven by his vision, he dismantled traditional social structures, abolished currency, and forced millions into agricultural labor camps.

The human cost of his worldview was devastating. Nearly 1.7 million people—almost a quarter of Cambodia's population—died from forced labor, mass executions, and famine. Families were torn apart, cultural traditions were erased, and entire communities were destroyed. Despite mounting evidence of widespread suffering, Pol Pot refused to adapt his policies, clinging instead to his narrow ideological identity. His obsession with reshaping society blinded him to the human consequences of his actions, prioritizing dogma over humanity.

By the time his regime collapsed in 1979, Cambodia was left in ruins, and Pol Pot's legacy became synonymous with destruction and brutality. His inflexible commitment to a singular identity not only decimated his people but also left a nation struggling to recover for decades.

Pol Pot's story vividly illustrates the dangers of ignoring Rule Seven. By confining himself to a narrow ideological identity, he prioritized rigidity over compassion, leading to unimaginable suffering. His life serves as a cautionary tale about the catastrophic consequences of clinging to restrictive labels, reminding us of the critical need to embrace broader perspectives and prioritize humanity over ideology.

Rule Eight: How People Treat You Is Their Choice; How You React Is Yours

"We are not disturbed by what happens to us, but by our thoughts about what happens."
—Epictetus, *The Enchiridion*

This rule emphasizes the importance of personal responsibility in how we respond to others' actions. While we cannot control how others behave, shaped by their beliefs and choices, we hold full responsibility for our reactions. Every interaction presents a choice: to perpetuate negativity or to respond with intention, guided by kindness, firmness, or a balance of both.

When faced with mistreatment or negativity, thoughtful reactions can transform challenges into opportunities for growth. Kindness often fosters understanding and diffuses tension, while firmness—rooted in values and integrity—upholds boundaries and addresses injustice. The key lies in aligning our responses with the person we aspire to be, ensuring they reflect our values and principles.

While mindful responses cultivate resilience, authenticity, and stronger relationships, this rule does not advocate passivity or aggression but emphasizes deliberate action that balances empathy with strength. By responding in ways that honor our integrity, we inspire understanding, foster growth, and remain true to ourselves, even in challenging interactions.

Rule Eight reminds us that every reaction is a reflection of our character. By responding with empathy, strength, and intentionality, we transform challenges into opportunities to grow, inspire, and live authentically.

EXAMPLE 1: THE DALAI LAMA (1935–)

Born as Lhamo Thondup in a small Tibetan village, the Dalai Lama was recognized as the reincarnation of the thirteenth Dalai Lama and became Tibet's spiritual and political leader at a young age. In 1950, during the Chinese occupation of Tibet, he assumed full political authority at just fifteen years old. A defining moment in his life came in 1959, when the Tibetan uprising failed, forcing him to flee to India and establish a government in exile.

Despite losing his homeland and witnessing the suffering of the Tibetan people, the Dalai Lama chose to respond with compassion, dialogue, and nonviolence. His Middle Way Approach exemplifies his values, advocating for genuine autonomy for Tibet within the Chinese Constitution rather than complete independence. This framework prioritizes preserving Tibet's culture, language, and spiritual heritage while fostering peaceful coexistence. Through this approach, the Dalai Lama has consistently sought resolution through understanding rather than retaliation, even in the face of provocation.

The Dalai Lama's life vividly illustrates Rule Eight. By responding to injustice with empathy, integrity, and a commitment to peace, he transformed adversity into an opportunity for dialogue and unity. His unwavering alignment with his values inspired global admiration and advanced the Tibetan cause. The Dalai Lama's story reminds us that how we react to challenges defines our character and has the power to inspire change, fostering resilience and hope even in the most difficult circumstances.

EXAMPLE 2: NICOLAE CEAUȘESCU (1918–1989)

Born in Scornicești, Romania, Nicolae Ceaușescu rose to power in 1965, initially earning a reputation as a reformer. Over time, his rule became increasingly oppressive, marked by censorship, propaganda, and repressive policies that caused widespread economic and social hardship. By the late 1980s, discontent with his regime was widespread, and public frustration was reaching a breaking point.

In December 1989, the Timișoara uprising began as a peaceful protest against the government's decision to evict a local pastor, László Tőkés. The demonstration quickly escalated into a broader outcry against Ceaușescu's regime. Rather than addressing the grievances of the protesters, Ceaușescu reacted with fear and rigidity. He deployed security forces to suppress the uprising, ordering a brutal crackdown that resulted in numerous deaths. The violence only fueled the unrest, sparking nationwide protests that culminated in the Romanian Revolution. Within days, Ceaușescu and his wife were captured, tried, and executed.

Ceaușescu's story vividly illustrates the dangers of ignoring Rule Eight. His impulsive and oppressive response to peaceful protests reflected fear and a refusal to adapt, alienating his people and accelerating his downfall. By reacting without thoughtfulness or empathy, he prioritized force over dialogue, creating division and instability. His story reminds us that reactions driven by fear and rigidity often lead to collapse, while mindful, deliberate responses have the power to foster trust and resolution.

Rule Nine: Align Your Knowledge with Your Actions

"Knowing is not enough; we must apply.
Willing is not enough; we must do."
—Johann Wolfgang von Goethe, *Wilhelm Meisters Wanderjahre*

In a world overflowing with knowledge, its true value emerges only when we transform it into deliberate action. Without action, knowledge becomes stagnant, leading to frustration, wasted potential, and missed opportunities for growth. The gap between knowing and doing limits our ability to create meaningful contributions in our lives and the world around us. Knowledge gains relevance and power only when applied with purpose and intention.

To bridge this gap, we must confront the barriers holding us back. Fear, procrastination, and unclear goals often prevent us from taking the first step. By practicing introspection, setting specific goals, and creating actionable plans, we build the momentum needed to move forward. Developing habits that consistently translate knowledge into action ensures our efforts are intentional, impactful, and aligned with our values.

Rule Nine reminds us that knowledge without action is potential wasted. By aligning what we know with what we do, we unlock our ability to grow, achieve, and inspire change. Transforming insights into deliberate steps allows us to lead fulfilling lives, achieve professional success, and leave a legacy defined by meaningful contributions to the world.

EXAMPLE 1: KAILASH SATYARTHI (1954–)

Born in Vidisha, India, Kailash Satyarthi grew up deeply disturbed by the sight of children working in hazardous conditions while being denied education. Determined to address this injustice, he left a promising career in electrical engineering to dedicate his life to championing children's rights. In 1980, he founded the Bachpan Bachao Andolan (Save the Childhood Movement), which has since rescued more than one hundred thousand children from bonded labor, trafficking, and exploitation.

Satyarthi's journey was far from easy. He faced violent resistance from those who profited from child labor, enduring threats and attacks while rescuing children from factories and brick kilns. Despite these risks, he remained unwavering in his commitment to turning knowledge into action. In 1998, he organized the Global March Against Child Labour, mobilizing millions across 103 countries to advocate for the adoption of ILO Convention No. 182, targeting the worst forms of child labor. His efforts also influenced India's Child

Labour (Prohibition and Regulation) Act, creating lasting policy changes to protect children.

In 2014, Satyarthi's tireless advocacy was recognized globally when he received the Nobel Peace Prize, jointly with Malala Yousafzai. His leadership not only freed thousands of children from exploitation but also inspired a global movement to protect future generations.

Kailash Satyarthi's life vividly illustrates Rule Nine. By aligning his knowledge of child exploitation with deliberate, informed action, he turned awareness into global advocacy and lasting reform. His story reminds us that knowledge alone is insufficient—it is the courageous application of that knowledge that creates meaningful change and a legacy of impact.

EXAMPLE 2: RAJAT GUPTA (1948–)

Born in Kolkata, India, Rajat Gupta rose to global prominence as the managing director of McKinsey & Company and a board member of prestigious corporations, including Goldman Sachs. Widely respected for his business acumen, Gupta's career symbolized success and influence. He was admired for his leadership and extensive knowledge of corporate governance, making his downfall all the more shocking.

In 2012, Gupta was convicted of insider trading after sharing confidential information about Goldman Sachs with a hedge fund manager. Driven by ambition and the allure of financial gain, Gupta violated ethical and legal standards, betraying the trust of colleagues and organizations who had placed immense faith in his leadership. His conviction led to a two-year prison sentence, the collapse of his career, and irreparable damage to his reputation.

Beyond the personal consequences, Gupta's actions undermined trust in the corporate world and highlighted the risks of eroding ethical principles in leadership. His choices not only tarnished his legacy but also raised broader concerns about the integrity of business practices.

Rajat Gupta's story vividly illustrates the dangers of ignoring Rule Nine. Despite his deep understanding of corporate ethics, he failed to align his actions with his knowledge, prioritizing personal gain over integrity. His downfall serves as a stark reminder that knowledge alone is insufficient—ethical action is essential to preserving trust, sustaining leadership, and building a meaningful legacy.

CHAPTER 4

Navigating Personal Growth

"We cannot become what we want by remaining what we are."

—Max De Pree, *Leadership Is an Art*

Rule One: Be Grateful for What You Have While Aspiring for More

"Do not dream of what you do not have; rather, reckon up the blessings you do possess and think how much you would wish for them if they were not yours."

—Marcus Aurelius, *Meditations*

In our pursuit of success, material possessions, and achievements, we often overlook the importance of gratitude. This rule reminds us to root our ambitions in appreciation, valuing what we have while striving for more.

Gratitude goes beyond acknowledging possessions. It involves appreciating our relationships, achievements, and personal qualities like resilience and creativity. Practices such as journaling or reflecting on blessings help cultivate a positive mindset, deepen relationships, and foster self-awareness.

Neglecting gratitude creates a scarcity mindset, focusing on what we lack rather than what we have. This fuels dissatisfaction, erodes self-worth, and amplifies stress, trapping us in negativity. Practicing gratitude alongside ambition shifts our focus to life's positives, helping us navigate challenges with strength drawn from our blessings.

Rule One emphasizes the harmony between gratitude and ambition. By grounding our aspirations in gratitude, we align present joy with future goals, ensuring our pursuit of success is both meaningful and fulfilling. Gratitude doesn't ignore challenges but empowers us to face them with resilience and a deeper appreciation for life's blessings.

EXAMPLE 1: A. P. J. ABDUL KALAM (1931–2015)

Born in the small island town of Rameswaram, India, A. P. J. Abdul Kalam grew up in a modest household, where he often helped his family make ends meet by delivering newspapers as a child. Despite financial struggles, Kalam maintained a profound sense of gratitude for the love and support of his parents, teachers, and community. Their encouragement instilled in him a respect for education and a burning desire to contribute to society.

Kalam's journey from a small-town boy to a world-renowned scientist and the eleventh president of India exemplifies the harmony between gratitude and ambition. As a scientist, his leadership in India's space and missile programs transformed the nation's technological landscape, earning him the title "Missile Man of India." Yet, even as he reached extraordinary heights, Kalam never lost sight of his humble beginnings.

One of his first acts as president was to invite his ninety-four-year-old elementary school teacher to the Presidential Palace—a heartfelt gesture of appreciation for the man who had nurtured his early curiosity. Similarly, he often spoke of his gratitude for the challenges that shaped him, viewing them as stepping stones to success.

A. P. J. Abdul Kalam's life vividly illustrates Rule One. By pairing gratitude with ambition, he created a legacy rooted in humility and progress. His story demonstrates how deeply appreciating one's blessings provides the foundation for greatness, inspiring others to pursue their dreams with purpose and humility. Kalam's life reminds us that when aspirations are grounded in gratitude, they not only enrich our journey but uplift everyone around us.

EXAMPLE 2: RAJ RAJARATNAM (1957–)

Born in Sri Lanka, Raj Rajaratnam rose to prominence as the founder of the Galleon Group, one of Wall Street's most successful hedge funds. Renowned for his sharp investment instincts, he managed billions of dollars and became one of the wealthiest figures in finance. However, despite his extraordinary success, Rajaratnam's relentless pursuit of greater wealth overshadowed any sense of gratitude for his achievements.

In 2009, his empire collapsed when he was arrested for insider trading. Investigations revealed that Rajaratnam had used confidential information to execute profitable trades, breaching ethical and legal standards. Driven by a scarcity mindset, he prioritized accumulation over integrity, betraying the trust of colleagues and investors. His conviction in 2011 led to an eleven-year prison sentence, millions of dollars in fines, and the loss of his reputation.

Beyond his personal ruin, Rajaratnam's actions had far-reaching consequences. His scandal shook Wall Street, eroded trust in financial institutions, and prompted stricter regulatory scrutiny. What could have been a legacy of innovation and leadership became a cautionary tale of ambition untempered by gratitude or ethics.

Raj Rajaratnam's story vividly illustrates the dangers of ignoring Rule One. His unchecked ambition, rooted in a scarcity mindset, led him to compromise ethics and betray trust. His downfall serves as a stark reminder that ambition without gratitude breeds dissatisfaction and destructive choices. Grounding our aspirations in gratitude ensures that success is built on integrity, creating a legacy of respect, fulfillment, and lasting impact.

Rule Two: Understand the Power of Your Choices

"Life is 10 percent what happens to us and 90 percent how we react to it."
—Charles R. Swindoll, *Strengthening Your Grip*

Life presents us with unpredictable challenges that test our emotions, beliefs, and decisions. While we cannot control everything that happens, we hold immense power in how we respond. Our thoughts, actions, and emotions shape our experiences, reflect our values, and influence how we navigate reality.

Understanding the power of choice begins with distinguishing what we can control from what we cannot. For situations within our control, we can choose positivity, take proactive steps, and align our actions with our goals. For circumstances beyond our control, acceptance becomes essential. Viewing setbacks as opportunities for growth helps us build resilience, focus on our strengths, and navigate uncertainties with confidence.

Failing to exercise this power leads to impulsive reactions, regrets, and strained relationships. Conversely, intentional choices break these cycles, fostering resilience and aligning actions with our principles. Cultivating self-awareness empowers us to make decisions that reflect who we are and who we aspire to become. A mindful approach to our choices transforms adversity into opportunities for self-improvement, enabling us to face life's challenges with integrity and purpose.

Rule Two emphasizes the transformative power of choice. By aligning our responses with our values and aspirations, we turn challenges into opportunities and build a life defined by authenticity, resilience, and meaningful growth.

EXAMPLE 1: VIKTOR FRANKL (1905–1997)

Viktor Frankl, a neurologist and psychiatrist from Vienna, Austria, endured unimaginable suffering as a prisoner in Nazi concentration camps during World War II. Stripped of his family, freedom, and dignity, Frankl discovered that while he could not control his circumstances, he retained the power to choose his attitude. This realization became his lifeline, helping him navigate the horrors around him and inspiring his groundbreaking psychological approach, logotherapy, which centers on finding meaning in all circumstances.

Frankl often recounted moments in the camps when he made deliberate choices to preserve his humanity. On one occasion, he shared his meager bread ration with another prisoner, finding purpose in offering compassion even amid despair. He described this ability to choose one's perspective as "the last of the human freedoms." By exercising this freedom, Frankl transcended unimaginable hardship, finding purpose in love, meaningful work, and the courage to endure suffering. After his liberation, he shared these insights with the world in *Man's Search for Meaning*, inspiring millions to view adversity as an opportunity for growth.

Viktor Frankl's life vividly illustrates Rule Two. By understanding the power of his choices, he transformed even the darkest challenges into opportunities for profound growth. His ability to align his responses with resilience and purpose demonstrates that intentional choices shape the quality and meaning of our lives, regardless of circumstances.

EXAMPLE 2: KAISER WILHELM II (1859–1941)

Kaiser Wilhelm II ascended to the German throne in 1888, driven by a grand vision of establishing Germany as a dominant global power. His reign was characterized by aggressive military policies and an unyielding ambition for prestige, often clouding his judgment.

A pivotal moment came in 1914 after the assassination of Archduke Franz Ferdinand. Wilhelm II, driven by pride and impulsivity, issued the infamous "blank check" assurance to Austria-Hungary, offering unconditional support in its conflict with Serbia. This reckless decision emboldened Austria-Hungary to escalate tensions, triggering a chain reaction among Europe's major powers and ultimately igniting World War I.

As the war progressed, Wilhelm II's refusal to adapt or reassess his strategies deepened Germany's struggles. His leadership, shaped by unchecked ambition and emotional reactions, left Germany isolated and weakened. Following Germany's defeat, Wilhelm II abdicated in 1918 and lived the rest of his life in exile. Reflecting on his choices, he reportedly expressed regret for his impulsive actions, acknowledging their catastrophic consequences for Germany and the world.

Kaiser Wilhelm II's story vividly illustrates the dangers of ignoring Rule Two. By failing to make thoughtful, value-driven decisions, Wilhelm II allowed impulsivity and unchecked ambition to dictate his actions, leading to devastating outcomes. His legacy serves as a cautionary tale, reminding us that choices made without reflection or responsibility can shape history in profoundly negative ways.

Rule Three: Take Personal Responsibility for Life's Direction

"I am not a product of my circumstances. I am a product of my decisions."
—**Yemisi Edun,** summarizing the ideas of
Stephen R. Covey, *The Guardian*

It is tempting to believe that our lives are shaped by circumstances beyond our control—external events, other people's actions, or sheer luck. While circumstances play a role, this perspective often leads to passivity and frustration. Rule Three reminds us that our happiness, success, and growth are determined more by our decisions and actions than by external forces. Taking responsibility for life's direction empowers us to actively shape our path with intention and purpose. To embrace personal responsibility, we must take the following steps:

1. **Take ownership of our circumstances:** Blaming others or external factors keeps us stuck. Acknowledging ourselves as the architects of our lives shifts our focus to solutions and fosters a sense of control.
2. **Engage in honest self-reflection:** Assessing how past decisions have shaped our current circumstances helps us identify areas for growth, set intentional goals, and make deliberate changes.
3. **Harness our inner strengths:** Recognizing the power of small, consistent actions aligned with our values enables us to create meaningful progress toward our aspirations.
4. **Focus on what we can control:** By directing energy toward what we can influence and accepting what we cannot, we foster resilience, uncover valuable lessons, and grow stronger.

Rule Three emphasizes that our decisions—not external circumstances—determine the quality and direction of our lives. By adopting a proactive mindset, reflecting on our journey, and focusing on what we can control, we actively shape a life aligned with our values, aspirations, and purpose.

EXAMPLE 1: CHRIS GARDNER (1954–)

Born in Milwaukee, Wisconsin, Chris Gardner grew up in poverty and instability. By the early 1980s, he found himself homeless while raising his young son alone. Nights spent in shelters, subway stations, and public restrooms became his reality. Despite these overwhelming challenges, Gardner made a pivotal decision: He would take full responsibility for creating a better future for himself and his son.

While working odd jobs to survive, Gardner discovered the world of finance and saw an opportunity to change his circumstances. With no guarantees of success, he enrolled in a competitive training program for stockbrokers. Juggling single parenthood, long working hours, and the emotional toll of homelessness, Gardner's determination and focus on his goals became the driving forces behind his transformation.

In 1987, after years of relentless effort, Gardner founded his own brokerage firm, Gardner Rich & Co., in Chicago. His story, later adapted into the critically acclaimed movie *The Pursuit of Happyness*, became a symbol of perseverance and determination.

Chris Gardner's life vividly illustrates Rule Three. By taking personal responsibility for his life's direction, Gardner demonstrated how intentional decisions and actions can transform even the most challenging circumstances. His journey reminds us that personal responsibility, paired with determination and resilience, is a powerful tool for shaping a meaningful and fulfilling future.

EXAMPLE 2: ELIZABETH HOLMES (1984–)

Elizabeth Holmes, born in Washington, DC, grew up in a well-connected family that nurtured her ambitious nature. At just nineteen, she founded Theranos, a company she claimed would revolutionize healthcare with groundbreaking blood-testing technology. Her vision captivated investors and the media, propelling Theranos to a valuation of $9 billion and making Holmes one of the youngest self-made billionaires.

Behind the scenes, however, Theranos's technology was deeply flawed. Employees raised concerns, but Holmes dismissed them, insisting on secrecy and continued growth. As failures mounted, she faced a critical choice: to confront the truth about Theranos's capabilities or double down on deception. Holmes chose the latter, promoting the technology publicly and raising millions in additional funding while knowing the devices could not deliver accurate results.

By 2015, whistleblowers and investigations exposed the extent of the fraud. Patients received incorrect diagnoses, investors lost millions, and Theranos collapsed under regulatory scrutiny. Holmes was charged with defrauding investors and, in 2024, was sentenced to over eleven years in prison. Her actions not only destroyed her career but also eroded trust in Silicon Valley startups, raising concerns about ethical failures in leadership.

Elizabeth Holmes's story vividly illustrates the dangers of ignoring Rule Three. By refusing to take responsibility for Theranos's failures, she prioritized ambition over accountability, betraying trust and ethical principles. Her downfall serves as a cautionary tale, showing that true leadership requires owning one's actions and aligning them with integrity. Without personal responsibility, even the most promising visions can crumble, leaving a legacy of failure and regret.

Rule Four: Master Your Emotions

"You have power over your mind—not outside events. Understand this, and you will find strength."

—**Marcus Aurelius,** *Meditations*

Our emotions shape how we perceive and respond to life's challenges. While they offer valuable insights, unmanaged emotions can cloud judgment and lead to impulsive actions. Mastering emotions means gaining control over our internal responses, enabling thoughtful decisions aligned with our values and long-term goals.

Emotional mastery begins with self-awareness. Recognizing that emotions often stem from internal conflicts helps us understand their roots and view them as signals pointing to deeper issues. Certain emotions, if left unchecked, can distort judgment:

- **Fear** amplifies challenges, leading to overreaction or paralysis. For example, fearing failure might prevent us from pursuing meaningful opportunities.
- **Anger** disrupts logical thinking, prompting hasty decisions. In a conflict, reacting out of anger may damage relationships rather than resolving issues constructively.
- **Joy** may blind us to risks or cause us to neglect responsibilities, such as overspending after a financial windfall.
- **Impatience** accelerates decision-making, often sacrificing better solutions, like rushing a project and compromising quality.

To manage emotions constructively, we can apply mindfulness, self-reflection, and deliberate action. Techniques like deep breathing ground fear, reflection tempers anger, gratitude balances joy, and patience counters impulsiveness. By aligning emotional responses with our principles, we cultivate resilience, strengthen relationships, and lead a life of intentionality.

Rule Four underscores that mastering emotions is essential for personal growth. By managing our internal responses thoughtfully, we ensure that emotions guide us toward growth and fulfillment rather than control us, empowering us to navigate life with strength, composure, and purpose.

EXAMPLE 1: LEE KUAN YEW (1923–2015) AND THE 1964 RACE RIOTS

Lee Kuan Yew, the founding father of modern Singapore, is celebrated for transforming the nation from a small port city into a global economic hub. After qualifying as a barrister at Cambridge, he became Singapore's first prime minister in 1959. His leadership emphasized multiracialism, meritocracy, and strict public order, principles that shaped the nation's stability and success.

In 1964, race riots between the Chinese and Malay communities erupted, threatening Singapore's fragile unity. Fear and anger gripped the streets as violent clashes left dozens dead and hundreds injured. Amid the chaos, Lee Kuan Yew faced immense pressure to act decisively. Despite the volatile situation, he displayed exceptional emotional mastery. In a televised address, Lee spoke directly to the nation, urging calm and unity. His tone was composed yet resolute, balancing empathy for the fear and anger in the communities with firmness to restore order.

Lee implemented immediate measures to stabilize the situation, such as curfews and security deployments, while initiating policies to address the underlying causes of the unrest. He promoted integrated housing and education initiatives to foster long-term racial harmony. By mastering his own fear and maintaining composure under pressure, Lee turned a volatile crisis into an opportunity to strengthen Singapore's commitment to unity and progress.

Lee Kuan Yew's leadership during the 1964 race riots vividly illustrates Rule Four. By mastering his emotions, he transformed fear and anger into constructive action, ensuring stability during a moment of crisis. His ability to align his responses with long-term goals and values demonstrates the importance of emotional control in effective leadership. Lee's story underscores that mastering emotions enables us to lead with strength, clarity, and purpose, even in the most challenging circumstances.

EXAMPLE 2: MAXIMILIEN ROBESPIERRE (1758–1794)

Maximilien Robespierre, a prominent leader of the French Revolution, initially gained recognition for his advocacy for the poor and opposition to the death penalty. However, as the revolution intensified, Robespierre's leadership became increasingly authoritarian. By 1793, during the Reign of Terror—a period marked by mass executions and extreme measures to eliminate perceived enemies of the revolution—Robespierre played a central role in shaping its policies.

Robespierre's unchecked emotions, particularly fear and paranoia, clouded his judgment and led to increasingly oppressive decisions. Convinced that dissent posed an existential threat to the revolution, he justified mass executions as necessary to protect its ideals. His paranoia escalated further as he began suspecting close allies of betrayal, ordering their executions despite a lack of evidence. These decisions alienated his supporters, deepened public discontent, and created an atmosphere of widespread fear.

As opposition grew, Robespierre refused to moderate his approach, believing harsher measures were the only path to revolutionary success. His emotional instability culminated in his arrest and execution on July 28, 1794, marking the end of the Reign of Terror. His inability to master his fear and paranoia not only led to his downfall but also caused immense suffering and upheaval across French society.

Robespierre's story vividly illustrates the dangers of failing to master emotions like fear and paranoia. His inability to control these emotions turned revolutionary ideals into tyranny, leading to destructive decisions with catastrophic consequences. His downfall underscores Rule Four's message: Mastering emotions is essential for rational decision-making and sustainable leadership, as emotional instability can lead to chaos, suffering, and personal ruin.

Rule Five: Be Aware of the Roots of Your Aggression and Arrogance

"No one is arrogant except out of humiliation he finds within himself."
—commonly attributed to Al-Ahnaf ibn Qays

Aggression and arrogance often appear as displays of strength or confidence. Yet, they frequently stem from deeper emotional struggles, such as insecurity or past humiliation. These behaviors often serve as overcompensations, masking inner fears with exaggerated responses. While they may offer temporary relief, they harm relationships, erode trust, and hinder meaningful communication.

Conversely, when we feel secure and grounded, our behavior becomes more positive, empathetic, and constructive.

To address these tendencies, we must look inward to uncover their origins. Recognizing triggers and patterns of insecurity is the first step toward meaningful change. By practicing humility, mindfulness, and empathy—along with techniques explored in this book—we can shift from defensive reactions to thoughtful responses. These practices nurture self-awareness and emotional balance, fostering authentic confidence and well-being.

Rule Five encourages us to confront the emotional roots of aggression and arrogance with introspection and kindness. By cultivating humility and empathy, we transform defensive behaviors into constructive actions, strengthening our relationships and unlocking deeper personal growth.

EXAMPLE 1: ADOLF HITLER (1889–1945)

Adolf Hitler, born in Braunau am Inn, Austria, rose to power as the führer of Nazi Germany, channeling early personal failures into an authoritarian and destructive leadership style. His strict upbringing under an abusive father and his repeated rejection by the Vienna Academy of Fine Arts left him with deep feelings of inadequacy and humiliation. These personal struggles, combined with the national humiliation Germany faced after World War I, fueled his aggressive personality and domineering ambitions. Hitler found solace in extreme nationalist ideologies, which reinforced his belief in racial superiority and the need for control and dominance.

As chancellor from 1933 and later as führer, Hitler's unchecked aggression and arrogance led to catastrophic decisions. He initiated World War II, seeking territorial expansion, and orchestrated the Holocaust, driven by his obsessive pursuit of racial purity. Rather than addressing his insecurities constructively, Hitler masked his vulnerabilities with authoritarianism and violence. His refusal to confront the emotional roots of his aggression and arrogance resulted in unimaginable suffering, devastating millions of lives and leaving a scar on global history.

Adolf Hitler's life vividly illustrates Rule Five. His failure to address the roots of his aggression and arrogance—stemming from personal humiliation and insecurity—demonstrates the catastrophic consequences of unexamined emotions. Hitler's story underscores the critical importance of resolving internal struggles, particularly for those in positions of power. Without self-awareness and emotional balance, unchecked aggression and arrogance can lead to destructive decisions that harm both individuals and society.

EXAMPLE 2: HARVEY WEINSTEIN (1952–)

Born in Queens, New York, Harvey Weinstein grew up in a modest, middle-class family. Alongside his brother Bob, he cofounded Miramax in 1979, a company named after their parents, Miriam and Max. The company rose to prominence by producing critically acclaimed films like *Pulp Fiction*, *Shakespeare in Love*, and *Good Will Hunting*. Weinstein's influence shaped the careers of countless actors and filmmakers, cementing his reputation as one of Hollywood's most powerful producers.

Beneath his professional success, however, lay a pattern of abusive behavior fueled by a need to assert control and dominance. Reports in 2017 revealed decades of sexual harassment, assault, and exploitation, exposing deep insecurities and emotional struggles that drove his actions. Weinstein often wielded his power to intimidate and manipulate others, masking his vulnerabilities behind displays of aggression and arrogance. His unchecked behavior created a toxic environment that silenced victims and enabled systemic abuse in the entertainment industry.

By 2020, Weinstein's actions caught up with him. Convicted of two felonies and sentenced to twenty-three years in prison, his dramatic fall from grace became a symbol of the consequences of unchecked aggression and arrogance. His downfall sparked the #MeToo movement, prompting global conversations about accountability and abuse of power.

Harvey Weinstein's story vividly illustrates Rule Five. His failure to address the emotional roots of his aggression and arrogance led to destructive behaviors that harmed others and destroyed his career. Weinstein's life underscores the importance of self-awareness, humility, and emotional balance in preventing harm and preserving integrity. True strength lies not in exploiting power but in confronting and resolving internal struggles constructively.

Rule Six: Conquer Your Inner Enemy

"The only enemy you have to deal with is yourself. If you can conquer yourself, no external force can harm you."

—inspired by an African proverb

In life, we often perceive external challenges as our greatest obstacles, blaming circumstances or others for our struggles. Yet the real battle lies within. Our doubts, fears, and negative thoughts often limit our potential for growth and happiness. Conquering these inner enemies requires intentional effort, self-awareness, and resilience. To master our inner conflicts, we can take the following steps:

1. **Identify negative patterns:** Through introspection, we uncover recurring thoughts or behaviors that hold us back. Recognizing triggers, such as self-doubt, allows us to take deliberate steps toward transformation.
2. **Replace negative thoughts:** Reframing negativity with affirmations like "I'll learn something valuable" instead of "I'll fail" rewires our mindset and fosters confidence.
3. **Confront fears gradually:** Facing fears incrementally—like practicing speeches in small groups before addressing larger audiences—reduces their power and builds courage over time.
4. **Regulate emotions:** Mindfulness and meditation help us manage emotions, allowing thoughtful responses instead of impulsive reactions during moments of frustration or anxiety.
5. **Reframe failure:** Viewing setbacks as opportunities for growth strengthens resilience. For example, seeing rejection as a stepping stone to improvement fosters perseverance.

By mastering these inner struggles, we cultivate peace, clarity, and self-confidence. Inner mastery empowers us to navigate external challenges with composure, make thoughtful decisions, and enhance overall satisfaction in life.

Rule Six reminds us that our most significant battles are within ourselves. By recognizing and addressing our inner fears, doubts, and conflicts, we unlock our potential for growth and fulfillment. This mastery transforms how we perceive challenges and engage with the world, leading to a life of clarity, balance, and purpose.

EXAMPLE 1: WINSTON CHURCHILL (1874–1965)

Winston Churchill, the United Kingdom's celebrated prime minister during World War II, became a symbol of resilience and determination during one of history's darkest periods. Behind his commanding public presence, however, Churchill fought a private battle with depression, which he referred to as his "black dog." This struggle was particularly intense during the Blitz, when relentless bombings devastated London and tested his leadership. Despite his internal turmoil, Churchill maintained composure, delivering stirring speeches that inspired hope and unity among the British people.

Churchill's ability to lead while confronting his inner struggles was rooted in self-awareness and emotional management. He found solace in creative pursuits like painting and writing, which allowed him to process his emotions and regain clarity. These activities were not mere distractions but essential tools for channeling his inner conflicts into constructive action. By acknowledging his emotions rather than suppressing them, Churchill transformed personal challenges into sources of strength and resilience, enabling him to guide the nation with unwavering resolve.

Winston Churchill's story vividly illustrates Rule Six: Conquering inner conflicts is critical to achieving external success. By addressing his struggles with self-awareness and constructive action, Churchill demonstrated that resilience and emotional mastery enable us to face external challenges with courage and purpose. His leadership during wartime serves as a timeless reminder that mastering our inner enemies transforms adversity into strength and clarity.

EXAMPLE 2: STEFAN ZWEIG (1881–1942)

Stefan Zweig, born in Vienna, Austria, rose to international fame as one of the most celebrated writers of the 1920s and 1930s. As a Jewish intellectual, Zweig fled Austria in 1934 to escape the rise of Nazism, leaving behind his homeland and cultural roots. Though he found temporary refuge in England, the United States, and finally Brazil, his sense of displacement and the horrors of World War II weighed heavily on him. In exile, his writings became darker, reflecting the anguish of losing his identity and witnessing the destruction of Europe. Zweig described himself as "a man without a homeland," revealing the depth of his inner turmoil.

Despite his literary acclaim, Zweig struggled to confront the despair caused by his exile and the global chaos. Isolated and consumed by hopelessness, he and his wife, Lotte, tragically took their own lives in Petrópolis, Brazil, on February 22, 1942. Instead of addressing his despair through self-reflection or seeking support, Zweig allowed his inner conflicts to overwhelm him, leading to his tragic decision. His inability to master his inner struggles turned the chaos around him into an insurmountable burden.

Stefan Zweig's story vividly illustrates Rule Six: Conquering inner enemies is essential for navigating life's challenges. His failure to confront his despair and find emotional resilience highlights the critical importance of self-awareness and inner strength. Zweig's life serves as a poignant reminder that inner peace and clarity are indispensable for overcoming external adversities and achieving personal fulfillment.

Rule Seven: Be Aware That Your Suffering and Pain Create Your Values and Experiences

"The wound is the place where the light enters you."

—commonly attributed to Rumi

In life, suffering and pain are not merely obstacles—they are profound teachers that shape our values, deepen our understanding of life, and fuel personal growth. Pain pushes us beyond our comfort zones, challenging us to confront fears and insecurities. These moments of struggle reveal the strength of our values, providing clarity about who we are and what we stand for. Through self-reflection, pain enhances self-awareness, helping us cultivate a more defined sense of self.

Suffering also cultivates resilience and empathy. By navigating hardships, we discover our inner fortitude and develop a greater capacity for compassion. These experiences deepen our relationships and heighten our appreciation for life's joys, creating a richer, more meaningful existence.

Embracing pain is essential for transforming it into wisdom and strength. This requires introspection, resilience, and a willingness to learn from challenges. By confronting struggles directly and exploring their roots, we convert hardships into opportunities for growth, self-improvement, and personal development.

Rule Seven reminds us that our most challenging moments hold the potential for profound self-discovery. By confronting and embracing pain, we unlock deeper wisdom, compassion, and resilience, enriching our journey and empowering us to navigate life's complexities with strength and empathy.

EXAMPLE 1: ALBERT CAMUS (1913–1960)

Albert Camus, the celebrated French-Algerian philosopher, author, and journalist, was born into poverty in Mondovi (now Dréan), Algeria. His father's death during World War I left his mother, a partially deaf housekeeper, to raise him in a working-class neighborhood. This profound loss, coupled with financial hardship, instilled in Camus an acute awareness of life's fragility. At age seventeen, he was diagnosed with tuberculosis, forcing him to abandon his passion for football and confront his physical limitations. These experiences deeply shaped his understanding of adversity and the human condition.

Rather than succumbing to despair, Camus used his suffering as a catalyst for transformation. Poverty taught him resilience and the value of perseverance, while his illness pushed him to confront the absurdity of life—the tension between humanity's search for meaning and the indifference of the universe. This philosophy of absurdism became central to his works. In *The Stranger* (1942), he examines the struggle to find purpose in a chaotic world, and in *The Plague* (1947), he celebrates solidarity and the courage to act in the face of suffering. Camus's involvement in the French Resistance during World War II further exemplified his ability to channel personal pain into action, fighting against oppression to uphold his values of justice and freedom.

Albert Camus's life vividly illustrates Rule Seven. By confronting his suffering with reflection and courage, he transformed adversity into wisdom, shaping his values and philosophical contributions. Camus's ability to turn personal pain into universal truths demonstrates that suffering is not merely an obstacle—it is a teacher that fosters resilience, clarity, and purpose. His journey reminds us that by embracing our struggles, we can uncover deeper meaning and create a legacy of growth and insight.

EXAMPLE 2: INGVAR KAMPRAD (1926–2018)

Ingvar Kamprad, born in Småland, Sweden, grew up in a rural farming community where financial hardship was a way of life. Witnessing the struggles of hardworking families who could not afford quality furniture deeply influenced his values of simplicity, practicality, and service. At seventeen, Kamprad founded IKEA with a vision of making stylish, functional furniture affordable for everyone. However, his entrepreneurial journey faced significant challenges.

In the 1950s, IKEA encountered a boycott from established Swedish furniture retailers, who pressured suppliers to sever ties with Kamprad. To overcome this obstacle, he drew inspiration from a colleague who removed the legs of a table to fit it into his car. This observation led to the idea of flat-pack furniture, a concept that reduced production and transportation costs while allowing customers to assemble the products themselves. This innovation not only solved the supply chain issues but also transformed the global furniture industry.

Kamprad later reflected, "Adversity creates innovation." His struggles, from rural poverty to supplier challenges, instilled in him resilience, creativity, and a commitment to serving others. These hardships became the foundation for IKEA's core values of affordability, accessibility, and sustainability.

Ingvar Kamprad's story vividly illustrates Rule Seven. By addressing adversity with ingenuity and determination, he transformed challenges into groundbreaking innovations that shaped IKEA's success. Kamprad's ability to turn obstacles into opportunities highlights how hardships can strengthen values, foster growth, and drive meaningful change.

Rule Eight: Mind Your Mind as a Garden

"I will not let anyone walk through my mind with their dirty feet."
—commonly attributed to Mahatma Gandhi

Our minds, much like gardens, thrive when tended with care. Each day, we encounter various influences—conversations, media, and experiences—that act like seeds in our mental soil. Positive influences plant enriching thoughts, while negative ones sow weeds that hinder growth. Cultivating a healthy mental environment requires consistent effort through the following practices:

- **Selective exposure:** Choose uplifting content and interactions, much like selecting the healthiest seeds for a thriving garden.
- **Regular reflection:** Dedicate time to identify and address negative thoughts, ensuring they don't take root, much like regularly weeding a garden.
- **Constructive engagement:** Approach challenges as opportunities for growth, enriching your mental space rather than overwhelming it.
- **Balanced information intake:** Strike a balance between staying informed and protecting your mental well-being,

much like providing plants with the right amount of water and sunlight.

These practices are essential for cultivating a resilient and productive mind. Just as gardens flourish with attentive care, our minds thrive when nurtured with positive influences and shielded from negativity.

Rule Eight reminds us to treat our minds with intentional care, fostering resilience, clarity, and growth. By curating the influences we allow in and nurturing positive thoughts, we create a mental environment that empowers us to grow, adapt, and thrive in all aspects of life.

EXAMPLE 1: SUSAN WOJCICKI (1968–2024)

Susan Wojcicki, as the CEO of YouTube, played a pivotal role in shaping the global digital media landscape. Beyond growing the platform into a global powerhouse, Wojcicki recognized the profound psychological influence digital content has on its users. She often compared YouTube's vast library to a garden, where the content acts as seeds planted in the minds of viewers. This analogy shaped her leadership philosophy: to cultivate a digital ecosystem that could inspire growth while preventing the spread of harmful weeds.

Under her leadership, YouTube faced significant challenges in balancing creativity with responsibility. Viral conspiracy theories, harmful trends, and misinformation threatened to erode trust and disrupt society. In response, Wojcicki championed initiatives to combat harmful content. For example, during the COVID-19 pandemic, she prioritized elevating credible sources like the WHO and CDC while combating misinformation about treatments and vaccines. She also launched campaigns promoting educational content, ensuring YouTube became a space for learning and empowerment.

Despite facing criticism for content moderation and concerns over free speech, Wojcicki remained steadfast. She believed in the need for mindful curation to protect users' mental well-being without stifling creativity. She encouraged creators to contribute positively, fostering a community rooted in inspiration, learning, and empathy.

Susan Wojcicki's leadership vividly illustrates Rule Eight. By intentionally curating content to promote positive influences and address harmful ones, she demonstrated the transformative power of tending to the mental garden. Her vision for a healthier digital ecosystem reminds us that curating what we consume shapes our thoughts, decisions, and emotional well-being. Wojcicki's approach teaches us that cultivating a flourishing mental environment requires vigilance, empathy, and action.

EXAMPLE 2: SOCIAL MEDIA CHALLENGES

Social media, with its vast reach and influence, has transformed how people connect, learn, and express themselves. Yet, it has also become fertile ground for harmful influences that can overwhelm mental well-being. For many young users, constant exposure to viral trends like body image filters, validation-seeking behaviors, and harmful ideologies is like planting weeds in their mental garden—content that distracts, distorts, and diminishes emotional health.

For instance, the widespread use of filters promoting unattainable beauty standards has fueled self-esteem issues, leaving many to question their worth and identity. Validation through likes and shares often becomes a substitute for authentic self-expression, creating anxiety and a constant need for external approval. Similarly, viral conspiracy theories or divisive political content can cloud judgment, replacing clarity and understanding with confusion and mistrust. Over time, these unchecked influences dominate mental space, leaving little room for positive or growth-oriented thoughts to flourish.

The mental toll of unfiltered digital engagement reflects the dangers of neglecting Rule Eight. Without vigilance, harmful content can overshadow constructive influences, much like weeds overtaking an untended garden. Participants in these trends often prioritize instant gratification and external validation over introspection and emotional balance, reinforcing unhealthy habits and distorting values.

The prevalence of these harmful digital trends vividly illustrates the consequences of failing to adhere to Rule Eight. By neglecting to curate the mental garden, users allow negativity to take root, fostering clutter and diminishing resilience. Rule Eight reminds us that by consciously removing harmful influences and nurturing positive content, we can cultivate mental clarity, self-esteem, and emotional well-being, ensuring that digital engagement enriches rather than erodes us.

Rule Nine: You Can't Give What You Don't Have

"You cannot pour from an empty cup. You must fill your own cup first."

—Unknown

In life, we often prioritize others—our family, friends, and colleagues—while neglecting our own needs. Rule Nine reminds us that supporting and uplifting others begins with nurturing ourselves. Without self-awareness and intentional care, our contributions lack the energy and authenticity needed to create a meaningful impact.

Self-care is not an indulgence—it is a foundation for meaningful relationships and effective support. When we are emotionally or mentally depleted, we cannot offer genuine empathy or guidance. Just as a tree provides shade only when its roots are nourished, we can only uplift others when we cultivate inner strength through self-care.

Self-reflection is central to this process. Examining our emotions, needs, and limitations allows us to identify areas for growth. Practices such as mindfulness, journaling, and engaging in activities that nurture mental, emotional, and physical well-being—like exercise, meditation, and creative pursuits—replenish our inner resources. These practices ensure we give with authenticity, purpose, and meaning.

Rule Nine teaches us that filling our own cup is not an act of indulgence but a responsibility. By nurturing ourselves, we create the strength, empathy, and clarity needed to build meaningful relationships. This process transforms our connections, enabling us to give from a place of abundance rather than depletion.

EXAMPLE 1: SATYA NADELLA (1967–)

Satya Nadella, who became CEO of Microsoft in 2014, is widely credited with transforming the company's culture and steering it toward unprecedented growth. However, the roots of his empathetic leadership style trace back to a deeply personal experience: the birth of his son Zain, who was diagnosed with cerebral palsy. This life-altering event reshaped Nadella's worldview, teaching him patience, understanding, and the importance of compassion. Caring for Zain was not just a personal challenge—it was a journey that required him to confront his own frustrations and cultivate resilience. These qualities became the foundation of his leadership philosophy.

Nadella often reflected on how supporting Zain helped him understand the value of empathy. This transformation was evident in his leadership at Microsoft, where he focused on building a more inclusive and collaborative culture. He championed accessibility in Microsoft's products, ensuring they addressed the needs of all users, including those with disabilities. For example, Nadella oversaw the development of tools like Immersive Reader and AI-driven accessibility features, inspired by his desire to make technology empowering for everyone. His efforts extended to reshaping Microsoft's workplace culture, encouraging teams to adopt a growth mindset and prioritize inclusion.

Satya Nadella's journey vividly illustrates Rule Nine. By embracing self-reflection and growth, he cultivated the qualities of empathy, resilience, and patience within himself, enabling him to lead authentically and meaningfully. His story reminds us that we cannot uplift or empower others without first nurturing these qualities within ourselves. Nadella's leadership demonstrates that personal growth is the foundation of authentic influence and impactful change.

EXAMPLE 2: TRAVIS KALANICK (1976–)

Travis Kalanick, cofounder of Uber, was instrumental in building the company into a global ride-sharing giant. Under his leadership, Uber revolutionized the transportation industry, achieving rapid growth and becoming synonymous with innovation. However, Kalanick's aggressive leadership style, coupled with a lack of emotional intelligence and self-awareness, created a culture of toxicity and controversy that jeopardized the company's success.

Kalanick's approach to leadership prioritized relentless growth and competitiveness over empathy and accountability. For example, in a widely publicized incident in 2017, a video emerged of Kalanick arguing with an Uber driver who criticized the company's fare policies. Instead of addressing the driver's concerns with empathy, Kalanick responded defensively, revealing a lack of emotional regulation. This incident became a symbol of Uber's broader issues under his leadership—an environment where workplace misconduct, sexual harassment, and discriminatory practices went unchecked.

Despite numerous warnings and public criticism, Kalanick resisted making meaningful changes. His inability to reflect on his leadership failures and address the needs of employees fostered distrust and alienation. By prioritizing short-term gains over long-term well-being, Kalanick allowed a toxic culture to take root, ultimately forcing his resignation as CEO in 2017 amid mounting scandals.

Travis Kalanick's story vividly illustrates the dangers of failing to adhere to Rule Nine. By neglecting to cultivate qualities like empathy, humility, and accountability within himself, Kalanick was unable to lead authentically or inspire trust. His downfall serves as a cautionary tale, reminding us that sustainable leadership and meaningful influence begin with self-awareness, personal growth, and alignment with core values. Without these, we risk eroding trust and undermining our ability to support and uplift others.

Rule Ten: Adopt a Playful Attitude in Life

"Life is far too important a thing ever to talk seriously about it."
—Oscar Wilde, *Lord Darlington*

In the pursuit of success and responsibility, we often overlook life's beauty and wonder. Rule Ten reminds us to embrace a playful attitude, where joy, curiosity, and spontaneity are essential elements of a meaningful life. A playful spirit reconnects us with our sense of wonder, shifting our focus from material achievements to the richness of experiences and relationships that truly define us.

A playful attitude fosters resilience and creativity. When we approach challenges with curiosity and humor, setbacks transform into opportunities for growth. Failure becomes a teacher, encouraging creative risks without fear of judgment. Playfulness also reduces stress and nurtures deeper connections—shared laughter can bridge divides, cultivate trust, and foster mutual respect.

Adopting a playful attitude does not mean trivializing responsibilities; rather, it involves approaching life with balance. Everyday problems—like misunderstandings or work setbacks—can be reframed as puzzles or adventures, encouraging creativity and adaptability. Meanwhile, deeper adversities, such as loss or failure, remind us to find lightness, explore possibilities, and embrace moments of growth amid hardship. Rediscovering joy in simple pleasures—such as storytelling, art, or time spent in nature—helps us stay connected to life's wonder, even in difficult times.

Rule Ten teaches us that while life demands responsibility, it is also meant to be savored. By embracing playfulness, we enrich our lives, inspire others, and transform how we grow, connect, and leave a lasting impact on the world.

EXAMPLE 1: RICHARD BRANSON (1950–)

Richard Branson, the celebrated founder of the Virgin Group, built his life and career on a foundation of curiosity, joy, and adventure. From launching Virgin Records in 1972 to pioneering space tourism with Virgin Galactic, Branson consistently approached challenges with a sense of playfulness. For him, life was more than a series of responsibilities—it was an exciting journey to explore and innovate.

Branson's playful attitude was not limited to business but defined how he faced challenges. In the early days of Virgin Atlantic, he personally drove a truck to deliver fuel when suppliers pulled out, using humor and determination to rally his team during a crisis. His daring exploits—like crossing oceans in hot air balloons—were not mere stunts but reflections of his belief that risk and playfulness fuel creativity and resilience. Even when ventures like Virgin Cola and Virgin Brides failed, Branson approached them with humor and curiosity, viewing these setbacks as opportunities to learn and refine his vision.

This mindset extended to the Virgin Group's workplace culture. Branson described business as "fun" and fostered an environment where creativity thrived. He encouraged his teams to take risks and collaborate openly, building trust and camaraderie through shared laughter and moments of joy. His playful leadership inspired innovation, turning challenges into stepping stones for growth.

Richard Branson's journey vividly illustrates Rule Ten: Adopting a playful attitude transforms challenges into opportunities, fuels creativity, and enriches life. Branson's story reminds us that by embracing curiosity, humor, and joy, we can navigate adversity with resilience, foster deeper connections, and uncover life's boundless possibilities.

EXAMPLE 2: SHONDA RHIMES (1970–)

Shonda Rhimes, the acclaimed creator of *Grey's Anatomy* and *Scandal*, transformed her life in 2014 with her "Year of Yes." This journey began during a family Thanksgiving dinner when her sister remarked that Rhimes rarely said yes to new opportunities. Struck by this observation, Rhimes reflected on how fear and routine had shaped her life, keeping her from embracing possibilities. Determined to change, she resolved to say yes to everything that intimidated her for an entire year.

Throughout this transformative period, Rhimes approached life with curiosity and openness, stepping far outside her comfort zone. She accepted public speaking engagements despite her fear, appeared in interviews she had long avoided, and even tried acting in a cameo role. Each "yes" became an adventure, reframing challenges as opportunities to grow and explore. One of the most defining moments came when she delivered a commencement address at Dartmouth College—a daunting experience that she later described as empowering and life-changing.

Rhimes's playful attitude toward fear and uncertainty reshaped her life. By adopting a mindset of curiosity and joy, she discovered newfound confidence, deepened her relationships, and expanded her professional horizons. Her willingness to embrace discomfort turned anxiety into empowerment, transforming life's obstacles into stepping stones for growth.

Shonda Rhimes's story vividly illustrates Rule Ten: A playful attitude invites growth, fosters resilience, and enriches life's experiences. By saying yes to life's possibilities, Rhimes transformed how she lived, worked, and connected with others. Her journey reminds us that approaching challenges with curiosity and openness leads to profound personal growth and a richer, more joyful life.

Rule Eleven: Don't Undermine the Impact of Small Actions

"Great things are not done by impulse, but
by a series of small things brought together."
—Vincent van Gogh, 1882 letter to Theo van Gogh

In a world that often glorifies grand gestures, we may overlook the quiet power of small actions. Rule Eleven reminds us that greatness is not born from singular moments but from countless small choices and deeds. Each small action—however insignificant it may seem—becomes a thread in the fabric of our lives and the world around us.

The butterfly effect, rooted in chaos theory, illustrates how minor actions can lead to profound outcomes. A kind word or a simple smile might seem trivial, yet these gestures can spark a chain reaction of positivity. The law of significance further teaches us that every contribution, no matter how small, holds value. Like brushstrokes in a masterpiece, our minor efforts collectively create the larger picture of our lives and society.

This perspective challenges us to rethink how we view our everyday choices. Small actions—checking in on a loved one, lending a helping hand, or expressing gratitude—build trust, deepen relationships, and foster a culture of kindness. They remind us that we hold the power to create meaningful change, one choice at a time.

Rule Eleven teaches us that small actions are not insignificant—they are foundational. By acting with intention, we embrace our role as architects of positive change. Each choice we make contributes to a greater whole, creating ripples of care and compassion that extend far beyond what we can see.

EXAMPLE 1: ROSA PARKS (1913–2005)

Rosa Parks, born in Tuskegee, Alabama, grew up witnessing the harsh realities of racial segregation. Her early experiences instilled in her a quiet resolve to challenge systemic injustice. On December 1, 1955, after a long day of work as a seamstress, Parks boarded a segregated bus in Montgomery, Alabama, and sat in the "colored" section. When ordered to give up her seat to a white passenger, Parks calmly but firmly refused.

This seemingly small act of defiance led to her arrest, but its impact reverberated far beyond that moment. Parks's decision, though deeply personal, became the spark for the Montgomery Bus Boycott, a 381-day protest led by Dr. Martin Luther King Jr. The boycott mobilized an entire community, highlighting the power of collective action and challenging the legality of segregation laws. Ultimately, it resulted in a Supreme Court ruling that declared bus segregation unconstitutional, marking a pivotal victory in the civil rights movement.

Rosa Parks's story vividly illustrates Rule Eleven: Her small yet courageous act of defiance created ripples that transformed history. Parks reminds us that even the simplest actions, when driven by purpose and conviction, can inspire collective change. Her journey demonstrates that no gesture is too small to make a difference, proving that every choice we make holds the potential to shape a better world.

EXAMPLE 2: GRETA THUNBERG (2003–)

Greta Thunberg, born in Stockholm, Sweden, developed a deep concern for the environment from a young age. After learning about climate change in school, she became profoundly aware of the urgency to act. At just fifteen years old, Thunberg began skipping school every Friday to protest outside the Swedish Parliament, holding a handmade sign that read "*Skolstrejk för klimatet*" ("School Strike for Climate"). Her solitary act of defiance, though seemingly small, was driven by an unwavering belief in the power of individual action.

What began as a personal protest quickly captured the world's attention. Young people across the globe resonated with her message, sparking the Fridays for Future movement, which mobilized millions of students in school strikes and climate demonstrations. Thunberg's determination and authenticity inspired global conversations about the climate crisis. Her small action grew into a platform that took her to high-profile events, such as the United Nations Climate Action Summit, where her impassioned speeches challenged world leaders to take accountability for the planet's future.

Greta Thunberg's journey vividly illustrates Rule Eleven: Even the smallest actions, like holding a protest sign, can ignite movements that transform the world. Her story reminds us that individual acts, when rooted in conviction and purpose, can inspire others and drive collective change. Thunberg's resolve demonstrates that no gesture is too insignificant to spark profound ripples, proving that every small step we take has the potential to shape a better, more sustainable future.

Rule Twelve: Avoid the Trap of Numbers

"Not everything that is counted counts, and
not everything that counts can be counted."
—William Bruce Cameron, *Informal Sociology*

In a world that often equates success with measurable metrics—like wealth, grades, or social media followers—it is easy to fall into the trap of defining our worth by numbers. Rule Twelve reminds us that while numbers are helpful for setting goals, they are inherently impersonal and infinite. Pursuing numerical achievements without balancing them with deeper values can lead to stress, burnout, and feelings of inadequacy.

Consider a professional who relentlessly chases higher income but sacrifices relationships and personal growth along the way. Despite financial success, they may feel unfulfilled because the most meaningful aspects of life—like joy, connection, and purpose—cannot be quantified. Numbers may track progress, but they cannot measure meaning.

This rule does not dismiss the value of numbers; instead, it calls for balance. Numbers can guide us, but they are not the ultimate measure of success or happiness. For every quantitative goal, we can pair a qualitative one, such as fostering deeper relationships, improving work-life balance, or pursuing creative passions. These intangible achievements provide purpose and satisfaction that numbers alone cannot deliver.

Rule Twelve teaches us that true fulfillment comes from balancing quantitative goals with qualitative values. This perspective transforms how we view success, allowing us to celebrate life's richness beyond measurable milestones. By aligning our actions with deeper values, we ensure that our journey is defined by purpose, connection, and enduring well-being.

EXAMPLE 1: NARAYANAN KRISHNAN (1981–)

Narayanan Krishnan, born in Madurai, India, dreamed of excelling in the culinary world. After graduating from a prestigious hotel management institute, he secured a coveted position with Taj Hotels in Bangalore and was offered a lucrative opportunity in Switzerland. This career path promised financial success and global recognition. However, during a visit to his hometown in 2002, a single encounter profoundly changed his life.

Krishnan saw an elderly homeless man scavenging for food and eating his own waste. Overwhelmed with empathy, he realized that his professional aspirations could not compare to the immediate need to help those in despair. This pivotal moment forced him to rethink his definition of success, transforming his priorities from personal accolades to serving others.

In 2003, Krishnan founded Akshaya Trust, a nonprofit organization that began by preparing and serving meals to a handful of homeless people. Over time, the initiative grew, and today, Akshaya Trust provides hundreds of meals daily to the destitute and homeless in Madurai. Beyond feeding the hungry, Krishnan expanded the organization's mission to include bathing, grooming, and providing medical care for those living on the streets. His efforts restored dignity and hope to countless individuals who had been forgotten by society.

Krishnan's work has been recognized globally, inspiring others to re-evaluate their own definitions of success. Despite receiving numerous awards, he remains focused on the intangible rewards of his mission—the gratitude of those he serves and the fulfillment of knowing he has made a difference.

Narayanan Krishnan's story vividly illustrates Rule Twelve: He chose to measure success not by financial milestones but by the unquantifiable impact of his actions on others. His journey reminds us that true fulfillment lies in aligning our actions with values that cannot be measured by numbers. By prioritizing compassion over metrics, Krishnan demonstrated that a meaningful life is built on service, connection, and purpose, proving that small, intentional acts can create ripples of profound change.

EXAMPLE 2: MARTIN SHKRELI (1983–)

Martin Shkreli, the son of immigrant parents, grew up in Brooklyn, New York, displaying a sharp intellect and a talent for finance from an early age. By his twenties, he had entered the competitive world of hedge funds and pharmaceuticals, quickly earning recognition for his financial acumen. However, Shkreli's relentless focus on profit soon overshadowed any ethical considerations. As CEO of Turing Pharmaceuticals in 2015, he made headlines for increasing the price of Daraprim—a life-saving medication for patients with compromised immune systems—by over 5,000 percent.

The move maximized profits but sparked widespread outrage. Patients and healthcare providers decried the decision as exploitative, accusing Shkreli of prioritizing financial gains over human lives. The backlash extended beyond the pharmaceutical industry, with Shkreli earning the nickname "Pharma Bro" and becoming a symbol of corporate greed. His controversial behavior on social media, including flaunting wealth and mocking critics, further cemented his public image as someone consumed by measurable achievements like profit and recognition.

This obsession came at a steep cost. Investigations into his business practices uncovered fraudulent activities, leading to his conviction for securities fraud in 2017 and a seven-year prison sentence. Shkreli's pursuit of quantifiable success—profits, accolades, and wealth—blinded him to the values of integrity, empathy, and social responsibility. His actions not only destroyed his career and reputation but also harmed countless patients who relied on the medication he exploited for profit.

Martin Shkreli's story serves as a cautionary tale for Rule Twelve: His fixation on measurable achievements came at the expense of ethical values and meaningful impact. By prioritizing profit over integrity, he undermined trust and caused harm, proving that true success requires balancing numbers with values that benefit society. His story reminds us that a legacy defined by numbers alone is ultimately hollow and unsustainable.

Rule Thirteen: Stop Complaining

"Complaining is like a rocking chair: It gives you something to do, but it gets you nowhere."
—Unknown

In life, it is easy to fall into the habit of complaining when things don't go as planned. We may blame others, external circumstances, or even ourselves. Yet, Rule Thirteen reminds us that complaining is counterproductive—it drains our energy without changing the situation. Instead, by embracing constructive action and active acceptance, we can approach challenges with clarity and purpose.

Constructive action involves taking practical steps to address the source of a complaint. For instance, someone dissatisfied with their health or income could transform their frustration into motivation. Instead of lamenting the situation, they could set specific goals, such as adopting healthier habits or upskilling to pursue better opportunities. By focusing on what we can control, we turn complaints into progress, empowering ourselves to create meaningful change.

Active acceptance, on the other hand, applies to situations beyond our control. Consider someone grieving the loss of a loved one. Complaining about the unfairness of life cannot alter the reality, but choosing acceptance allows them to redirect their energy toward honoring the person's memory, finding support, or fostering gratitude for shared experiences. Acceptance brings peace, resilience, and the strength to move forward.

Rule Thirteen teaches us that letting go of unproductive complaining frees us to approach life with resilience and creativity. By prioritizing action and acceptance over blame, we empower ourselves to grow, strengthen relationships, and uncover opportunities for progress. True growth lies not in what happens to us, but in how we choose to respond.

EXAMPLE 1: NICK VUJICIC (1982–)

Nick Vujicic, born in Melbourne, Australia, with tetra-amelia syndrome, faced immense physical and emotional challenges growing up. Without arms or legs, everyday tasks like eating, writing, and moving required extraordinary effort. At school, bullying and isolation deepened his struggles, leaving him feeling powerless and alone. By his early teens, Vujicic battled depression, often questioning his purpose and the fairness of his circumstances.

A turning point came when Vujicic realized that while he could not change his condition, he could change his response to it. Inspired by his faith and the stories of others overcoming adversity, he shifted his mindset from one of frustration to one of purpose. He began focusing on what he could do rather than what he lacked. With determination, he learned to write, type, swim, and even surf. Each small victory reinforced his belief that challenges could be transformed into opportunities for growth.

This mindset propelled Vujicic to share his journey with others. He started speaking to small prayer groups and eventually addressed international audiences, inspiring millions with his message of hope and resilience. Through his organization, NickV Ministries, he continues to support individuals with disabilities, demonstrating that physical limitations do not define potential.

Nick Vujicic's journey vividly illustrates Rule Thirteen: Rather than dwelling on complaints about his condition, he chose to embrace acceptance and action. His life reminds us that by shifting from negativity to purpose, we can transform challenges into opportunities for growth and inspiration, proving that progress lies in how we respond to life's difficulties.

EXAMPLE 2: BOBBY FISCHER (1943–2008)

Bobby Fischer, widely regarded as one of the greatest chess players in history, became a global icon in 1972 when he defeated Boris Spassky to claim the World Chess Championship. Fischer's unmatched brilliance symbolized intellectual triumph during the Cold War. However, despite his extraordinary talent, Fischer's career and legacy were overshadowed by chronic complaints and unproductive grievances.

Even at the height of his success, Fischer became notorious for his criticisms of tournament conditions, including lighting, seating, and camera placement. While some concerns were valid, his combative and uncompromising approach alienated tournament organizers, sponsors, and supporters. Instead of seeking constructive solutions, Fischer fixated on grievances, creating unnecessary conflicts that strained his relationships within the chess community.

In 1975, Fischer refused to defend his world title, demanding changes to the World Chess Federation's (FIDE) rules that many deemed unreasonable. When his demands were not met, he forfeited the championship and withdrew from competitive chess. Over time, his isolation deepened, and his public appearances were dominated by conspiracy theories and bitter complaints about perceived mistreatment. Fischer's inability to let go of negativity ultimately tarnished his reputation and severed his ties with the very community that had once celebrated his brilliance.

Bobby Fischer's story vividly illustrates the dangers of failing to adhere to Rule Thirteen. By allowing chronic complaints to dominate his mindset, Fischer limited his opportunities and alienated those around him. His story serves as a cautionary tale, reminding us that unproductive negativity can overshadow even the greatest achievements and isolate us from the connections that enrich our lives.

Rule Fourteen: Live Every Day as if It's Your First

"Life is understood by looking back, but
it must be lived by looking forward."
—commonly attributed to Søren Kierkegaard

In life, we often carry the weight of past mistakes and worries about the future, allowing them to overshadow the present.

Rule Fourteen invites us to approach each day with the wonder and curiosity of experiencing life for the first time. By letting go of regret and anxiety, we can focus on the richness of the present moment. Treating each day as a fresh opportunity opens the door to personal growth, discovery, and joy.

Living with this mindset begins with reflecting on the past, not as a source of regret, but as a guide for better decisions and greater confidence. Embracing change helps us view uncertainty as an opportunity for growth rather than a cause for fear, enabling us to adapt and evolve. Cultivating gratitude allows us to appreciate the abundance in daily life, shifting our perspective toward positivity and helping us find joy in the simplest moments. Practicing mindfulness further grounds us in the present, allowing us to savor life's ordinary experiences and approach each day with full attention and appreciation.

Living each day as if it's our first does not mean ignoring the past or neglecting future plans. Instead, it means embracing the lessons we've learned while approaching the future with optimism and hope. By staying present and open to the possibilities of each moment, we uncover the beauty, joy, and potential in every day.

Rule Fourteen reminds us that by transcending regret and fear, we can create a life filled with growth, gratitude, and boundless possibility. This mindset invites us to live with curiosity and openness, transforming the ordinary into the extraordinary and making each day a meaningful part of our journey.

EXAMPLE 1: ZEN BUDDHISM AND "BEGINNER'S MIND" (*SHOSHIN*)

Zen Buddhism, which originated in the sixth century, emphasizes the principle of "beginner's mind," or *shoshin*, as a central practice. *Shoshin* embodies a mindset of curiosity and openness, where each moment is experienced as if for the first time—free from preconceptions or expectations. Zen masters often liken *shoshin* to a child's perspective: unburdened by past failures or successes and eager to explore without bias.

This philosophy encourages practitioners to approach every moment as an opportunity to begin anew. For example, a Zen student may practice *shoshin* by brewing tea with complete focus, immersing themselves in the textures, sounds, and sensations of the process. By cultivating this awareness, they release the "expert's mind," which often clings to rigid expectations, and instead rediscover the beauty and simplicity of the present moment.

Historically, *shoshin* has been central to fostering wisdom and clarity in Zen teachings. Zen master Shunryu Suzuki famously said, "In the beginner's mind there are many possibilities, but in the expert's mind there are few." This perspective frees practitioners from dwelling on regrets or fearing the unknown, allowing them to fully engage with life as it unfolds.

Shoshin mirrors Rule Fourteen by championing curiosity, wonder, and engagement with the present. It reminds us that by letting go of past burdens and future anxieties, we can uncover the beauty in even the simplest experiences. By living each day as if it's our first, we open ourselves to growth, joy, and endless possibilities, creating a life of discovery and fulfillment.

EXAMPLE 2: JON KABAT-ZINN (1944–)

Jon Kabat-Zinn, a pioneer in mindfulness, has transformed how people approach stress, health, and daily living. With a PhD in molecular biology from MIT, Kabat-Zinn founded the Mindfulness-Based Stress Reduction (MBSR) clinic at the University of Massachusetts Medical School in 1979. His work bridged Eastern mindfulness practices with Western medicine, promoting mindfulness as a tool for managing life's complexities and finding joy in the present moment.

Kabat-Zinn's philosophy emphasizes that each day offers a fresh start. He encourages individuals to embrace the present moment fully, rather than being weighed down by past regrets or future worries. In his bestselling book *Full Catastrophe Living*, he explores how mindfulness helps us navigate life's messiest moments with resilience and clarity. Through simple practices like focusing on the breath or observing the world with fresh eyes, Kabat-Zinn inspires people to break free from habitual patterns of regret or anxiety, fostering gratitude and openness instead.

Millions of individuals have adopted his teachings, discovering that mindfulness transforms not only how they navigate challenges but also how they experience life's everyday beauty. By grounding themselves in the present, they uncover the richness of small moments—like the warmth of the sun, the sound of laughter, or the simple act of breathing.

Kabat-Zinn's teachings vividly embody Rule Fourteen: By encouraging us to embrace each day with renewal and curiosity, he shows us how to transcend regret and fear. His work reminds us that by focusing on the present, we create opportunities for growth, joy, and transformation, living fully in the richness of each moment.

Rule Fifteen: Be Formless and Adaptable

"Water can flow, or it can crash. Be water, my friend."
—Bruce Lee, 1971 interview, *The Pierre Berton Show*

Rule Fifteen invites us to embody the adaptability and resilience of water—fluid in our approach yet steadfast in our values. Like water, which carves through stone or takes the shape of any container, we can navigate life's challenges by adjusting to circumstances without losing our essence.

Living with this mindset begins with embracing change. Just as water flows around obstacles, we can transform challenges into opportunities by shifting paths and perspectives. Approaching life with curiosity and open-mindedness allows us to replace outdated beliefs with fresh insights, unlocking new possibilities. Resilience, like water's persistence against resistance, enables us to reframe setbacks as stepping stones and adapt strategies to keep moving forward.

Self-reflection also plays a critical role in cultivating adaptability. Like water reflecting its surroundings, we can draw lessons from our experiences without being defined by past failures or external influences. This mental fluidity encourages creative problem-solving and fosters innovation, helping us move beyond rigid patterns and embrace dynamic solutions.

Striking balance is equally important. Water finds its level naturally, whether calm like a still pond or forceful like a crashing wave. Similarly, we can adapt our actions to suit each situation, knowing when to act decisively and when to remain steady and composed.

By embodying these qualities, we become better equipped to handle uncertainty and thrive in dynamic environments. Adapting to change helps us pivot during unforeseen challenges, resilience transforms setbacks into growth opportunities, and open-mindedness reveals fresh paths forward. Together, these traits foster creativity, adaptability, and continuous learning, enabling us to live with clarity and purpose.

Living by Rule Fifteen means breaking free from rigid patterns and embracing uncertainty with a flexible mindset. By embodying the qualities of water, we navigate life with resilience, grace, and creativity, thriving in a world of constant change.

EXAMPLE 1: NETFLIX

Netflix, founded in 1997 by Reed Hastings and Marc Randolph, began as a DVD rental service that revolutionized the traditional video rental industry. Customers could browse an extensive catalog online and have DVDs delivered to their doorsteps, eliminating the inconvenience of in-store visits. This innovative model disrupted the market and established Netflix as a forward-thinking company.

By the mid-2000s, the entertainment landscape was shifting rapidly with the rise of digital technology. Recognizing the potential of streaming, Netflix launched its streaming platform in 2007. This pivot involved abandoning its highly profitable DVD rental business and embracing an untested technology, a decision that carried significant risks. Skepticism abounded, and Netflix faced backlash from customers who were reluctant to move away from DVDs. However, the company's willingness to adapt positioned it as a pioneer in digital entertainment, redefining how audiences consumed media.

Netflix's adaptability didn't stop there. In 2013, it made another bold move by entering content production with original series like *House of Cards* and *Orange Is the New Black*. Transitioning from distributor to creator allowed Netflix to differentiate itself, control its content pipeline, and set a new industry standard. Despite fierce competition, Netflix has continued to evolve, embracing data-driven strategies and expanding globally to maintain its leadership.

Netflix's journey vividly illustrates Rule Fifteen: By embodying the adaptability of water, the company transformed challenges into opportunities. Netflix's willingness to take risks, anticipate trends, and reinvent itself demonstrates the power of being formless and adaptable. Its story reminds us that resilience and flexibility are essential for thriving in a dynamic world.

EXAMPLE 2: KODAK

Kodak, founded by George Eastman in 1888, was a trailblazer in photography. Its easy-to-use cameras and dominance in the film market made it a household name for much of the twentieth century. Kodak was even a pioneer in innovation: In 1975, one of its engineers invented the first digital camera, a groundbreaking advancement that could have positioned the company as a leader in the future of photography.

However, as digital photography gained traction in the 1990s and 2000s, Kodak clung to its film-centric strategies, fearing that embracing digital technology would cannibalize its lucrative film business. While competitors like Sony and Canon embraced the digital revolution, Kodak hesitated, believing that its traditional products would remain dominant. Although it introduced the Kodak EasyShare line in 2001, these efforts were reactive and insufficient to compete in a rapidly evolving market.

The consequences were devastating. By prioritizing short-term profits over innovation, Kodak's market share dwindled, and its reputation as an industry leader eroded. The company, once synonymous with photography, was unable to adapt to the changing landscape and filed for bankruptcy in 2012. Despite having the technology and expertise to lead the digital revolution, Kodak's resistance to change left it unable to thrive in a digital world.

Kodak's downfall vividly illustrates the dangers of failing to adhere to Rule Fifteen. By clinging to outdated strategies and resisting innovation, Kodak missed critical opportunities for growth and relevance. Its story serves as a cautionary tale, reminding us that adaptability and openness to change are essential for long-term success. Without the fluidity to navigate evolving landscapes, even the most iconic legacies can be swept away by the currents of time.

CHAPTER 5

Navigating Dreams and Aspirations

"The future belongs to those who believe in the beauty of their dreams."

—Eleanor Roosevelt, *It Seems to Me: Selected Letters of Eleanor Roosevelt*

Rule One: Prime Your Mind and Document Your Dreams

"Write the vision, and make it plain upon tables, that he may run that readeth it."

—The Bible, Habakkuk 2:2 (KJV)

In our pursuit of dreams, we must combine the psychological power of mental priming with the practical act of documenting aspirations, creating a transformative approach to achieving success.

Mental priming involves visualizing goals as if they are already achieved, cultivating a mindset of success. This practice fosters motivation, builds confidence, and creates an emotional connection to aspirations, making them feel tangible and attainable. By focusing on the emotions tied to achieving our dreams, we prepare ourselves mentally to embrace opportunities and tackle challenges with purpose and optimism.

Documenting dreams complements mental priming by providing structure and clarity. Writing down goals transforms abstract ideas into concrete objectives and helps uncover the deeper values behind them. By asking solution-focused questions like "What steps can we take today to move closer to our dreams?" we shift from inspiration to actionable planning, bridging the gap between imagination and execution. A written vision serves as a visual reminder of commitment, reinforcing focus and determination. For instance, envisioning a milestone—like publishing a book or launching a project—while outlining actionable steps makes the journey exciting and achievable. Together, mental priming and documentation create a dynamic strategy for success. Priming keeps us inspired, while documentation turns dreams into actionable roadmaps.

Rule One teaches us that mental readiness and strategic planning are essential for turning aspirations into reality. By fostering a proactive mindset and clearly defining our goals, we align our actions with our vision, empowering us to grow, achieve, and live intentionally.

EXAMPLE 1: BRUCE LEE (1940–1973)

Bruce Lee, an iconic martial artist and actor, revolutionized both fields with his unparalleled talent and groundbreaking philosophy. Born in the United States and raised in Hong Kong, Lee faced significant racial prejudice when he sought to break into

Hollywood during the 1960s and 1970s. Despite his exceptional skills, he was repeatedly told that an Asian actor could not succeed as a leading man in the US film industry. Determined to defy these limitations, Lee made a pivotal decision in January 1969 to write a letter to himself titled "My Definite Chief Aim."

In this letter, Lee boldly declared his goal of becoming the highest-paid Asian superstar in the United States. He wrote, "I will live the way I please and achieve inner harmony and happiness." This act of documentation wasn't just aspirational; it became a guiding document that Lee revisited during moments of doubt. When faced with rejection and limited opportunities, his words reminded him of his vision, keeping him motivated and focused.

Lee's commitment drove him to intensify his training, acting, and filmmaking skills. He worked tirelessly, producing iconic films like *Enter the Dragon*, which shattered stereotypes and redefined the global perception of Asian actors. By 1973, Lee had achieved his dream, becoming a cultural icon whose influence extended far beyond martial arts and film.

Bruce Lee's journey vividly illustrates Rule One: By articulating his aspirations through mental priming and documenting his vision, he aligned his actions with his dreams. His letter served as both a motivational anchor and a strategic guide, helping him navigate challenges and transform his ambitions into reality. Lee's story demonstrates the transformative power of committing to one's dreams with clarity and purpose.

EXAMPLE 2: JIM CARREY (1962–)

Jim Carrey, a celebrated comedic actor, rose from humble beginnings marked by hardship and unshakable ambition. Born in Ontario, Canada, Carrey faced financial struggles early in life, living with his family in a van and working as a janitor to help make ends meet. Despite these challenges, he clung to his dream of becoming a successful actor, believing deeply in his potential.

In 1985, during a particularly challenging period of rejection and uncertainty in Hollywood, Carrey performed a symbolic act of faith: He wrote himself a check for $10 million for "acting services rendered" and postdated it for Thanksgiving 1995. He carried the check in his wallet, treating it as a physical manifestation of his aspirations. This act of visualization became a daily source of inspiration, reminding him of what was possible even during moments of doubt and discouragement.

Over the next decade, Carrey worked relentlessly, transitioning from stand-up comedy to acting roles. He landed a breakthrough spot on *In Living Color*, which catapulted him into Hollywood's spotlight. By 1994, he had become a household name, starring in blockbuster films like *Ace Ventura: Pet Detective*, *The Mask*, and *Dumb and Dumber*. His earnings from these films far exceeded the amount on the check, fulfilling his vision just shy of his target date.

Jim Carrey's story vividly illustrates Rule One: Writing the check was a deliberate exercise in mental priming and documenting his aspirations. This symbolic act aligned his mindset and actions, turning his dreams into reality. Carrey's journey highlights the power of visualization and documentation in transforming even the loftiest ambitions into achievable goals.

Rule Two: Realize the Only Limit You Have in Your Life Is You

"If you hear a voice within you saying, 'You are not a painter,' then by all means paint, boy, and that voice will be silenced."
—**Vincent van Gogh,** as quoted in *Van Gogh's Letters*

Throughout our lives, external influences—family, teachers, society, and peers—shape our beliefs about what we can achieve. These narratives often create a framework of self-doubt and perceived limitations. Yet, many of the barriers we face are self-imposed, born from internal fears and insecurities.

The first step in overcoming these limitations is introspection. By reflecting on whether our reactions to challenges stem from real constraints or unfounded fears, we can begin to dismantle the mental barriers holding us back. For instance, someone hesitant to pursue public speaking might discover that their fear originates not from a lack of ability but from a single moment of past embarrassment. Recognizing this distinction empowers us to approach challenges with curiosity and resilience.

The second step is redefining setbacks. Instead of viewing them as failures, we can embrace them as opportunities to grow. A stumble during a presentation, for example, becomes a chance to refine communication skills and build confidence. By reframing obstacles as stepping stones, we foster perseverance and adaptability, turning challenges into catalysts for growth.

Rule Two teaches us that the only true limits in life are the ones we impose on ourselves. By fostering introspection and resilience, we reshape our beliefs and actions, unlocking the potential to grow, achieve, and redefine what's possible.

EXAMPLE 1: TAHA HUSSEIN (1889–1973)

Taha Hussein, a towering figure in modern Arabic literature, overcame immense challenges to leave an indelible mark on intellectual and cultural history. Born in a poor village in Egypt and blinded at the age of three, Hussein's early years were marked by immense hardship. Living in a society with limited opportunities for the disabled, he faced prejudice and skepticism about his abilities. Yet, Hussein refused to let his blindness define his future or limit his dreams.

Determined to pursue education, Hussein mastered braille and developed an extraordinary memory, using them as tools to overcome his physical challenges. His relentless pursuit of knowledge led him to enroll in Al-Azhar University in Cairo, where he often struggled against traditional teaching methods. Undeterred, he sought broader intellectual horizons and eventually earned a scholarship to the Sorbonne in France. There, Hussein earned a PhD, becoming one of the first Egyptians to study at the prestigious institution.

Hussein's contributions extended far beyond academics. Through groundbreaking novels, criticism, and autobiographies, he challenged societal norms, advocated for equal access to education, and championed enlightenment and reform. For his efforts, he was nominated multiple times for the Nobel Prize in Literature and was awarded the United Nations Prize in the Field of Human Rights in 1973. His work reshaped Arabic literature and modern Egyptian intellectual life, proving that personal limitations could be transformed into strengths.

Taha Hussein's life vividly illustrates Rule Two: By refusing to accept limitations imposed by his blindness and societal expectations, he demonstrated that true barriers are often internal. Through introspection, resilience, and an unrelenting commitment to his goals, Hussein transformed challenges into stepping stones. His journey is a testament to the power of breaking through self-imposed and external limitations to achieve greatness and inspire generations.

EXAMPLE 2: STEPHEN HAWKING (1942–2018)

Stephen Hawking, one of the greatest theoretical physicists of our time, demonstrated extraordinary resilience in the face of overwhelming challenges. Diagnosed with amyotrophic lateral sclerosis (ALS) at the age of twenty-one, Hawking was told he had just a few years to live. The diagnosis, which progressively robbed him of his physical abilities, could have defined his life. However, Hawking refused to let his condition dictate his potential or extinguish his passion for uncovering the universe's mysteries.

At first, the diagnosis left him in despair, questioning the value of pursuing his ambitions. But over time, his love for physics reignited his determination. Instead of focusing on his limitations, he chose to embrace his intellectual potential. Remaining at the University of Cambridge, Hawking developed groundbreaking theories on black holes and the Big Bang, reshaping our understanding of modern cosmology. Using a speech-generating device, he overcame communication barriers to share his revolutionary ideas. His book, *A Brief History of Time*, became a global bestseller, making complex scientific concepts accessible to millions and solidifying his role as a public intellectual.

Despite his physical challenges, Hawking earned numerous accolades, including the prestigious Lucasian Chair of Mathematics at Cambridge, a position once held by Sir Isaac Newton. His life was a testament not only to his intellectual brilliance but also to his resilience, humor, and unyielding belief in human potential.

Stephen Hawking's journey vividly illustrates Rule Two: By refusing to let his diagnosis define him, he demonstrated that true barriers are often self-imposed. His determination to transcend his physical limitations and focus on his intellectual strengths is a powerful reminder that mindset, not circumstances, determines what is possible. Hawking's story inspires us to embrace resilience and redefine what we believe we are capable of achieving.

Rule Three: Understand That There Is No Such Thing as Failure

"Success is not final, failure is not fatal:
It is the courage to continue that counts."
—John C. Maxwell, *Sometimes You Win—Sometimes You Learn*

Rule Three challenges us to redefine failure, viewing setbacks on the path to achieving our dreams and aspirations not as defeats but as essential steps toward growth and success. Every obstacle encountered during this journey offers valuable lessons that refine our strategies, deepen our understanding, and strengthen our resilience. By embracing these moments as opportunities for learning, we cultivate a growth mindset—an outlook that sees challenges as stepping stones rather than barriers.

A crucial part of this mindset is overcoming the fear of failure, which often prevents us from taking risks or pursuing bold aspirations. Recognizing that setbacks are intrinsic to the process of achieving meaningful goals diminishes this fear, empowering us to act with courage and persistence. Whether or not we achieve the desired outcome, every attempt provides insights that guide our next steps, helping us refine our approach and stay aligned with our vision.

Rule Three teaches us that success is not a single destination but a continuous journey of learning and growth. By reframing setbacks on the path to our aspirations as opportunities for evolution, we navigate challenges with resilience and purpose. This mindset transforms failure into a powerful tool for progress, paving the way for personal and professional fulfillment.

EXAMPLE 1: THOMAS EDISON (1847–1931)

Thomas Edison, one of history's most influential inventors, revolutionized modern life with innovations that spanned numerous fields. Born in Milan, Ohio, Edison faced financial hardships and had limited formal education, but his relentless curiosity and determination drove him to experiment tirelessly. His most iconic achievement, the electric light bulb, exemplifies his ability to redefine failure as progress.

Edison famously conducted thousands of experiments before arriving at a practical design for the light bulb. Each unsuccessful attempt presented unique challenges, from materials that couldn't withstand heat to filaments that burned out too quickly. Despite these repeated setbacks, Edison refused to be discouraged. Instead, he viewed each experiment as a valuable lesson. Reflecting on his persistence, Edison remarked, "I have not failed. I've just found 10,000 ways that won't work." This mindset of resilience and curiosity transformed his obstacles into opportunities for refinement and growth.

In 1880, after years of tireless effort, Edison patented his successful light bulb design, revolutionizing the world by bringing electric light to homes and businesses. His ability to persevere through failure not only reshaped modern life but also cemented his legacy as "The Wizard of Menlo Park."

Thomas Edison's story vividly illustrates Rule Three: By redefining failure as progress, he demonstrated that setbacks are not defeats but necessary steps toward success. Edison's relentless determination to learn from each obstacle reminds us that persistence and a growth mindset can turn challenges into stepping stones to achieving our aspirations. His journey teaches us that failure is not an endpoint—it is part of the path to greatness.

EXAMPLE 2: SOICHIRO HONDA (1906–1991)

Soichiro Honda, born in rural Japan, began his career working in a garage, where he developed a passion for automotive mechanics. Determined to enter the growing automotive industry, Honda applied for a position at Toyota Motor Corporation. However, he faced a pivotal setback when Toyota rejected his application, a moment that could have defined his career.

Initially disheartened, Honda used the rejection as motivation to forge his own path. Reflecting on the rejection, he decided to channel his frustration into creating something innovative. In 1948, with limited resources and immense postwar challenges, he founded Honda Motor Company, starting with motorized bicycles to address Japan's fuel scarcity. These products quickly gained recognition for their efficiency and reliability, setting Honda apart in the market.

Under his leadership, Honda Motor Company grew from a small startup to a global leader in the automotive industry.

The company expanded into motorcycles and later cars, gaining worldwide acclaim for innovation and quality. Honda often credited the Toyota rejection as the spark that fueled his determination to succeed. Rather than allowing the setback to define him, he embraced it as a stepping stone to greatness.

Soichiro Honda's journey vividly illustrates Rule Three: By redefining rejection as an opportunity, he demonstrated that setbacks are not failures but lessons that guide us toward success. Honda's resilience, ingenuity, and growth mindset turned what seemed like failure into the foundation for a globally successful company. His story reminds us that challenges on the path to our dreams are not defeats but catalysts for innovation and progress.

Rule Four: Transcend Life's Unfairness to Achieve Your Dreams

"Life is never fair . . . and perhaps it is a good thing for most of us that it is not."
—Oscar Wilde, *Lord Goring* in *An Ideal Husband*

Life's inherent unpredictability often presents significant challenges, especially in our pursuit of dreams. Rule Four emphasizes the importance of transcending these challenges through commitment, resilience, consistency, and extraordinary effort. Recognizing that struggles are part of the broader human experience helps us persevere with determination and purpose. To navigate life's volatility and unfairness while pursuing our dreams, we must embody four key attributes:

- **Commitment:** Dedication to our aspirations is essential. Commitment involves staying focused and determined, even when external circumstances are discouraging. For instance, an athlete training for a major competition must remain steadfast through injuries and setbacks, viewing obstacles as temporary detours rather than insurmountable barriers.

- **Resilience:** The ability to recover and adapt in the face of difficulties is critical. Resilience allows us to transform setbacks into opportunities for growth. A failed business venture, for example, can provide invaluable lessons that pave the way for future success.
- **Consistency:** Progress is built on steady, disciplined effort. Consistency ensures we maintain momentum, even during challenging times. Small, consistent actions, like practicing a skill daily, compound over time to create significant achievements.
- **Extraordinary effort:** Achieving dreams often requires going beyond the ordinary. Extraordinary effort means embracing creativity, innovation, and the courage to step outside our comfort zones, striving to reach heights that once seemed unattainable.

Rule Four teaches us that while we cannot control life's unfairness, we can control how we respond to it. By embodying commitment, resilience, consistency, and extraordinary effort, we transform life's unpredictability into opportunities for growth. This mindset empowers us to rise above challenges, turn setbacks into stepping stones, and turn our dreams into reality.

EXAMPLE 1: MADAM C. J. WALKER (1867–1919)

Madam C. J. Walker, born Sarah Breedlove in Delta, Louisiana, overcame extraordinary adversity to become one of the first female self-made millionaires in the United States. The daughter of formerly enslaved parents, Walker was orphaned at seven, married at fourteen, and widowed by twenty, leaving her to support herself and her young daughter. Her early life was marked by poverty, racial discrimination, and a scalp ailment that caused severe hair loss—a personal challenge that would inspire her life's work.

Determined to find a solution, Walker developed her own line of hair care products tailored to the needs of African American women. She started with door-to-door sales, facing skepticism and rejection, but remained committed to her vision. Through resilience and consistent effort, she refined her products and built trust among her customers. By 1905, she had founded the Madam C. J. Walker Manufacturing Company, employing thousands of African American women as sales agents and creating unprecedented economic opportunities.

Beyond her business achievements, Walker demonstrated extraordinary effort by using her influence to advocate for racial and gender equality. She funded scholarships, supported civil rights organizations, and empowered others through her philanthropy and activism. Her story exemplifies how life's inherent unfairness can be transformed into opportunities for growth and impact.

Madam C. J. Walker's journey exemplifies Rule Four: By embodying commitment, resilience, consistency, and extraordinary effort, she overcame life's inherent unfairness and turned adversity into achievement. Her story inspires us to approach challenges as stepping stones to greatness, reminding us that perseverance and purpose can transform even the harshest circumstances into lasting success.

EXAMPLE 2: MOHED ALTRAD (1948–)

Born into a Bedouin tribe in the Syrian desert, Mohed Altrad faced profound hardships from an early age. Orphaned as a young child, he grew up in extreme poverty, often lacking basic resources like food and education. Despite these obstacles, Altrad developed a love for learning, attending a poorly equipped school where he excelled academically. His dedication and hard work earned him a scholarship to study in France, a daunting transition that required him to adapt to a new culture, language, and way of life.

While pursuing a PhD in computer science, Altrad faced numerous challenges, including financial struggles and the isolation of being far from home. Yet, his resilience and commitment to his education carried him through. After completing his studies, he worked in various roles before taking a bold step in 1985: acquiring a failing scaffolding company. The company was burdened with financial difficulties and a demoralized workforce, but Altrad saw potential where others saw failure.

Through extraordinary effort and consistent innovation, Altrad transformed the business into the Altrad Group, a global leader in construction and industrial services with operations in over fifty countries. Beyond his business success, he never forgot his roots, using his wealth to support education initiatives and promote social equality.

Mohed Altrad's journey exemplifies Rule Four: By embodying

commitment, resilience, consistency, and extraordinary effort, he transcended life's inherent unfairness and turned adversity into achievement. His story reminds us that even the greatest obstacles can be overcome with purpose and determination, transforming challenges into opportunities for lasting success.

Rule Five: Don't Wait for the Perfect Moment to Leave Your Comfort Zone

"Do not wait; the time will never be 'just right.'"
—Napoleon Hill, *Think and Grow Rich*

Rule Five emphasizes the importance of acting in the pursuit of our dreams without waiting for ideal conditions. Waiting for the perfect moment often leads to hesitation, missed opportunities, and unfulfilled potential. Progress requires stepping beyond comfort and familiarity, embracing challenges, and acting despite uncertainty. To embody this rule, five key principles are essential:

- **Overcoming excuses:** Growth begins by identifying and challenging the excuses that hold us back. By shifting our mindset from limitations to solutions, we transform roadblocks into opportunities and build resilience.
- **Cultivating a proactive mindset:** Transitioning from dreamer to doer requires energy, focus, and commitment. A proactive mindset empowers us to take ownership of our aspirations and steadily work toward them.
- **Acting in the present:** Progress is built by seizing current opportunities rather than waiting for an elusive "perfect time." The present moment is our most powerful tool for change.

- **Adopting an action-oriented approach:** Achieving our dreams demands active involvement. Setting specific goals, embracing continuous learning, and breaking routines create momentum and open new possibilities.
- **Embracing discomfort:** Growth lies outside our comfort zones. Tackling new challenges builds skills and insights essential for progress. For instance, a writer who fears rejection might submit their work anyway, gaining valuable feedback and opportunities.

Rule Five reminds us that progress is not about waiting but about acting with courage and persistence. By embracing these principles, we transform hesitation into growth, creating a life defined by bold choices and meaningful achievements.

EXAMPLE 1: HARRIET TUBMAN (1822–1913)

Harriet Tubman, born into slavery in Maryland, United States, overcame extraordinary challenges to become one of history's most iconic figures of freedom and justice. In the mid-nineteenth century, the United States was deeply divided over the institution of slavery, especially between the northern states (which opposed slavery) and the southern states (where slavery was legal and widespread). Tubman's journey began in 1849 when she made the courageous decision to escape slavery. Guided by the Underground Railroad—a secret network of safe houses and abolitionists who helped enslaved people escape to freedom—she traversed dangerous terrain with the constant threat of capture and severe punishment.

Her escape was just the beginning. Over the next decade, Tubman risked her life by returning to the southern states approximately thirteen times to guide about seventy enslaved individuals to freedom. Known as a "conductor" on the Underground Railroad, Tubman relied on her resourcefulness, courage, and an unyielding commitment to justice. Her bravery earned her the nickname "Moses," symbolizing her role as a liberator, leading others to freedom.

During the American Civil War (1861–1865), a conflict fought primarily over slavery and the preservation of the Union, Tubman served as a scout, nurse, and spy for the Union Army. Despite the dangers, she continued to push beyond her comfort zone, contributing to the broader fight for justice and equality. Later in life, she became an advocate for women's suffrage, inspiring others to challenge injustice and pursue freedom.

Harriet Tubman's journey exemplifies Rule Five: She did not wait for ideal circumstances but acted boldly, stepping into the unknown to create transformative change. Tubman's story reminds us that progress often requires immediate action and the courage to embrace uncertainty, inspiring us to leave our comfort zones in the pursuit of meaningful goals.

EXAMPLE 2: HOWARD SCHULTZ (1953–)

Howard Schultz, raised in a Brooklyn housing project, grew up surrounded by financial hardship but fueled by ambition and a desire to create a better life. His journey began in 1982 when he joined Starbucks, a small company selling coffee beans and equipment. A year later, during a business trip to Milan, Italy, Schultz experienced a revelation. Inspired by the vibrant coffee culture of Italian espresso bars, he envisioned Starbucks as more than a coffee retailer—a welcoming space where people could connect over expertly brewed coffee.

However, Schultz's vision was met with resistance from Starbucks's founders, who didn't share his ambitious plans. Rather than waiting for ideal circumstances or abandoning his dream, Schultz made the bold decision to leave Starbucks in 1985 to start his own company, Il Giornale. This leap into uncharted territory carried significant risks, including financial uncertainty and skepticism from investors about his unconventional ideas. Despite the challenges, Schultz persisted, refining his vision and building his business with extraordinary effort and innovation.

Two years later, Schultz returned to acquire Starbucks, merging it with Il Giornale. This marked the beginning of Starbucks's transformation into a global brand. Schultz introduced specialty drinks, created a warm café atmosphere, and redefined coffee culture worldwide. His ability to embrace discomfort, act decisively, and adapt his approach turned his dream into a reality, making Starbucks synonymous with coffee, culture, and connection.

Howard Schultz's journey exemplifies Rule Five: He didn't wait for the perfect moment but acted boldly, stepping outside his comfort zone to pursue his vision. Schultz's story reminds us that transformative success often begins with courage, persistence, and a willingness to embrace uncertainty, proving that action is the key to progress.

Rule Six: Cherish Your Dreams, However Unlikely They May Be

"All our dreams can come true—if we have the courage to pursue them."
—Walt Disney, *Imagination Unlimited*

Rule Six inspires us to cherish our dreams, even when the paths toward their realization seem unclear or improbable.

Every significant achievement begins with a dream—a spark of inspiration that propels us into the realms of imagination and possibility.

Dreams, by nature, are elusive and uncertain, and this very unpredictability is what makes them transformative. If dreams came with clear, predictable steps, they would cease to be dreams and instead become routine tasks. It is this uncertainty that turns dreams into journeys of growth, creativity, and discovery. History is filled with visionaries who embraced the unknown to achieve what once seemed impossible.

Disregarding our dreams leaves them as distant fantasies, while pursuing them challenges us to believe in our potential and cultivate resilience through continuous learning. Progress often begins with small, deliberate steps. Breaking dreams into manageable goals enables us to approach them with persistence and diligence, celebrating each milestone. Setbacks, rather than failures, serve as lessons that refine our strategies and strengthen our resolve.

Rule Six teaches us that dreams are not just aspirations—they are the foundation of meaningful achievements. By cherishing our dreams and pursuing them with courage, persistence, and a belief in our potential, we transform even the most unlikely aspirations into reality.

EXAMPLE 1: ORVILLE WRIGHT (1871–1948) AND WILBUR WRIGHT (1867–1912)

Orville and Wilbur Wright, brothers from Dayton, Ohio, cherished a dream of achieving powered human flight, a concept many in their time dismissed as impossible. With no formal education in engineering, the brothers relied on their curiosity, creativity, and skills as bicycle mechanics to design and build their flying machines.

Their path to success was far from smooth. Aviation was an untested field, and their experiments were met with widespread skepticism and ridicule. In the dunes of Kitty Hawk, North Carolina—chosen for its strong winds—they endured countless crashes, injuries, and equipment failures. Each setback tested their resolve, but instead of abandoning their dream, the Wright brothers treated every failure as an opportunity to learn. They meticulously documented their experiments and refined their designs, improving their understanding of flight mechanics with each attempt.

Their breakthrough came with the invention of a three-axis control system, which allowed pilots to steer and stabilize an aircraft. After years of perseverance, their dream became a reality on December 17, 1903. The Wright Flyer completed the first powered, controlled flight, lasting twelve seconds and covering 120 feet. Though brief, this historic moment marked the birth of modern aviation and demonstrated the transformative power of persistence.

The Wright brothers' journey exemplifies Rule Six: They cherished their dream of flight, even when success seemed improbable and the path was uncertain. By embracing failure, learning from setbacks, and persisting with courage and innovation, they turned an unlikely aspiration into reality. Their story reminds us that dreams, no matter how ambitious, can reshape the world when pursued with unwavering determination.

EXAMPLE 2: KIRAN MAZUMDAR-SHAW (1953–)

Kiran Mazumdar-Shaw, born in Bangalore, India, cherished a dream of transforming biotechnology into a tool for affordable healthcare. In 1978, she founded Biocon in a rented garage, determined to make her vision a reality despite overwhelming challenges. At the time, biotechnology was an unfamiliar concept in India, and Mazumdar-Shaw faced skepticism not only for her ambitious ideas but also as a woman entrepreneur in a male-dominated field.

Her journey was filled with obstacles. Banks refused to fund her startup, citing biotechnology as too risky and unconventional. Professionals hesitated to join her venture, doubting its viability. Rather than being discouraged, Mazumdar-Shaw broke her dream into achievable goals. She began by focusing on producing industrial enzymes, a manageable starting point that laid the foundation for Biocon's growth. Her breakthrough came when Biocon became the first Indian company to export enzymes to the United States, earning credibility and international recognition.

Building on this success, Mazumdar-Shaw expanded Biocon's vision to biopharmaceuticals, developing affordable treatments for diabetes and cancer. In 2004, Biocon became the first biotechnology company in India to go public, with its IPO making Mazumdar-Shaw the richest self-made woman in the country at the time. Today, Biocon is valued at over $4 billion and is a global leader in biotechnology, revolutionizing healthcare access for millions worldwide.

Kiran Mazumdar-Shaw's journey exemplifies Rule Six: She cherished her dream despite overwhelming skepticism and uncertainty. By embracing challenges, breaking her vision into manageable steps, and pursuing her goals with determination, she proved that even the most unlikely dreams can inspire transformative change. Her story reminds us that courage, persistence, and innovation are the keys to turning aspirations into groundbreaking realities.

Rule Seven: Find Your Gift

"Your work is to discover your world and then with all your heart give yourself to it."
—commonly attributed to Buddha

In our quest to achieve our dreams, discovering and nurturing our unique talents is essential. Each of us possesses a personal gift—a distinct ability or passion—that can guide us toward fulfillment and purpose. This journey is not just about reaching goals but about uncovering what gives our lives meaning and direction.

Our gifts manifest in diverse ways, reflecting the richness of our personalities and abilities. They may include creativity, empathy, technical expertise, or leadership skills. Often, these talents lie dormant, waiting to be uncovered through introspection and awareness. Reflecting on questions like "What activity makes me lose track of time and brings joy, regardless of external rewards?" can help reveal these hidden abilities. For instance, a teacher who thrives on helping others succeed may discover their gift in mentoring and empowering people.

Once we identify our gift, nurturing it becomes vital. Growth requires consistent effort and alignment with our innate abilities. By practicing regularly and embracing opportunities to use our gifts, we cultivate purpose and resilience. This alignment reduces fear of failure and enhances satisfaction, helping us reach our potential while inspiring others.

Rule Seven encourages us to embark on this journey of self-discovery. By uncovering and nurturing our gifts, we unlock our personal potential and contribute meaningfully to the world. Fully realized gifts are not only tools for fulfillment but also the seeds of a lasting legacy.

EXAMPLE 1: MILTON HERSHEY (1857–1945)

Milton Hershey, born in Pennsylvania, discovered his passion for confectionery as a fifteen-year-old apprentice in a candy shop. However, his journey to success was far from smooth. Hershey faced repeated failures—his candy shops in Philadelphia, Chicago, and New York all closed due to financial struggles. Each setback tested his resolve, but Hershey's unshakable belief in his craft kept him moving forward.

Returning to Lancaster, Pennsylvania, Hershey began experimenting tirelessly with caramel recipes, driven by a vision to create something exceptional. In 1886, his perseverance paid off with the founding of the Lancaster Caramel Company, marking his first major success. Yet Hershey wasn't content with his achievements. Fascinated by the potential of milk chocolate, he made a bold decision to sell his caramel company in 1900 to focus exclusively on chocolate production—a move many saw as risky.

By 1903, Hershey had built the world's largest chocolate manufacturing plant, determined to make high-quality milk chocolate affordable for the masses. His innovation didn't just transform the chocolate industry, it created opportunities for others. Hershey founded a model town, complete with schools, parks, and housing for his employees, reflecting his belief in using his gift to uplift lives. Today, the Hershey brand stands as a testament to his vision and generosity.

Milton Hershey's journey exemplifies Rule Seven: He discovered his gift for confectionery and nurtured it with unwavering determination and purpose. By aligning his talent with a vision to create joy and opportunity, Hershey revolutionized an industry and built a legacy that continues to inspire. His story reminds us that finding and nurturing our gifts can transform not only our own lives but also the world around us.

EXAMPLE 2: STEVE HARVEY (1957–)

Steve Harvey, born in West Virginia and raised in Ohio, discovered his gift for comedy early in life, despite facing significant challenges. Growing up, he struggled with financial hardship and a debilitating stutter, making his dream of performing on stage seem far-fetched. Even his mother humorously doubted his abilities, telling him she didn't think he was funny. But Harvey's passion for making others laugh remained unwavering, giving him confidence and a sense of purpose.

Before dedicating himself to comedy, Harvey worked a series of jobs, including as a boxer, factory worker, and carpet cleaner. In his late twenties, he made the bold decision to pursue comedy full-time—a choice that brought immense challenges. With little income from performances, he faced homelessness, often sleeping in his car and showering at gas stations. Despite these hardships, Harvey remained committed to his gift, performing in small clubs across the country, honing his craft, and gaining confidence with each show.

In 1990, Harvey's breakthrough came when he reached the

finals of the Second Annual Johnnie Walker National Comedy Search. This pivotal moment opened doors to hosting opportunities and led to *The Steve Harvey Show*, which ran successfully for six seasons. Over time, he expanded his career to include acting, writing, and hosting, eventually penning the book *Jump*, where he encourages others to discover and pursue their own gifts. Today, he uses his platform to inspire millions, sharing his journey of resilience and faith to help others embrace their potential.

Steve Harvey's journey exemplifies Rule Seven: By discovering his natural talent for comedy and nurturing it with persistence and purpose, he transformed his life and built a lasting legacy. Harvey's story reminds us that finding and embracing our gifts, even in the face of doubt and adversity, can lead to extraordinary success and inspire others to do the same.

Rule Eight: Guard Your Dreams by Silence and Selective Sharing

"You can't tell big dreams to small-minded people."

—Steve Harvey, *X* (formerly Twitter), July 3, 2022

In the pursuit of our dreams, it's essential to protect them with care and intention. Like delicate seeds, dreams need the right environment to grow. Sharing aspirations prematurely can expose them to negativity, skepticism, or doubt—often rooted in others' fears or limitations. These reactions can plant seeds of hesitation, disrupting our focus and draining our motivation.

This rule does not discourage sharing entirely but emphasizes discernment. Surrounding ourselves with supportive individuals who uplift and encourage us is key to nurturing our dreams.

Sharing aspirations with experienced mentors, who can offer constructive feedback and relevant insights, can also provide invaluable guidance. However, being selective about who we confide in ensures that our dreams are fostered in an environment of belief and positivity.

Rule Eight encourages us to guard our dreams until they are resilient enough to withstand external pressures. By sharing selectively and seeking support from the right people, we protect our aspirations from unnecessary doubt and empower ourselves to pursue them with confidence. This thoughtful approach ensures our dreams grow into realities, supported by trust, focus, and unwavering belief.

EXAMPLE 1: LEONARDO DA VINCI (1452–1519)

Leonardo da Vinci, born in Vinci, a small town in Tuscany, became one of the most celebrated figures of the Italian Renaissance. Renowned for his brilliance in anatomy, engineering, and painting, da Vinci's ideas often transcended the knowledge of his time. However, he lived in an intensely competitive era, where rivalries among artists, scientists, and inventors were fierce, and misappropriation of ideas was common. Da Vinci understood that protecting his groundbreaking concepts was as crucial as developing them.

To safeguard his innovations, da Vinci employed ingenious strategies. One of his most famous methods was reverse writing, where his notes were legible only with a mirror. This simple yet effective technique deterred casual readers and competitors. Additionally, he deliberately scattered his concepts across multiple notebooks, ensuring that even if one fell into the wrong hands, the entirety of his work could not be easily deciphered or replicated. These measures not only protected his ideas but also allowed him the freedom to refine them privately, free from interference or premature criticism.

Da Vinci's discernment extended to sharing his work selectively. He presented his ideas only to trusted patrons or collaborators who shared his vision, ensuring his concepts were nurtured in a supportive environment. This thoughtful approach enabled him to focus on innovation and leave a legacy of creativity and discovery.

Leonardo da Vinci's journey exemplifies Rule Eight: He guarded his dreams through strategic secrecy and selective sharing, creating the space to nurture his ideas until they were ready to leave a lasting impact. His story reminds us that protecting our aspirations from premature exposure allows them to grow stronger, ensuring their realization and enduring significance.

EXAMPLE 2: WALT DISNEY (1901–1966)

Walt Disney, born in Chicago, Illinois, grew up to become one of the most influential visionaries in entertainment history. In the early 1950s, he conceived a groundbreaking idea: a theme park where visitors could immerse themselves in the worlds of his animated characters. At the time, such a concept was unheard of, and Disney recognized the risks of sharing his vision too soon. Premature disclosure could invite skepticism, imitation, or financial hurdles, threatening the viability of his dream.

To protect his vision, Disney employed meticulous strategies. One of his most remarkable moves was acquiring land in Anaheim, California, using dummy corporations to maintain anonymity. This secrecy prevented landowners from inflating prices, ensuring the project remained financially viable. Additionally, Disney limited discussions about Disneyland's development to a trusted inner circle of engineers—later known as Imagineers—and close collaborators. By controlling the flow of information, he shielded his team from external pressures, allowing them to focus entirely on creativity and problem-solving.

Disney refrained from publicly announcing Disneyland until every element of his vision had been carefully refined and planned. This approach not only protected his dream from premature criticism but also ensured that the park was launched with precision and clarity. The success of Disneyland, which opened in 1955, transformed the entertainment industry and solidified Disney's legacy as an innovator.

Walt Disney's journey exemplifies Rule Eight: By sharing his vision selectively and exercising strategic discretion, he safeguarded his dream and nurtured it in the right environment. His ability to protect his vision while fostering creativity demonstrates the power of selective sharing in turning ambitious ideas into transformative realities.

Rule Nine: Remember That Your Dreams and Success Are Both Unique

"Success is to be measured not so much by the position that one has reached in life as by the obstacles which he has overcome."
—Booker T. Washington, *Up from Slavery: An Autobiography*

In the pursuit of our dreams, it is vital to embrace the truth that every path is unique. Our cultural, social, and economic backgrounds shape not only the challenges we face but also the aspirations we pursue. These differences make each journey distinct and deeply personal, reflecting the diversity of human experience.

Success, too, is subjective. For some, it may mean professional achievements or financial security, while for others, it lies in personal growth, creative expression, or community impact. The key to fulfillment is defining success on our terms, guided by our values and aspirations rather than external expectations. Questions like "What brings me purpose and joy?" or "What kind of legacy do I want to leave?" help uncover what success truly means to us.

The journey to our dreams often includes obstacles that test our resilience and deepen our character. These struggles give meaning to our achievements, turning success into more than just a destination. Comparing our progress to others diminishes the value of our own experiences. Instead, reflecting on how far we've come and the lessons we've learned helps us honor the growth and perseverance that define our unique paths.

Rule Nine teaches us to embrace the individuality of our journeys and define success as a deeply personal concept. True success lies not in external benchmarks but in honoring the growth, purpose, and resilience that shape our lives. By celebrating our unique paths, we build a foundation for authentic and fulfilling success.

EXAMPLE 1: ZAHA HADID (1950–2016)

Zaha Hadid, born in Baghdad, Iraq, broke barriers in the male-dominated field of architecture with her bold and visionary designs. After studying at the Architectural Association in London, she embraced a deconstructivist style that defied conventional norms. Early in her career, Hadid faced intense skepticism—her designs were often labeled "unbuildable" and impractical by critics. The rejection of her winning Cardiff Bay Opera House design due to political controversy was a particularly painful setback.

Rather than conforming to traditional expectations, Hadid doubled down on her individuality. She continued to refine her vision, using challenges as opportunities to innovate. Her breakthrough came with projects like the Vitra Fire Station in Germany and the Rosenthal Center for Contemporary Art in Cincinnati, Ohio, which showcased her fluid, futuristic designs. These works not only redefined architecture but also silenced critics who doubted her approach. In 2004, Hadid became the first woman to receive the Pritzker Architecture Prize, cementing her legacy as a trailblazer in her field. Throughout her career, Hadid aligned her success with her values, prioritizing creativity over conformity. She proved that success is not about meeting external expectations but about staying true to one's vision.

Zaha Hadid's journey exemplifies Rule Nine: She redefined success by embracing the individuality of her dreams and staying committed to her vision. Her story reminds us that true success lies in aligning our aspirations with our values, celebrating the uniqueness of our paths, and overcoming challenges with unwavering determination.

EXAMPLE 2: MUHAMMAD YUNUS (1940–)

Muhammad Yunus, born in Chittagong, Bangladesh, revolutionized the concept of microfinance, turning it into a transformative tool for poverty alleviation. After earning a PhD in economics from Vanderbilt University, Yunus returned to his homeland, deeply moved by the extreme poverty he witnessed. Determined to make a difference, he began offering small loans to low-income individuals in rural communities—especially women—who lacked access to traditional banking. Using his own funds, Yunus empowered these individuals to start small businesses, improve their livelihoods, and break free from cycles of poverty.

Yunus's approach faced significant skepticism. Financial institutions dismissed his idea, arguing that lending to marginalized communities was too risky and unsustainable. Critics doubted whether borrowers, particularly women with limited resources, could repay their loans. Undeterred, Yunus founded the Grameen Bank in 1983, prioritizing group-based lending and focusing on financial empowerment. Despite resistance, he remained committed to his vision of redefining banking as a tool for social good rather than profit alone.

Over time, the Grameen Bank proved its critics wrong, uplifting millions of families and demonstrating the power of financial inclusion. By 2006, Yunus's groundbreaking efforts were recognized with the Nobel Peace Prize, solidifying his legacy as a pioneer of social innovation and economic justice.

Muhammad Yunus's journey exemplifies Rule Nine: He redefined success by aligning his dreams with his values, prioritizing social impact over conventional metrics. His story reminds us that true success lies in pursuing distinctive dreams that create meaningful change. Yunus's path highlights the importance of embracing individuality and leaving a transformative legacy.

Rule Ten: Be Patient While Pursuing Your Dreams

"Patience is bitter, but its fruit is sweet."

—John Chardin, *Voyages en Perse et autres lieux de l'Orient*

Patience is a cornerstone of achieving meaningful dreams and aspirations. In a world obsessed with instant gratification, it is easy to feel discouraged when progress seems slow or challenges arise. Yet, nothing of true value can be obtained instantly. Success requires persistence, resilience, and the courage to stay committed, even when the journey becomes difficult.

The pursuit of dreams often tests our patience through setbacks and obstacles. These challenges are not signs of failure but opportunities to grow stronger and refine our strategies. Like a sculptor chiseling stone, every effort shapes us closer to our vision. Patience enables us to stay focused, learn from difficulties, and keep moving forward with purpose.

Dreams that are built with patience often carry the most significance. Whether it's mastering a skill, building a career, or creating meaningful change, lasting achievements are forged through steady, deliberate effort. Challenges encountered along the way enrich our resilience and make the final accomplishment all the more rewarding.

Rule Ten reminds us that patience is not merely waiting but persevering with purpose and determination. By staying committed to our dreams and embracing the lessons in each difficulty, we transform obstacles into stepping stones. Patience teaches us to see our journey not as a race but as a process of growth and fulfillment, where each step brings us closer to achieving our aspirations.

EXAMPLE 1: COLONEL HARLAND SANDERS (1890–1980)

Colonel Harland Sanders, born in Henryville, Indiana, faced numerous challenges before founding Kentucky Fried Chicken (KFC). His early career included a series of jobs—steamboat pilot, insurance salesman, and gas station operator—none of which brought lasting success. In the 1930s, his passion for cooking led him to open a dining service at a gas station in Corbin, Kentucky. There, he developed the fried chicken recipe that would later define KFC. However, the construction of an interstate highway diverted traffic away from his restaurant, forcing its closure.

At sixty-five years old, Sanders decided to franchise his chicken recipe. The process was far from easy. Over two years, he pitched his idea to numerous potential partners and endured over a thousand rejections. Despite repeated setbacks, Sanders remained steadfast, driven by his belief in the quality of his recipe. Eventually, he secured his first franchise agreement, marking the beginning of KFC's expansion.

Today, KFC is a global fast-food giant with over twenty-seven thousand restaurants in more than one hundred fifty countries, generating billions of dollars in annual revenue. What started as a single recipe became a worldwide phenomenon, demonstrating the transformative power of persistence and vision.

Colonel Sanders's journey exemplifies Rule Ten: His patience and resilience allowed him to overcome repeated obstacles and stay committed to his dream. By enduring challenges and focusing on long-term goals, Sanders built a legacy that continues to thrive. His story reminds us that meaningful success requires patience, persistence, and the courage to persevere through difficulties.

EXAMPLE 2: MALCOLM GLADWELL (1963–)

Malcolm Gladwell, born in Hampshire, England, and raised in Ontario, Canada, rose to prominence as one of the most influential thinkers in modern social science. In his bestselling book *Outliers*, Gladwell explored the factors that shape extraordinary success. One of the book's central concepts, the "10,000-hour rule," posits that mastery in any field requires approximately ten thousand hours of deliberate practice—a significant investment of time and patience.

Gladwell supported this theory with compelling examples. He highlighted the Beatles, who performed relentlessly in Hamburg for years before achieving global fame. Their grueling performance schedule allowed them to refine their musical skills, laying the foundation for their success. Similarly, he examined Bill Gates, who as a teenager spent countless hours programming on early computers, gaining the expertise that later helped him found Microsoft. Another example featured Canadian hockey players, whose additional practice opportunities—linked to their birth months—helped them gain a competitive edge.

These stories dismantled the myth of overnight success, emphasizing that greatness stems not from innate talent alone but from sustained effort and persistence. Gladwell's analysis showed that while raw talent might spark interest, it is long-term dedication that truly leads to mastery.

Malcolm Gladwell's exploration in *Outliers* perfectly illustrates Rule Ten: Success is not achieved through shortcuts but through patience, persistence, and time. The "10,000-hour rule" reminds us that meaningful progress requires consistent effort and a willingness to embrace the long journey toward mastery and achievement.

Rule Eleven: Be Wary of "Turn Back" Moments

"Many of life's failures are people who did not realize how close they were to success when they gave up."

—commonly attributed to Thomas A. Edison

In the pursuit of our dreams, we often encounter "turn back" moments—times when obstacles feel overwhelming and doubt clouds our resolve. These moments test our commitment and demand introspection. Asking questions like "Does stepping back align with my values and bring peace?" or "Will abandoning my dream lead to regret?" helps us evaluate our path with clarity. If stepping back feels aligned and brings genuine peace, it may be the right choice. However, if the thought of giving up stirs regret or self-doubt, perseverance becomes essential.

Navigating these moments requires more than endurance—it demands a mindset that views challenges as opportunities for growth. Obstacles, though daunting, often serve as stepping stones that refine our character and approach. Keeping long-term goals in focus helps us maintain perspective, reminding us that while challenges are temporary, the fulfillment of achieving our dreams lasts.

Rule Eleven teaches us that perseverance is not just a means to success but a transformative process that shapes our purpose and resilience. By embracing obstacles and remaining committed to our aspirations, we not only move closer to our goals but also grow as individuals, turning challenges into stepping stones for lasting success.

EXAMPLE 1: STEVEN SPIELBERG (1946–)

Steven Spielberg, born in Cincinnati, Ohio, developed a fascination with filmmaking at an early age, using his family's 8mm camera to create amateur films. Determined to pursue his dream of becoming a director, Spielberg applied to the University of Southern California's School of Cinematic Arts but faced multiple rejections. Undeterred, he began making short films and secured an unpaid internship at Universal Studios, where he observed professionals and gained invaluable experience.

Spielberg's breakthrough came with his short film *Amblin'*, which impressed Universal executives and earned him a directing contract. Early in his career, he directed television episodes and TV movies, including *Duel* (1971), a suspenseful thriller that showcased his talent. His defining moment came with *Jaws* (1975), a film plagued by technical issues and delays. Spielberg's persistence turned it into a groundbreaking blockbuster, redefining modern cinema. Over the decades, he delivered iconic films such as *E.T. the Extra-Terrestrial* (1982), *Jurassic Park* (1993), and *Schindler's List* (1993), earning multiple Academy Awards and cementing his status as one of Hollywood's most influential directors.

Steven Spielberg's journey exemplifies Rule Eleven: His ability to persevere through rejections and early career challenges highlights the importance of resilience during critical moments. By staying committed to his dream despite setbacks, Spielberg transformed obstacles into opportunities for extraordinary achievements. His story reminds us that perseverance through challenges often brings us closer to success than we realize.

EXAMPLE 2: SYLVESTER STALLONE (1946–)

Sylvester Stallone, born in New York City, faced adversity from the start. A birth complication caused partial paralysis in his face, resulting in a slurred voice and distinctive appearance—features that initially hindered his acting aspirations. Despite his passion for acting, Stallone encountered relentless rejection, with casting agents repeatedly dismissing him for his unconventional look and voice.

Stallone's challenges extended beyond professional setbacks. At one point, he was homeless, spending nights in a bus station. In desperation, he sold his beloved dog, Butkus, for $50 to afford food. Channeling his struggles into creativity, Stallone wrote the screenplay for *Rocky*, inspired by his resilience and determination. When the script garnered attention, Stallone faced a critical "turn back" moment. Producers offered him significant money for the screenplay but refused to cast him in the lead role. Turning down these offers, Stallone risked immediate financial relief to pursue his dream of playing Rocky.

His gamble paid off. Stallone was ultimately cast in the film, which became a cultural phenomenon, earning ten Academy Award nominations and winning Best Picture in 1977. Stallone's performance launched his career, transforming him into a global icon and a symbol of perseverance.

Sylvester Stallone's journey exemplifies Rule Eleven: His ability to persist through rejection, financial despair, and pivotal "turn back" moments demonstrates the transformative power of resilience. Stallone's unwavering belief in his vision turned overwhelming obstacles into extraordinary success, reminding us that perseverance during critical moments often leads to the fulfillment of our dreams.

Rule Twelve: Pursue Your Dreams Passionately While Practicing Nonattachment to Their Outcome

"Set thy heart upon thy work, but never on its reward."

—Bhagavad Gita

In the pursuit of our dreams, we must balance passionate effort with nonattachment to specific outcomes. This rule encourages us to pour our energy into meaningful aspirations while embracing life's unpredictability. By focusing on the journey and valuing the process, we ensure that our dreams enrich our lives regardless of their ultimate result.

Passion drives us to give our best, sustain resilience through challenges, and stay motivated in the face of obstacles. Yet, when outcomes fall short of expectations, disappointment often follows. Practicing nonattachment in these moments allows us to accept what we cannot control while adapting when change is possible. This approach fosters emotional balance, preventing discouragement and helping us grow from every experience.

Failures and setbacks, though painful, are often opportunities to refine our dreams. Nonattachment helps us see these moments not as endpoints but as stepping stones to greater clarity and purpose. By valuing effort and growth over fixed outcomes, we transform the pursuit of our dreams into a meaningful journey of self-discovery.

Rule Twelve teaches us to pursue our dreams with passion while remaining serene in uncertainty. By focusing on effort, growth, and adaptability, we ensure our aspirations enrich our lives, regardless of the results. This balance helps us find resilience, fulfillment, and deeper purpose along the way.

EXAMPLE 1: LUDWIG VAN BEETHOVEN (1770–1827)

Ludwig van Beethoven, born in Bonn, Germany, displayed extraordinary musical talent from an early age, becoming a virtuoso pianist and composer. His career took off in Vienna, where he earned recognition for his innovative compositions and exceptional performances. However, in his mid-twenties, Beethoven faced a devastating challenge: He began losing his hearing. For a musician, this seemed like an insurmountable obstacle, one that could have ended his career. Yet, Beethoven was determined to continue his work.

As his hearing deteriorated, Beethoven developed creative ways to adapt. He relied on vibrations, memory, and his profound understanding of music to compose some of his greatest works. Despite near-total deafness, he produced masterpieces such as the *Ninth Symphony* and his late string quartets, which broke musical conventions and pushed the boundaries of classical music. These compositions not only solidified his legacy but also redefined the possibilities of what music could achieve.

Beethoven's journey exemplifies Rule Twelve: He pursued his dreams passionately while practicing nonattachment to their outcomes. Rather than fixating on how his work might be received or on his physical limitations, Beethoven focused on the creative process itself. His story reminds us that by channeling our passion into meaningful pursuits and letting go of rigid expectations, we can transcend obstacles and achieve greatness.

EXAMPLE 2: VINCENT VAN GOGH (1853–1890)

Vincent van Gogh, born in Zundert, Netherlands, discovered his passion for painting after a series of failed attempts at other careers. His artistic journey was fraught with challenges, including severe mental illness, financial instability, and social isolation. Despite these hardships, Van Gogh's dedication to his craft never wavered. With the support of his brother, Theo, he poured his emotions into his work, creating vivid, emotive pieces that redefined artistic expression.

Van Gogh's unique style, characterized by bold colors and intense brushstrokes, produced masterpieces such as *Starry Night* and *Sunflowers*. However, during his lifetime, his work was largely unrecognized. He sold only a handful of paintings and lived in poverty, often battling despair and feelings of failure. Yet, Van Gogh continued to paint, driven by an inner need to create rather than by the pursuit of fame or fortune. His art became his solace and voice, allowing him to communicate what words could not.

Vincent van Gogh's story exemplifies Rule Twelve: He pursued his dreams with unwavering passion while practicing nonattachment to recognition or material success. By focusing on the creative process rather than external rewards, Van Gogh found fulfillment in his work. His posthumous acclaim underscores the unpredictability of success, reminding us that true fulfillment lies in embracing the journey and staying committed to our passions, regardless of outcomes.

CHAPTER 6

Navigating Life's Challenges

"Every problem is a gift—without problems, we would not grow."

—**Tony Robbins,** *Awaken the Giant Within*

Rule One: Navigate Life's Challenges with Ten-Year and Deathbed Perspectives

"Rule number one is don't sweat the small stuff. Rule number two is it's all small stuff."

—**Dr. Robert S. Eliot,** as popularized by Richard Carlson in *Don't Sweat the Small Stuff . . . and It's All Small Stuff*

Successfully navigating life's challenges requires adopting a long-term perspective. By assessing difficulties through two distinct lenses—their potential impact over a decade and their relevance at the end of life—we gain clarity on their true significance.

These perspectives enable us to prioritize our responses, focusing energy on what truly matters.

When faced with obstacles, it's easy to overestimate their importance, leading to stress and clouded judgment. Reflective questions such as "Will this matter in ten years?" and "Will this hold significance in my final moments?" help discern the challenge's weight. If the answer to either question is yes, it signals a need for thoughtful action—whether to strategize solutions or accept what is beyond our control. If the answer to both is no, we conserve energy by addressing the issue calmly and proportionately.

This rule is not about dismissing challenges but understanding their true importance. The ten-year and deathbed perspectives shift our focus to what genuinely affects the trajectory of our life. By approaching challenges strategically, we conserve emotional energy, make wiser decisions, and prioritize what shapes our journey.

Rule One encourages us to view life's challenges through these lenses, fostering clarity, balance, and resilience. By focusing on what truly matters, we navigate life with intention and create a more meaningful and fulfilling path.

EXAMPLE 1: NELSON MANDELA (1918–2013)

Nelson Mandela, born in the rural village of Mvezo, South Africa, grew up under the oppressive system of apartheid, where racial injustice was a daily reality. Witnessing systemic inequality fueled his commitment to the anti-apartheid movement. As a young lawyer and activist, Mandela joined the African National Congress (ANC), dedicating himself to the fight for racial equality. His activism came at a great personal cost. Arrested multiple times, Mandela faced his greatest challenge at the 1964 Rivonia Trial, where he delivered an iconic speech affirming his readiness to die for justice and equality.

Mandela was sentenced to twenty-seven years in prison, much of it spent in the harsh conditions of Robben Island. Despite the isolation and physical toll, Mandela refused to let his circumstances define him. He chose to view his imprisonment through a long-term lens, focusing on how his time behind bars could contribute to the broader fight against apartheid. Instead of succumbing to despair, Mandela used his imprisonment strategically—building relationships with fellow inmates, maintaining communication with activists, and refining his vision for a democratic South Africa. By anchoring his resolve in the belief that his sacrifices would have lasting significance, Mandela turned what could have been years of despair into a foundation for transformation.

Nelson Mandela's life exemplifies Rule One: He navigated the immense challenges of imprisonment by adopting a ten-year and deathbed perspective. Mandela viewed his time in prison not as an endpoint but as a stepping stone toward a greater purpose. This reflective mindset allowed him to focus on the long-term impact of his actions, empowering him to persevere and ultimately reshape the destiny of a nation. His story reminds us that adopting a long-term perspective transforms even the greatest adversities into meaningful achievements.

EXAMPLE 2: THE PIG WAR (1859)

In 1859, a seemingly trivial incident between an American farmer and a British settler nearly escalated into a war between the United States and Britain. On San Juan Island, a disputed territory between British Canada and the United States, tensions simmered due to ambiguous territorial agreements. The conflict began when Lyman Cutlar, an American farmer, found a pig owned by Charles Griffin, a British settler and employee of the Hudson's Bay Company, rooting in his potato patch. Frustrated, Cutlar shot and killed the pig.

What could have been a minor property dispute quickly escalated. Griffin demanded compensation for the pig, but Cutlar refused, arguing that the pig had trespassed. When British authorities threatened Cutlar with arrest, US military forces were sent to the island. Britain responded by deploying warships, turning the incident into an international standoff. For weeks, tensions mounted as both sides mobilized forces, risking war over a single pig. Eventually, cooler heads prevailed, and the crisis was resolved through negotiation, avoiding bloodshed. The dispute over San Juan Island was later peacefully settled through arbitration, with the territory awarded to the United States.

The Pig War illustrates the dangers of failing to apply Rule One. Had both sides paused to consider whether the pig's death would matter in ten years—or on their deathbeds—they might have resolved the issue proportionately without risking conflict. This example underscores how reflective thinking and long-term perspectives can prevent small issues from escalating into unnecessary crises. It reminds us that maintaining clarity and proportionality in our responses ensures more thoughtful, measured decisions.

Rule Two: Realize That Life's Challenges Often Arise from Your Desires and Dissatisfaction

"He who is not contented with what he has will not be contented with what he wishes to have."
—commonly attributed to Socrates

Many of life's challenges originate not from external circumstances but from within, shaped by our desires and dissatisfaction. These internal forces influence how we perceive obstacles, often creating situations we label as challenges—even when others might not view them as such. This subjectivity highlights the need to evaluate our desires and dissatisfaction carefully, ensuring they are proportionate and not exaggerated.

Our desires reflect our longing for material possessions, success, fulfilling relationships, or health we do not have. While they can inspire growth, they often lead to frustration, stress, and anxiety when paired with feelings of inadequacy. Similarly, dissatisfaction arises from displeasure with hardships, financial difficulties, or personal setbacks. Left unchecked, these emotions magnify minor inconveniences into significant challenges, preventing us from addressing their root causes constructively. To navigate these challenges effectively, a mindful approach is essential:

1. **Recognition:** Acknowledge desires and dissatisfaction as natural experiences. Self-awareness helps us distinguish genuine challenges from exaggerated perceptions.
2. **Acceptance:** Embrace the reality of our current situation. Acceptance is not resignation but a step toward thoughtful and constructive action.

3. **Gratitude:** Shift our focus from what we lack to what we have. Gratitude transforms dissatisfaction into contentment, fostering resilience and balance.
4. **Proactive change:** From a place of clarity and gratitude, take deliberate actions to address challenges within our control, or practice acceptance when change is not possible.

Rule Two teaches us to evaluate our desires and dissatisfaction carefully, ensuring they do not distort our perspective or magnify life's challenges. By approaching difficulties with mindfulness and balance, we empower ourselves to overcome obstacles and create a life defined by growth, resilience, and contentment.

EXAMPLE 1: FRIDA KAHLO (1907–1954)

Frida Kahlo, born in Coyoacán, Mexico, is celebrated as one of the most influential artists of the twentieth century. Her life was marked by extraordinary physical and emotional challenges. At six years old, she contracted polio, leaving her with a permanent limp. At eighteen, a catastrophic bus accident caused severe spinal and pelvic injuries, confining her to bed for long periods and shattering her dreams of becoming a doctor. Kahlo's longing for health and a normal life clashed with her reality, fueling frustration and dissatisfaction.

Kahlo's personal life added to her struggles. Her tumultuous marriage to Diego Rivera, marked by infidelities, deepened her longing for stability and fulfillment. Despite these challenges, she refused to let her dissatisfaction consume her. Turning to painting as a form of self-expression, she transformed her physical and emotional pain into art. Her self-portraits explored themes of identity, femininity, and resilience, capturing both her struggles and gratitude for her inner strength.

Kahlo's ability to channel her challenges into her art brought her extraordinary success. Her works gained international acclaim during her lifetime, with exhibitions in New York, Paris, and Mexico City. Today, her paintings—like *The Two Fridas* and *Self-Portrait with Thorn Necklace and Hummingbird*—are celebrated as masterpieces, and her legacy continues to inspire millions.

Frida Kahlo's story exemplifies Rule Two. By recognizing her unmet desires, accepting her struggles, and transforming them through gratitude and purposeful action, she turned life's challenges into a legacy of resilience and artistic brilliance. Kahlo's journey reminds us that when we manage desires and dissatisfaction with balance and clarity, we unlock the potential to create meaningful contributions that endure far beyond our challenges.

EXAMPLE 2: ADOLF MERCKLE (1934–2009)

Adolf Merckle, born in Dresden, Germany, was one of Europe's wealthiest industrialists, overseeing a vast business empire that included pharmaceuticals, construction, and manufacturing. Despite his immense success, Merckle struggled with dissatisfaction and an unrelenting desire to expand his wealth and influence. His inability to find contentment in his accomplishments drove him to take increasingly risky financial ventures, including a speculative short sale of Volkswagen shares during the 2008 global financial crisis.

Merckle's life challenge emerged when his gamble backfired.

Volkswagen's stock prices surged unexpectedly, leading to catastrophic financial losses for his company. As his empire faced mounting debts, threats of bankruptcy, and the erosion of investor confidence, Merckle's dissatisfaction magnified the situation. Instead of focusing on the substantial successes he still retained, he became consumed by his losses, tying his identity and self-worth to his financial standing. Overwhelmed by despair and unable to accept his circumstances, Merckle tragically ended his life in early 2009.

Adolf Merckle's story illustrates the dangers of failing to adhere to Rule Two. His inability to practice gratitude for his achievements and his relentless dissatisfaction drove him to magnify life's challenges unnecessarily. By allowing unchecked desires to distort his perspective, Merckle missed the opportunity to address his struggles constructively. His story serves as a poignant reminder that recognizing and managing desires with balance and gratitude can prevent challenges from escalating, fostering clarity, resilience, and fulfillment even in the face of adversity.

Rule Three: Remember That Life's Challenges Are Angels in Disguise

"Perhaps you hate a thing and it is good for you; and perhaps you love a thing and it is bad for you."
—**The Quran,** Surah Al-Baqarah 2:216

Life often confronts us with challenges that feel overwhelming and distressing. Yet, as the verse reminds us, what appears undesirable may carry hidden blessings, while what seems desirable might not truly serve us. By reframing our perspective, we can view life's challenges not as obstacles but as opportunities—angels in disguise—that shape our character, deepen our resilience, and expand our understanding of life.

Challenges, though painful, are pivotal moments for self-discovery and growth. They push us to confront discomfort, explore uncharted paths, and uncover strengths we may not have realized we possessed. Setbacks such as losing a job or facing rejection may initially feel devastating but often lead to unexpected clarity, personal transformation, or new opportunities. The impact of a challenge lies not in the event itself but in how we respond to it. Reacting with fear or resistance can amplify stress and anxiety. However, when approached with curiosity, determination, and openness, challenges become guides that build resilience and foster growth. Engaging constructively with our emotions and extracting wisdom from adversity fortifies us for future trials.

Rule Three teaches us to embrace life's challenges as catalysts for growth. By recognizing their hidden blessings and approaching them with resilience and curiosity, we transform adversity into strength, uncover new capabilities, and lay the foundation for profound personal fulfillment.

EXAMPLE 1: ARIANNA HUFFINGTON (1950–)

Arianna Huffington, born in Athens, Greece, grew up with a deep appreciation for intellectual pursuits, nurtured by her mother's encouragement to think boldly and embrace challenges. Her early success as an author hinted at a promising future, but she faced significant obstacles along the way. After achieving recognition for her first book, Huffington's second manuscript was rejected by thirty-six publishers. This setback could have ended her aspirations, but she used it as motivation to explore new opportunities.

Huffington chose to expand her vision beyond traditional publishing, venturing into the digital space. In 2005, she cofounded *The Huffington Post*, an innovative platform blending traditional journalism with blogging and community discussions. Building the site required navigating a rapidly evolving digital landscape and overcoming skepticism from critics. Yet, Huffington drew strength from her earlier experiences with rejection, which had taught her resilience and adaptability.

Her perseverance paid off. *The Huffington Post* became a groundbreaking success, redefining digital journalism and earning Huffington global recognition. In 2011, the platform was acquired by AOL for $315 million, cementing its impact and her legacy as a pioneer in digital media.

Arianna Huffington's story exemplifies Rule Three. Her early rejections, though difficult, became opportunities in disguise, guiding her toward innovation and success. By reframing setbacks as opportunities and approaching challenges with determination, she transformed obstacles into milestones. Her journey reminds us that life's challenges often conceal blessings, leading us to paths we may not have initially envisioned.

EXAMPLE 2: GABRIEL GARCÍA MÁRQUEZ (1927–2014)

Gabriel García Márquez, born in Aracataca, Colombia, grew up immersed in the rich storytelling traditions of his grandparents and the political unrest of his country. These early influences laid the foundation for his distinctive narrative style, blending reality with magical realism. However, Márquez's path to literary success included significant personal and professional challenges.

One of Márquez's most defining challenges came in his youth when he was diagnosed with tuberculosis, a feared disease that required lengthy isolation. For many, such a diagnosis would have led to despair, but for Márquez, this period of solitude became a sanctuary for creativity. Removed from daily distractions, he immersed himself in storytelling, experimenting with themes and characters that would later define his masterpieces. It was during this time of stillness that the seeds for *One Hundred Years of Solitude* began to take root.

His struggles extended beyond his health. Early in his career, Márquez faced rejection from publishers who doubted whether his distinctive style, blending fantasy and reality, would resonate with readers. Yet, he persisted, drawing from his cultural heritage and personal experiences to craft narratives that eventually captivated the world. When his works gained recognition, they redefined global literature, earning him the Nobel Prize in Literature in 1982.

Gabriel García Márquez's life exemplifies Rule Three. His battle with tuberculosis and initial rejections, though daunting, became angels in disguise. By embracing his challenges with resilience and curiosity, Márquez transformed adversity into creative brilliance. His story reminds us that life's harshest moments can become catalysts for extraordinary achievements when approached with determination and an open mind.

Rule Four: Assess Your Emotions Before Reacting to Life's Challenges

"Between stimulus and response there is a space.
In that space is our power to choose our response.
In our response lies our growth and our freedom."
—commonly attributed to Viktor E. Frankl

Navigating life's challenges requires mastering our emotional responses. Emotions, while natural and valuable, can amplify obstacles, distorting our perception and clouding judgment. Rule Four emphasizes the importance of pausing to assess our emotions before reacting, enabling us to approach challenges with clarity and purpose. Emotions such as fear, anger, and impatience often distort our responses to life's difficulties:

- **Fear** magnifies obstacles, making them seem larger than they truly are. This can lead to avoidance, hesitation, and missed opportunities for constructive action.
- **Anger** distorts our perception of events and escalates conflicts. Reacting impulsively often creates unnecessary tension, overshadowing opportunities for resolution.
- **Impatience** drives hasty decisions that magnify challenges unnecessarily, leading to avoidable mistakes or further complications.

To master emotions, we can pause and ask reflective questions:

- "What am I truly feeling right now, and why?"
- "Is my reaction addressing the situation or fueled by my emotions?"
- "How can I respond in a way that aligns with my long-term values and goals?"

Emotional assessment is not about suppressing feelings but understanding them. By engaging constructively with our emotions, we transform them into tools for growth rather than barriers to progress. This mindful approach allows us to navigate challenges with composure, align our actions with our values, and make thoughtful decisions that reflect clarity and purpose.

Rule Four teaches us that mastering our emotional responses is essential for navigating life's complexities. By pausing to assess our emotions, we transform challenges into opportunities for growth, ensuring our decisions reflect clarity, purpose, and resilience.

EXAMPLE 1: KWAME NKRUMAH (1909–1972) AND THE INDEPENDENCE OF GHANA

Kwame Nkrumah, born in Nkroful, Ghana (then the Gold Coast), grew up witnessing the injustices of colonial rule. Determined to fight for independence, he became a leading figure in Ghana's nationalist movement. In 1948, protests against British colonial authorities turned violent, leading to the deaths of several protesters. Nkrumah and his colleagues were accused of inciting violence and imprisoned.

This period of incarceration tested Nkrumah's emotional resilience. Anger and frustration toward the British authorities could have driven him to adopt divisive rhetoric or retaliatory actions, jeopardizing the unity of the independence movement. Instead, he chose to pause and assess his emotions, recognizing that impulsive reactions would undermine the larger goal of freedom. From his prison cell, Nkrumah inspired his supporters to remain peaceful and focused on their shared vision for independence. He used this time to refine his strategy, uniting diverse factions and fostering a spirit of nonviolent resistance.

Upon his release, Nkrumah's leadership gained momentum. Through grassroots mobilization, diplomacy, and emotional discipline, he guided Ghana to a peaceful transition to independence. In 1957, Ghana became the first sub-Saharan African country to achieve independence, marking a historic victory against colonialism. Nkrumah's leadership not only freed his nation but also inspired anticolonial movements across Africa.

Kwame Nkrumah's life exemplifies Rule Four. By managing his emotions during critical moments, he avoided impulsive reactions and maintained focus on long-term goals. His ability to assess his anger and frustration allowed him to lead with wisdom and strategy, turning challenges into opportunities for transformative change. His story highlights the power of emotional mastery in achieving meaningful and lasting progress.

EXAMPLE 2: IVAN IV OF RUSSIA (1530–1584) AND THE OPRICHNINA

Ivan IV, later known as Ivan the Terrible, was crowned Tsar of Russia at age sixteen, becoming the first ruler to hold the title "Tsar of All Russia." His reign began with promise, marked by reforms that modernized governance and expanded Russian territory. However, his early life, shaped by neglect and abuse as an orphaned child, left him deeply mistrustful and emotionally volatile. These unresolved struggles later influenced how he reacted to life's challenges.

In 1565, Ivan IV faced growing tensions with the boyars (nobility), whom he suspected of conspiring against him. Russia had long followed a traditional governance system where the boyars wielded significant local power, controlling resources and administration in their regions. Distrustful of their influence, Ivan IV reacted emotionally, introducing the Oprichnina, a policy that divided Russia into two regions: one directly controlled by Ivan IV and the other governed by traditional structures led by the boyars. To enforce his control, Ivan IV created the Oprichniki, a personal militia with unchecked authority to suppress opposition.

This decision, driven by paranoia and anger, led to mass repression. The Oprichniki unleashed widespread terror, carrying out executions, land confiscations, and acts of brutality. Entire villages were destroyed, the economy weakened, and trust between the tsar and his people disintegrated. What began as a reaction to perceived conspiracies escalated into a reign of terror, leaving a legacy of fear and instability.

Ivan IV's reaction to this challenge illustrates the dangers of failing to assess emotions before acting. By allowing paranoia and fear to dictate his decisions, Ivan IV magnified the challenge, destabilizing his rule and the country. His story highlights the importance of emotional awareness in leadership, demonstrating how unchecked emotions can escalate manageable situations into crises with lasting consequences.

Rule Five: Be Aware That Life's Challenges Are Temporary

"This too shall pass."

—Persian proverb

Life often presents us with challenges that feel overwhelming and difficult to endure. In such moments, it's easy to believe that our struggles will last forever. However, no matter how daunting they may seem, life's challenges are like storms: powerful and unsettling in the moment but always passing to reveal clearer skies. This reminds us that the adversity we face today is not a permanent fixture in our lives.

When we recognize that obstacles are temporary, we can begin to see them as opportunities for growth, learning, and self-discovery. Instead of being consumed by fear or frustration, we can focus on the lessons these moments offer. Although difficult, these experiences often leave us stronger, more resilient, and better equipped for the future.

This perspective also helps lighten the emotional burden of adversity. By reducing the stress and anxiety that challenges bring, we can approach them with greater clarity and composure. Shifting our focus to solutions and personal growth allows even the toughest situations to become stepping stones for development.

Rule Five reminds us that struggles are temporary phases of life. Facing them with resilience and grace not only strengthens us but also prepares us for the future. By understanding this truth, we can navigate life's ups and downs with optimism, finding meaning and strength even in our darkest moments.

EXAMPLE 1: THE GREAT DEPRESSION (1929–1930s)

The Great Depression, which began with the Wall Street Crash of October 1929, was a catastrophic economic crisis that disrupted lives across the globe. Banks failed, industries halted production, and unemployment reached unprecedented levels. In the United States, nearly a quarter of the workforce was left jobless, while similar struggles unfolded in Europe and beyond. Families lost their homes, savings were wiped out, and hunger became a harsh reality for millions. The crisis pushed societies into survival mode, with many questioning whether recovery was even possible.

Despite the widespread despair, people found ways to endure and rebuild. Communities came together to share resources and support each other, while governments introduced policies aimed at stabilizing economies. In the United States, President Franklin D. Roosevelt's New Deal initiated public works programs, social security systems, and financial reforms. These measures helped restore confidence, provided employment, and set the stage for gradual recovery. By the late 1930s, economic conditions had improved, industries were revitalized, and hope began to return.

The story of the Great Depression demonstrates Rule Five. What initially seemed like an unending period of despair eventually transitioned into a time of rebuilding and renewal. Resilience, adaptability, and collective effort were key in overcoming this crisis. The recovery serves as a reminder that even the most severe challenges can be temporary when met with determination and collaboration.

EXAMPLE 2: THE COVID-19 PANDEMIC (2019–2023)

The COVID-19 pandemic, which began in late 2019, was one of the most disruptive global crises in recent history. The virus spread rapidly across continents, overwhelming healthcare systems and causing widespread economic shutdowns. Lockdowns, travel restrictions, and social distancing measures altered daily life for billions. Families were separated, businesses shuttered, and mental health issues surged as fear and uncertainty became dominant. The pandemic highlighted vulnerabilities in global systems, leaving many wondering how or when life would return to normal.

In response, humanity displayed remarkable resilience and ingenuity. Scientists worldwide worked together to develop vaccines in record time, leading to mass immunization efforts. Healthcare workers braved the frontlines, often risking their own health to save others. Communities adapted by finding new ways to stay connected, using technology to support relationships and maintain social bonds. Governments implemented economic support packages to help businesses and individuals cope with the financial impact. By 2023, vaccination rates had risen, treatments had improved, and the World Health Organization declared the public health emergency over, signaling the beginning of recovery.

The global response to COVID-19 is a powerful demonstration of Rule Five. What began as an overwhelming and seemingly endless crisis ultimately highlighted humanity's capacity for innovation, collaboration, and perseverance. The pandemic's eventual resolution serves as a reminder that even the most daunting challenges can be overcome when met with determination, unity, and a focus on solutions.

Rule Six: Choose Between Action and Acceptance in Response to Life's Challenges

"God grant me the serenity to accept the things I cannot change, the courage to change the things I can, and the wisdom to know the difference."
—Reinhold Niebuhr, *The Book of Prayers and Services for the Armed Forces*

Life often confronts us with challenges that test our patience and clarity. Rule Six offers a practical approach: Take action when change is possible, and practice acceptance when circumstances are beyond our control. This balance, rooted in teachings like Stoicism, is not about resignation but about making deliberate choices that conserve our energy and maintain our peace of mind. To apply this rule, we can follow three key steps:

1. **Identify the problem:** Assess the nature of the challenge objectively. Ask "Is this within our power to influence, or is it beyond our control?" This distinction sets the foundation for how we respond. Without clarity, we risk wasting energy on the unchangeable or overlooking areas where we can make a meaningful difference. Recognizing what is within our reach is not a sign of defeat; it is the first step toward a thoughtful response.
2. **Manage emotions:** Emotional reactions are inevitable but can cloud judgment if left unchecked. By managing our emotions constructively, we create the mental clarity needed to make sound decisions. This doesn't mean suppressing how we feel but rather acknowledging our emotions and ensuring they guide, rather than dictate, our actions. A balanced mindset allows us to respond to challenges with composure and intention.
3. **Choose action or acceptance:** Once we've identified the problem and achieved emotional balance, we can decide how to proceed. If the situation is within our control, we can act deliberately to create change. If it is beyond our influence, acceptance is the wiser choice. Acceptance is not passive; it is an active decision to release resistance, conserve energy, and focus on areas where we can make an impact.

Rule Six provides a powerful framework for navigating life's complexities. By aligning our responses with the realities of each situation, we reduce unnecessary stress and channel our energy toward meaningful actions. This mindset equips us to face challenges with resilience and clarity, transforming obstacles into opportunities for growth and fulfillment.

EXAMPLE 1: MUHAMMAD ALI (1942–2016) AND THE VIETNAM WAR

Born in Louisville, Kentucky, Muhammad Ali, originally Cassius Marcellus Clay Jr., was celebrated as one of the greatest boxers in history. However, Ali's legacy goes far beyond his achievements in the ring. In 1967, at the height of his career, Ali made the controversial decision to refuse induction into the US military during the Vietnam War. Citing his religious beliefs and moral opposition to the war, Ali declared, "I ain't got no quarrel with them Viet Cong."

This statement reflected Ali's deep conviction that he had no personal or moral justification to fight in a war against the Vietnamese people, who had not wronged him or his community. Ali viewed the war as unjust and expressed that his true fight was at home, standing against the systemic racism and inequality faced by African Americans. His words resonated with many who questioned the war and inspired others to consider the broader implications of justice, both abroad and domestically.

Ali's decision came with heavy consequences. He was stripped of his world heavyweight title, banned from professional boxing, and faced a potential five-year prison sentence.

These punishments threatened to derail his career during its peak. Yet, instead of succumbing to despair, Ali used this time to redefine his purpose. He became an outspoken advocate for civil rights and antiwar movements, traveling across the United States to speak about social justice and the principles behind his refusal. While banned from boxing, he continued to train diligently, preparing for the day he might return to the ring.

In 1971, after years of personal and professional sacrifices, the US Supreme Court overturned Ali's conviction, allowing him to resume his career. His return to the ring marked the beginning of a historic chapter in sports, with legendary matches such as the Rumble in the Jungle and the Thrilla in Manila solidifying his status as an icon. Ali's resilience during these years not only restored his career but also elevated him as a global symbol of integrity and perseverance.

Muhammad Ali's life exemplifies Rule Six: His decision to refuse the draft was a deliberate action aligned with his values, demonstrating courage in the face of immense opposition. At the same time, Ali practiced acceptance by focusing on what he could control—his advocacy, his training, and his personal growth—despite being banned from the sport he loved. This balance of action and acceptance allowed him to overcome adversity with integrity and leave a lasting impact on the world.

EXAMPLE 2: CHARLES I OF ENGLAND (1600–1649)

Born into the House of Stuart, Charles I ascended to the English throne in 1625, inheriting a nation already divided by political and religious tensions. His firm belief in the divine right of kings, which asserted his authority as absolute, placed him at odds with Parliament's growing demands for a greater role in governance. During his Personal Rule (1629–1640), Charles I dissolved Parliament and ruled alone, imposing unpopular taxes and enforcing religious conformity. These actions alienated many of his subjects, deepening mistrust and resentment.

As tensions escalated, Charles I faced critical challenges, including financial instability, public dissent, and the Bishops' Wars with Scotland. He was presented with opportunities to act decisively by negotiating with Parliament or to accept the limitations of his authority to preserve national stability. Instead, he refused to compromise, clinging to his vision of absolute power. This rigidity intensified divisions, culminating in the outbreak of the English Civil War (1642–1651). Defeated in the war, Charles I was captured, tried, and executed in 1649. His downfall ended the monarchy temporarily and led to republican rule under Oliver Cromwell, marking a profound shift in England's political landscape.

Charles I's reign demonstrates the consequences of ignoring Rule Six: By failing to act constructively or accept the changing realities of his time, he escalated tensions and ultimately sealed his fate. His story serves as a stark reminder that an unwillingness to balance action and acceptance can turn challenges into irreversible conflict.

Rule Seven: Apply the ABCD Method When Challenges Arise

"We don't see things as they are, we see them as we are."
—popularized by Anaïs Nin, *Seduction of the Minotaur*

When life presents us with challenges, our perceptions and responses play a crucial role in shaping the outcome. Rule Seven introduces the ABCD method, a cognitive strategy designed to help us reframe unhelpful thoughts and respond constructively. By challenging irrational beliefs and fostering healthier perspectives, this method equips us to handle difficulties with greater emotional balance and resilience. The ABCD method consists of four steps:

1. **A—Action:** Identify the event or situation triggering our response. This could be an external event, such as receiving criticism, or an internal thought or feeling.
2. **B—Belief:** Examine how we interpret the event. Are our beliefs rational and grounded in fact, or are they influenced by assumptions, fears, or distortions?
3. **C—Consequence:** Reflect on the emotional and behavioral outcomes of our beliefs. Irrational beliefs often lead to negative consequences, such as frustration, anxiety, or defensiveness.
4. **D—Disputation:** Challenge irrational beliefs by questioning their validity. Replace them with rational and constructive perspectives to foster healthier emotional and behavioral responses.

For example, imagine receiving unexpected criticism (Action). If we interpret the feedback as a personal attack (Belief), this may lead to anger, defensiveness, or withdrawal (Consequence). By disputing this belief, we can consider alternative interpretations, such as viewing the feedback as an opportunity for growth or recognizing that it may not be valid. This shift allows us to respond calmly, seek clarification, or let go of unnecessary negativity (Disputation).

Rule Seven provides a transformative framework for navigating challenges. By applying the ABCD method, we cultivate self-awareness, rational thinking, and emotional resilience. This approach not only helps us manage immediate difficulties but also strengthens our ability to thrive in the face of future challenges, fostering long-term growth and emotional intelligence.

EXAMPLE 1: ABRAHAM LINCOLN (1809–1865)

Born in a log cabin in Kentucky, Abraham Lincoln faced numerous obstacles long before becoming the sixteenth president of the United States. His political career was marked by a series of defeats, including his loss in the 1858 Senate race against Stephen Douglas despite his widely acclaimed debate performances. Earlier, he failed to secure the vice-presidential nomination in 1856, and in total, he lost eight elections. These public setbacks could have discouraged him from pursuing politics further.

However, Lincoln's ability to reassess and reframe these defeats was pivotal to his success. Rather than internalizing beliefs of inadequacy, he remained committed to his purpose and values. He viewed each setback as an opportunity to refine his strategies and strengthen his resolve. This perspective ultimately paid off when, in 1860, he was elected president, guiding the nation through the Civil War and leading efforts to abolish slavery. Lincoln's approach aligns seamlessly with the ABCD method:

1. **A—Action:** The repeated electoral defeats served as the triggering events.
2. **B—Belief:** Lincoln rejected irrational beliefs of failure or

inadequacy, focusing instead on his purpose and ability to lead.

3. **C—Consequence:** His constructive belief system enabled him to persevere and continue his political journey despite challenges.
4. **D—Disputation:** Lincoln critically reassessed his responses to each setback, challenging unproductive thoughts and identifying lessons that strengthened his resolve and adaptability.

Abraham Lincoln's story embodies Rule Seven. By applying the ABCD method, he transformed repeated challenges into opportunities for growth and perseverance. His ability to evaluate his beliefs, reframe his mindset, and maintain focus on his goals highlights the power of this approach in fostering resilience and clarity.

EXAMPLE 2: MAO ZEDONG'S GREAT LEAP FORWARD (1958–1962)

Born in Shaoshan, China, Mao Zedong rose to prominence as the leader of the People's Republic of China in 1949. By the late 1950s, Mao faced significant challenges as China sought to recover from colonial exploitation, war, and economic instability. To address these issues, he launched the Great Leap Forward, an ambitious campaign to rapidly transform China into an industrialized global power through collectivization and large-scale economic reforms.

However, Mao's unwavering commitment to his vision, combined with his refusal to reassess his strategies, led to catastrophic outcomes. Policies such as the establishment of People's Communes and excessive grain requisitions destabilized the economy and caused widespread famine, resulting in millions of deaths. Despite mounting evidence of failure, Mao suppressed dissent and doubled down on his approach, deepening the crisis. Mao's leadership during the Great Leap Forward illustrates a failure to apply the ABCD method:

1. **A—Action:** Mao's response to the challenge of rebuilding China's economy was the Great Leap Forward, an overly ambitious and poorly executed campaign.
2. **B—Belief:** Mao's rigid belief in his vision and communist ideology prevented him from considering alternative approaches or adapting to changing circumstances.
3. **C—Consequence:** These unyielding beliefs led to famine, economic collapse, and widespread suffering, marking one of the darkest periods in modern Chinese history.
4. **D—Disputation:** Mao failed to critically assess his beliefs or adapt his strategies, rejecting opportunities for corrective action and silencing those who questioned him.

Mao Zedong's leadership during the Great Leap Forward underscores the dangers of ignoring Rule Seven. His inability to reassess his response, challenge irrational beliefs, or adapt to reality turned a monumental challenge into a devastating crisis. His story serves as a stark reminder of the importance of critical reflection and adaptability when navigating life's complexities.

CHAPTER 7

Navigating Forgiveness

"Forgive others, not because they deserve forgiveness, but because you deserve peace."
—commonly attributed to Jonathan Lockwood Huie

Rule One: Forgive and Let Go of Resentment

"Resentment is like drinking poison and then hoping it will kill your enemies."
—commonly attributed to Nelson Mandela

Throughout life, others will inevitably cause us harm, leading to feelings of resentment and anger. While it may seem natural to hold on to these emotions, they often harm us more than those who wronged us. Resentment drains our emotional energy and clouds our peace of mind. Rule One emphasizes that forgiveness is not about excusing or forgetting wrongdoing; it is about freeing ourselves from negativity and reclaiming control over our emotional well-being.

Forgiveness is a deliberate choice to let go of bitterness. Left unchecked, resentment can harm our mental and physical health, creating a cycle of stress and unhappiness. By forgiving, we acknowledge that the past cannot be changed and choose to focus on the present and future instead. It empowers us to prioritize healing and resilience while maintaining emotional clarity.

The impact of forgiveness extends beyond our own healing. Forgiving someone, such as a family member after a prolonged conflict, can restore trust and rebuild relationships, creating a more compassionate environment. Forgiveness also enhances emotional intelligence, allowing us to navigate challenges with empathy and ensure that our actions reflect our values rather than the behavior of others.

Rule One reminds us of the profound liberation that forgiveness brings. By letting go of resentment, we break free from negativity and open the door to healing, connection, and fulfillment. Forgiveness is a tool for personal growth, enabling us to lead more peaceful, meaningful lives.

EXAMPLE 1: GORDON WILSON (1927–1995)

Gordon Wilson, a resident of Enniskillen, Northern Ireland, experienced a devastating loss on November 8, 1987, during the annual Remembrance Day parade. At the time, Northern Ireland was embroiled in a decades-long conflict known as the Troubles, a period marked by sectarian violence between unionists, primarily Protestant and loyal to the United Kingdom, and nationalists, primarily Catholic and seeking a united

Ireland. The violence included bombings, assassinations, and armed clashes, resulting in widespread fear and division.

During the parade, a bomb planted by the Irish Republican Army (IRA) exploded, killing eleven people and injuring dozens. Among the victims was Wilson's twenty-year-old daughter, Marie, who was critically injured. Trapped under the rubble together, Wilson held Marie's hand as they waited for rescue. Despite her injuries, Marie expressed her love for her father in their final moments together before succumbing to her wounds shortly after being freed.

In the wake of this tragedy, Wilson made the extraordinary decision to publicly forgive the bombers. He stated that harboring anger would not bring his daughter back and that forgiveness was the only way to move forward. This act of forgiveness, made during a period of intense violence and polarization, challenged the prevailing cycle of retaliation and hatred that defined the Troubles.

Wilson's forgiveness became the foundation of his efforts as a peace advocate. He worked tirelessly with political and community leaders to promote dialogue and reconciliation in Northern Ireland. His actions inspired many, offering a vision of hope and the possibility of healing in a deeply divided society. While the Troubles continued for years, Wilson's commitment to peace served as a powerful reminder of the potential for change, even in the most difficult circumstances.

Gordon Wilson's response reflects Rule One. By forgiving the bombers, he avoided the emotional harm caused by resentment and redirected his energy toward advocating for peace. His decision not only brought him personal healing but also demonstrated how forgiveness can inspire collective reconciliation, proving its transformative power even in times of great adversity.

EXAMPLE 2: IMMACULÉE ILIBAGIZA (1972–)

Immaculée Ilibagiza was born in Rwanda, a country that experienced one of the most devastating genocides in modern history. In 1994, ethnic tensions between the Hutus and Tutsis escalated into mass violence, resulting in the deaths of nearly one million Tutsis in ninety-one days. To survive, Ilibagiza and seven other women hid in a small bathroom measuring three feet by four feet. For ninety-one days, they lived in silence, surviving on minimal food and water, while the Hutu militia searched nearby homes to kill any Tutsis they found.

When the genocide ended, Ilibagiza learned that her parents, two brothers, and many relatives had been killed. Overwhelmed by anger and grief, she struggled to cope with the scale of her loss. While living in a refugee camp, she began to reflect on how resentment and hatred were affecting her. She turned to prayer, asking for the strength to forgive those responsible for the killings. Over time, she realized that holding on to anger would only harm her further and prevent her from rebuilding her life.

Her commitment to forgiveness was tested when she came face-to-face with one of her family's killers. Despite the difficulty of the moment, she chose to forgive him, understanding that forgiveness was not about excusing his actions but about releasing herself from the burden of resentment. This decision helped her find emotional freedom and move forward with her life. Ilibagiza shared her experience in her memoir, *Left to Tell*, where she documented the genocide and her decision to forgive. Her story has since inspired millions, encouraging others to let go of anger and use forgiveness as a tool for healing.

Immaculée Ilibagiza's journey reflects Rule One: She freed herself from the emotional weight of hatred and found a way to heal. Her experience shows how forgiveness can help individuals rebuild their lives after loss, offering a path to resilience and recovery even in the most challenging circumstances.

Rule Two: Forgive, Revenge Will Not Heal You

"Without forgiveness, there's no future."
—**Desmond Tutu,** *No Future Without Forgiveness*

When wronged, it is natural to feel anger and the urge for revenge, believing it will bring justice or closure. However, revenge rarely delivers the healing we seek. Instead, it perpetuates cycles of pain and anger, leaving us emotionally stuck. Forgiveness, on the other hand, is a choice to break free from this cycle. It allows us to let go of resentment and prioritize our emotional well-being, creating the space needed for healing and inner peace.

Forgiveness does not mean excusing harm or abandoning accountability. It is about releasing ourselves from the grip of anger and retribution, choosing instead to focus on personal recovery. This decision requires strength and emotional maturity, particularly in a world that often glorifies revenge. By forgiving—not for the wrongdoer's benefit, but for our own—we reclaim control over our emotions and create the foundation for lasting healing.

Forgiveness also has a broader impact. It fosters healthier relationships and can break cycles of retaliation, contributing to trust and understanding within communities. While justice may still be pursued, forgiveness ensures that our emotional energy is not consumed by anger, allowing us to move forward with clarity and purpose.

Rule Two reminds us that forgiveness is essential for healing and self-discovery. By choosing to let go of anger and resentment, we free ourselves from the weight of revenge. This choice fosters emotional resilience, enabling us to move forward with clarity and peace. Forgiveness transforms adversity into an opportunity for growth, leading to a life of greater meaning and fulfillment.

EXAMPLE 1: POPE JOHN PAUL II (1920–2005)

Born Karol Józef Wojtyła in Wadowice, Poland, Pope John Paul II led the Catholic Church from 1978 to 2005. On May 13, 1981, Mehmet Ali Ağca, a Turkish gunman, shot the pope in Saint Peter's Square, critically injuring him. The attack shocked the world, and the pope required extensive surgery to survive.

Two years later, Pope John Paul II took the unusual step of visiting Ağca in prison. Sitting face-to-face with the man who had tried to kill him, the pope offered him forgiveness. This act was deeply personal, stemming from his belief that anger and revenge would only perpetuate harm. Instead, he chose to approach the situation with compassion, focusing on his commitment to mercy and reconciliation.

The pope's decision not only demonstrated his own emotional strength but also sent a message to others that forgiveness can lead to healing. By refusing to harbor resentment, he showed how letting go of anger can promote peace and understanding, even in the face of serious harm.

Pope John Paul II's actions exemplify Rule Two: By forgiving his attacker, he broke the cycle of anger and resentment, choosing compassion and mercy instead. His decision demonstrated that forgiveness is a powerful act of strength, with the potential to foster healing and inspire reconciliation.

EXAMPLE 2: ARCHBISHOP DESMOND TUTU (1931–2021)

Born in Klerksdorp, South Africa, Archbishop Desmond Tutu witnessed the injustices of apartheid firsthand. This system of racial segregation caused widespread suffering and created deep divisions within the country. After apartheid ended, Tutu was tasked with one of the most difficult roles in South Africa's history: chairing the Truth and Reconciliation Commission (TRC) in 1995.

The TRC brought together victims and perpetrators of apartheid-era crimes to uncover the truth and promote healing. Tutu emphasized forgiveness and restorative justice, arguing that revenge would only worsen the divisions apartheid had created. Instead, the commission encouraged accountability and dialogue, allowing people to share their experiences in a safe environment. Although the process was painful, it helped many begin to let go of their anger and focus on rebuilding their lives and communities.

Tutu's leadership during this period demonstrated the strength required to reject revenge in favor of reconciliation. By prioritizing forgiveness, he provided a pathway for South Africa to confront its past and move toward unity. His work inspired others worldwide to consider forgiveness as a way to address conflicts and create lasting peace.

Archbishop Desmond Tutu's leadership reflects Rule Two: Through forgiveness and dialogue, he helped South Africa confront its painful past and move toward healing. His work showed that forgiveness is essential not only for personal peace but also for rebuilding divided communities.

Rule Three: When You Make a Mistake, Forgive Yourself, Then Seek Forgiveness

"Forgiving yourself is an act of self-love and self-acceptance."
—commonly attributed to Louise Hay

When we make a mistake, whether it's a small lapse in judgment or a significant error with lasting effects, it's natural to feel guilt and self-criticism. Rule Three reminds us that the first step is to forgive ourselves. Self-forgiveness is not about excusing harm or avoiding accountability—it is about acknowledging our imperfections, reflecting on what went wrong, and committing to learn from the experience. By letting go of guilt, we regain the clarity and emotional strength needed to move forward constructively.

Once we have forgiven ourselves, the next step is to seek forgiveness from those we have hurt. This involves recognizing how our actions impacted others, expressing sincere regret, and taking meaningful steps to rebuild trust. Seeking forgiveness goes beyond an apology; it requires accountability, consistent effort, and a commitment to change. By addressing the harm we caused, we not only repair relationships but also demonstrate integrity and mutual respect.

Rule Three teaches us that our mistakes can be valuable opportunities for growth when approached with humility and responsibility. By forgiving ourselves and seeking forgiveness from others, we develop resilience, empathy, and deeper self-awareness. This process not only helps us heal but also fosters stronger relationships, enabling us to move forward with greater purpose and compassion.

EXAMPLE 1: KING ASHOKA (304–232 BC)

Ashoka, the third ruler of the Mauryan Empire, was known for his ambition and military conquests. In 261 BC, he waged the Kalinga War, a campaign that caused immense destruction, leading to over one hundred thousand deaths and the displacement of countless others. The aftermath of the war left Ashoka deeply disturbed by the suffering his actions had caused, prompting a profound transformation in his leadership.

Ashoka turned to Buddhism for guidance, adopting its teachings on compassion, nonviolence, and moral responsibility. He expressed deep regret for the harm caused by his conquests and redirected his efforts toward promoting peace and welfare. Ashoka implemented reforms that prioritized social harmony, humane governance, and care for all living beings. His edicts, carved into stone across the empire, encouraged kindness, tolerance, and accountability, signaling his commitment to repair the damage caused by his earlier actions.

Ashoka's response reflects Rule Three. While history does not record whether Ashoka explicitly forgave himself, his actions demonstrate a recognition of his past mistakes and a determination to atone for them. Through his reforms, he sought to address the harm he had caused and rebuild trust within his empire. Ashoka's journey illustrates how acknowledging wrongdoing and taking responsibility can lead to meaningful change and a lasting positive legacy.

EXAMPLE 2: JOHN NEWTON (1725–1807)

John Newton, born in Georgian London, spent much of his early life participating in the transatlantic slave trade. In 1748, during a dangerous sea voyage, a violent storm threatened to sink his ship. This life-threatening experience led Newton to re-evaluate his actions and begin reflecting on his role in one of history's greatest injustices.

In the years that followed, Newton came to terms with his past. Acknowledging the harm he had caused, he forgave himself for his participation in the slave trade, recognizing the importance of taking responsibility for his actions. This self-forgiveness allowed him to redirect his life. He left the slave trade and dedicated himself to addressing the harm he had once supported.

Newton became a minister and an abolitionist, using his writings and influence to condemn the slave trade. His pamphlet *Thoughts Upon the African Slave Trade* detailed the atrocities he had witnessed and expressed his deep regret. His hymn "Amazing Grace" reflected his journey, serving as a personal expression of repentance and forgiveness. Newton's efforts significantly contributed to Britain's abolitionist movement and helped shift public opinion on slavery.

John Newton's transformation reflects Rule Three: By forgiving himself, he found the clarity to take responsibility for his actions and seek forgiveness through meaningful efforts to address the harm he caused. His life demonstrates how mistakes, when met with accountability and change, can lead to personal growth and positive societal impact.

Rule Four: Stop the Cycle of Blame and Shame with Forgiveness

"We are all full of weakness and errors;
let us mutually pardon each other our follies."

—Voltaire, *Letters on the English*

Life often places us in situations where mistakes—our own or others'—create cycles of blame and shame. These emotions, while understandable, can trap us in negativity, harming our self-esteem, straining relationships, and stalling personal growth. Rule Four reminds us that forgiveness is the key to breaking this cycle and moving forward.

Forgiveness begins with recognizing that mistakes often arise from ignorance, limited understanding, or misjudgment. This perspective fosters empathy, helping us view situations with greater compassion. By forgiving ourselves, we release guilt and self-criticism, allowing room for healing and growth. Forgiving others helps us move past resentment, focusing instead on reconciliation and building stronger connections.

Forgiveness is not about excusing harm or avoiding accountability. It involves acknowledging mistakes and taking responsibility for addressing the consequences. Self-forgiveness may include reflecting on what went wrong and committing to change, while forgiving others may involve open communication and empathy. By prioritizing forgiveness over blame, we transform mistakes into opportunities for trust, growth, and understanding.

Rule Four highlights the transformative power of forgiveness. Choosing forgiveness frees us from emotional burdens, fosters resilience, and strengthens relationships. By embracing mistakes as chances to learn and grow, we create pathways to deeper empathy, personal development, and emotional well-being.

EXAMPLE 1: BILAL IBN RABAH (580–640)

Born in Ethiopia and enslaved in Mecca, Bilal ibn Rabah endured years of brutal treatment. His conversion to Islam intensified his suffering, as his master, Umayyah ibn Khalaf, subjected him to relentless persecution. Bilal was tortured under the scorching desert sun, with heavy stones placed on his chest, in an attempt to force him to renounce his faith. Despite this, Bilal remained steadfast, repeatedly declaring "Ahad, Ahad" (One God), a proclamation of his unwavering belief.

Bilal's circumstances changed after the Muslim conquest of Mecca, where he gained prominence in the city that had once oppressed him. Now in a position of influence, Bilal had the power to retaliate against his former tormentors, including Umayyah. However, he chose forgiveness over vengeance. This decision required immense emotional strength, as it meant letting go of resentment and prioritizing peace over personal retribution. Bilal's forgiveness not only freed him from the weight of bitterness but also set an example for others, fostering reconciliation and unity within a divided community.

Bilal ibn Rabah's life vividly reflects Rule Four: By choosing forgiveness, he broke free from the cycle of blame and resentment, using his influence to promote healing and harmony. His actions demonstrate that forgiveness is not just a personal choice but a powerful tool for societal transformation, showing how letting go of anger can pave the way for understanding and peace.

EXAMPLE 2: PROPHET MUHAMMAD (570–632)

Born in Mecca, Prophet Muhammad endured years of persecution as he preached the message of Islam. His teachings challenged the societal and religious norms of his time, leading to hostility from Mecca's elite. Over the years, he and his followers faced economic boycotts, physical violence, and social ostracism, ultimately forcing them to migrate to Medina in 622. This migration marked a turning point, as it allowed Prophet Muhammad to establish a community grounded in justice, equality, and faith.

In 630, after years of conflict, Prophet Muhammad and his followers peacefully re-entered Mecca in the event known as the Conquest of Mecca. Presented with the opportunity for retribution against those who had persecuted him and his followers, he chose forgiveness instead. Declaring a general amnesty, he pardoned his former enemies, including those who had inflicted significant harm. In a society where revenge was the norm, this act of forgiveness set a new standard for leadership and moral strength.

Prophet Muhammad's decision to forgive was not merely an act of mercy; it was a deliberate effort to end cycles of blame and violence. His forgiveness allowed the people of Mecca to move past old grievances, fostering unity and reconciliation in a previously fractured society. By prioritizing compassion over retaliation, he established a foundation for lasting peace in the region.

Prophet Muhammad's actions during the Conquest of Mecca exemplify Rule Four: By choosing forgiveness over revenge, he demonstrated that true strength lies in the ability to let go of resentment and focus on reconciliation. His actions not only brought healing to his community but also set a lasting example of how forgiveness can pave the way for unity, understanding, and progress.

Rule Five: Imagine the Unreceived Apology and Forgive

"To forgive is to set a prisoner free and discover that the prisoner was you."
—Lewis B. Smedes, *Forgive and Forget*

In life, we often face situations where we are wronged but never receive an apology. These moments challenge our emotional resilience, particularly when those responsible fail to acknowledge their actions. Rule Five introduces the practice of visualization as a tool for healing. By imagining a heartfelt apology from those who hurt us, we create an internal sense of closure, helping us release unresolved pain and move forward.

Visualization is not about excusing wrongdoing or changing the past. Instead, it shifts the focus inward, allowing us to let go of resentment and regain control of our emotional well-being. While this process may feel difficult or unnatural at first, it fosters empathy and understanding, even when reconciliation is not possible.

It is important to recognize that visualization is not a universal solution or a replacement for therapy in cases of profound trauma or distress. Rather, it is a complementary practice that supports other forms of healing and self-reflection. By finding peace within ourselves, we free ourselves from the emotional weight of past wrongs and cultivate resilience and clarity.

Rule Five reminds us that forgiveness is an internal journey. By practicing visualization, we liberate ourselves from the grip of resentment and embrace a future of emotional freedom and growth. Forgiveness through visualization empowers us to let go of the past and live with greater peace and purpose.

EXAMPLE 1: CBT AND GUIDED IMAGERY

Cognitive behavioral therapy (CBT) often incorporates visualization exercises to help individuals navigate feelings of anger, resentment, or guilt. A common practice involves imagining a conversation with someone who has caused harm, including visualizing an apology that was never received. This mental exercise allows individuals to confront their emotions, process their pain, and achieve closure, even in the absence of a real apology.

Guided imagery, another therapeutic approach, focuses on creating positive mental scenarios to support emotional healing. For self-forgiveness, individuals might visualize their younger selves expressing regret for past mistakes and their present selves responding with compassion and forgiveness. This internal dialogue, conducted in a safe mental space, helps break cycles of self-blame and fosters emotional resilience. Both techniques empower individuals to shift their focus inward, reclaiming control over their emotional well-being.

Visualization aligns seamlessly with Rule Five: It underscores that forgiveness begins internally, independent of external validation. By practicing visualization, individuals can process unresolved emotions, release resentment, and cultivate empathy and understanding. This transformative tool demonstrates that emotional freedom and growth come from within, even in the absence of external apologies.

EXAMPLE 2: LOUISE HAY (1926–2017)

Louise Hay, born in Los Angeles, overcame significant personal challenges to become a pioneer in the self-help movement. Her early life was marked by trauma, including abuse and sexual violence, which left her with deep emotional scars. Later in life, a cancer diagnosis added another layer of adversity. Determined to heal, Hay explored various techniques, with visualization playing a central role in her journey toward forgiveness and recovery.

In her book *You Can Heal Your Life*, Hay described how she used visualization to imagine conversations with those who had hurt her. By picturing heartfelt apologies and responding with forgiveness, she created a sense of closure that had been missing in reality. This practice allowed her to process long-held anger and resentment, which she believed were contributing to her emotional and physical distress. Through visualization, Hay was able to release the burden of unresolved pain, fostering empathy and self-compassion.

Hay's teachings extended far beyond her personal journey. Her approach to forgiveness and visualization inspired millions to address their own unresolved emotions. By imagining unreceived apologies, she empowered others to break free from the emotional grip of past wrongs and embrace forgiveness as a tool for healing and self-acceptance.

Louise Hay's practice of visualization reflects Rule Five: By using visualization to create closure, she demonstrated that forgiveness is an internal process, independent of external validation. Her life and teachings show how visualization can transform unresolved pain into emotional freedom and resilience, paving the way for personal growth and well-being.

Rule Six: Visualize Those Who Wronged You as Children, Then on Their Deathbed

"If we could read the secret history of our enemies, we should find in each man's life sorrow and suffering enough to disarm all hostility."
—Henry Wadsworth Longfellow, *Driftwood*

Forgiveness can be one of life's most challenging emotional journeys, especially when the pain caused by others runs deep. Rule Six offers a transformative approach: visualizing those who wronged us in two contrasting stages of life—childhood innocence and deathbed vulnerability. This practice shifts our perspective from resentment to compassion, fostering emotional liberation and healing. The visualization process involves five steps:

1. **Childhood innocence:** Picture the person as a four-year-old child—innocent and untainted by life's hardships. This perspective reminds us that their harmful behaviors were shaped by experiences, not inherent malice. Recognizing their early innocence helps soften feelings of anger.
2. **Vulnerability at life's end:** Visualize the person on their deathbed, reflecting on their life. This image highlights their humanity and fragility, reminding us that they, like us, have faced joys, regrets, and struggles.
3. **Acknowledgement of our pain:** Reflect on how their actions impacted us, using journaling, meditation, or silent contemplation. This step allows us to process and release our emotions, preparing us for forgiveness.
4. **Contemplation of their perspective:** Consider the circumstances that may have shaped their behavior.

Understanding the complexities of their choices fosters empathy without excusing their actions.

5. **Forgiveness as liberation:** Forgiveness is not about condoning harm but about freeing ourselves from resentment. By forgiving, we choose to heal, grow, and reclaim our emotional peace.

It is important to recognize that visualization is not a universal solution or a replacement for professional therapy, particularly in cases of profound trauma or deep emotional distress. Instead, it is a complementary practice that supports healing and self-reflection. By finding peace within ourselves through this process, we can release the emotional weight of past wrongs and cultivate clarity, resilience, and compassion.

Rule Six reminds us that forgiveness is a journey of perspective and empathy. By visualizing others at their most human—innocent and vulnerable—we move from bitterness to compassion. This practice not only fosters emotional healing but also strengthens our ability to approach life with greater understanding and peace.

EXAMPLE 1: METTA MEDITATION IN BUDDHISM

Metta meditation, a central practice in Buddhist traditions, offers a profound method for cultivating empathy and forgiveness. Rooted in teachings that emphasize compassion for all beings, it guides practitioners to extend kindness even to those who have caused harm. This practice becomes particularly transformative when it involves visualizing adversaries at vulnerable stages of life, such as childhood and old age, fostering a shift in perspective.

Metta meditation begins with directing kindness toward oneself and gradually expanding it to loved ones, acquaintances, and those who have wronged us. Practitioners visualize an individual who has caused pain as an innocent child, free from malice and before being shaped by life's experiences. They also imagine the same person at the end of their life, reflecting on their joys, regrets, and struggles. These visualizations highlight shared humanity, encouraging forgiveness by replacing resentment with compassion. While powerful, this process is not without challenges. Confronting anger and pain requires emotional effort and patience, as forgiveness is seldom immediate. Yet, by persevering, practitioners find that Metta meditation transforms their view of adversaries, helping them release resentment and achieve inner peace.

Metta meditation perfectly aligns with Rule Six: By encouraging a perspective shift through visualization, it empowers individuals to break cycles of anger and bitterness. This practice nurtures not only personal healing but also a culture of empathy and reconciliation, demonstrating the transformative power of forgiveness.

EXAMPLE 2: THERAPEUTIC VISUALIZATION FOR FORGIVENESS

Therapeutic visualization is a widely used tool for fostering forgiveness and emotional healing. Similar to Metta meditation, it encourages individuals to visualize those who have wronged them at two contrasting life stages: as a young child and on their deathbed. This method deepens empathy and understanding, paving the way for forgiveness and emotional freedom. The visualization process unfolds in three steps:

1. **Guided visualization:** Practitioners begin by imagining the person as a small child—innocent, curious, and untainted by life's hardships. Next, they visualize the same person on their deathbed, reflecting on their life's joys, regrets, and struggles. These images highlight the shared humanity and fragility that connect us all.
2. **Emotional reflection:** Through these visualizations, individuals confront their own pain while recognizing that hurtful actions often stem from unresolved struggles and suffering in others. This step helps replace anger with compassion, fostering emotional clarity.
3. **Forgiveness and release:** With this newfound perspective, individuals are able to release resentment and embrace forgiveness. Forgiveness becomes not just an act of compassion but a pathway to personal healing and emotional liberation.

This therapeutic approach aligns perfectly with Rule Six: By humanizing those who have hurt us, therapeutic visualization enables a shift from bitterness to compassion. This process fosters resilience and promotes personal growth, showing that forgiveness is not about excusing harm but about reclaiming our emotional peace and moving forward with clarity.

Rule Seven: Forgive Others, as They May Be Facing Struggles Unknown to You

"Be pitiful, for every man is fighting a hard battle."
—John Watson (Ian Maclaren), *The British Weekly*

Life often conceals the struggles others endure when they wrong us. Behind even the most hurtful actions may lie unseen emotional, physical, or mental battles. Rule Seven encourages us to forgive by recognizing that people's behaviors are often shaped by challenges we cannot see. This shift in perspective—from judgment to empathy—helps us approach others with understanding and compassion, fostering healthier relationships and inner peace.

Forgiveness rooted in empathy begins with the recognition that mistakes are part of the shared human experience. People's actions are rarely rooted in malice; more often, they stem from personal struggles, ignorance, or poor judgment. Stepping into others' shoes and considering their circumstances bridges the gap between perceived harm and the complexities of human behavior.

This rule does not advocate excusing harm but emphasizes the importance of releasing anger and resentment. Forgiveness is a conscious act of letting go, freeing ourselves from emotional burdens and reclaiming inner peace. Whether or not we communicate forgiveness, this practice nurtures emotional resilience, strengthens relationships, and fosters a culture of understanding and patience.

Rule Seven reminds us that forgiveness is a path to freedom and transformation. By responding with empathy and compassion, we enrich our emotional strength and contribute to a more understanding world. This perspective enables us to navigate life's challenges with grace, fostering healing and deeper connections.

EXAMPLE 1: EVA KOR (1934–2019)

Born in Romania, Eva Kor and her twin sister, Miriam, were just ten years old when they were transported to Auschwitz in 1944. Upon arrival, they were separated from their family, whom they would never see again. The twins became subjects of Josef Mengele's inhumane medical experiments, enduring daily injections, blood draws, and procedures without anesthesia. Eva described how Mengele often smiled while conducting his experiments, which added to the psychological torment. She was forced to watch Miriam suffer, all while grappling with her own physical pain and the haunting knowledge that her parents and siblings had perished in the gas chambers.

Despite surviving Auschwitz, Eva carried the scars of her experiences for decades. The weight of anger and resentment consumed her, tethering her emotionally to the trauma of her past. In 1995, during the fiftieth anniversary of the liberation of Auschwitz, Eva made a groundbreaking public declaration of forgiveness. At a Holocaust commemoration event in Boston, she stunned attendees by announcing her decision to forgive the Nazis, including Mengele. This act was not about excusing their actions but about reclaiming her emotional freedom. Eva explained that forgiveness allowed her to release the hold that anger had over her, giving her the strength to heal and move forward.

This decision was deeply personal but had a profound ripple effect. Eva channeled her experiences into advocacy, founding the CANDLES Holocaust Museum and Education Center in Indiana in 1995. Through public speaking, educational initiatives, and her documentary *Forgiving Dr. Mengele*, she inspired others to explore forgiveness as a path to healing. Her message emphasized that forgiveness, rooted in empathy, is a choice that liberates the one who forgives.

Eva Kor's journey exemplifies Rule Seven: By recognizing the systemic forces and ideologies that shaped her oppressors, she chose to view them through the lens of human complexity rather than pure malice. Her courage to forgive not only liberated her from the weight of anger but also inspired countless others to embrace forgiveness as a tool for personal and societal healing. Eva's life demonstrates that forgiveness, rooted in empathy, has the power to transform pain into a force for reconciliation and understanding.

EXAMPLE 2: STEVE SAINT (1951–)

Steve Saint was just five years old when his father, Nate Saint, was killed by members of the Waorani tribe in Ecuador. In 1956, Nate and four other missionaries attempted to reach the Waorani, a historically isolated and defensive community. Misunderstandings and long-standing fears led to a tragic confrontation, resulting in the missionaries' deaths.

As a child, Steve struggled to make sense of his father's death. Years later, seeking closure, he returned to Ecuador to engage directly with the Waorani. Immersing himself in their culture, Steve built relationships with tribe members, including those involved in his father's death. Through these interactions, he came to understand the historical conflicts, cultural isolation, and fears that had shaped the Waorani's actions. This shift in perspective allowed him to see beyond his pain and resentment, fostering empathy for the community.

Rather than harboring anger, Steve chose forgiveness. He recognized the Waorani's humanity and worked alongside them to build trust and improve their living conditions. He shared their story with the world, helping others understand the complexities of their culture and the circumstances that led to the tragic events of 1956. His journey of forgiveness not only brought him personal healing but also contributed to reconciliation and mutual understanding between the Waorani and the outside world.

Steve Saint's story exemplifies Rule Seven: By acknowledging the hidden struggles and fears that influenced the Waorani's actions, he demonstrated the power of empathy and forgiveness. His ability to move beyond judgment and embrace understanding highlights how forgiveness can transform grief into healing and build bridges across even the deepest divides.

Rule Eight: Choose Kindness over Being Right and Forgive

"I have always found that mercy bears richer fruits than strict justice."
—Abraham Lincoln, as quoted in *Lincoln Memorial*

Life often places us in situations where others wrong us or act unjustly. In these moments, we face a choice: prioritize being right and defending our perspective or choose kindness and forgiveness. Rule Eight encourages us to favor the latter—not by abandoning truth or principles, but by responding with empathy and understanding. This choice reflects a recognition of human imperfection, including our own, and fosters emotional growth and reconciliation.

Choosing kindness and forgiveness is not a sign of weakness; it is a demonstration of strength and emotional maturity. By responding with compassion, we shift the focus from the wrongdoing to mutual understanding, creating opportunities for constructive dialogue and healing. This approach allows us to move forward without being consumed by anger or the need for vindication.

It is important to recognize that forgiveness is not always immediate or straightforward, particularly in cases of severe harm or ongoing injustice. Practicing kindness does not mean tolerating abuse, ignoring systemic issues, or excusing harmful behavior. Instead, it requires a balanced response—one that upholds truth and justice while releasing anger and resentment. Kindness and forgiveness must coexist with accountability, ensuring that justice and integrity are not compromised.

Rule Eight reminds us that kindness and forgiveness are not just acts of compassion but tools for transformation. By balancing empathy with accountability, we create a culture of harmony and fairness. This approach helps us navigate life's challenges with grace, fostering healing and deeper connections while enriching both ourselves and those around us.

EXAMPLE 1: JOSÉ "PEPE" MUJICA (1935–)

Born in Uruguay, José "Pepe" Mujica grew up witnessing social inequalities that fueled his desire for change. In the 1960s and 1970s, he joined the left-wing Tupamaros guerrilla movement, advocating for political and social reform. As a result of his activism, Mujica was captured and imprisoned multiple times. His longest incarceration began in 1972, when he was held under extreme conditions for more than a decade. During this time, he endured physical abuse, solitary confinement, and years of near-total isolation, often confined in darkness or silence.

When Uruguay transitioned back to democracy in 1985, Mujica was released along with other political prisoners. Despite his suffering, he made a remarkable decision: He chose to forgive those who had imprisoned and mistreated him. Mujica recognized that holding on to anger would tether him to the past, preventing him from contributing to his country's future. Instead, he redirected his energy toward reconciliation and democratic politics, believing that unity and empathy were essential for societal healing.

In 2010, Mujica became president of Uruguay, gaining international recognition for his humility and progressive policies. Known as "the world's poorest president," he lived in his modest farmhouse, drove an old Volkswagen Beetle, and donated most of his salary to social causes. His leadership reflected his deep commitment to understanding and compassion. Mujica advocated for social welfare, environmental protection, and equality, often emphasizing the importance of forgiveness and unity in overcoming division.

José Mujica's journey exemplifies Rule Eight: By choosing compassion and reconciliation over vengeance, he demonstrated immense emotional strength and maturity. His ability to forgive those who had wronged him allowed him to lead with empathy, fostering personal healing and societal progress. Mujica's life reminds us that prioritizing kindness over being right can transform both individuals and communities, creating a lasting impact and meaningful change.

EXAMPLE 2: KIM PHUC (1963–)

Born in Vietnam, Kim Phuc became a global symbol of the Vietnam War's devastation when she was photographed as a nine-year-old fleeing a napalm attack on Trang Bang village in 1972. Severely burned and left with deep physical scars, Kim endured years of painful surgeries and chronic pain. Yet beyond her physical injuries, she also carried the emotional burden of anger and resentment toward those responsible for her suffering.

For years, Kim struggled with her hatred, feeling tethered to the trauma of her past. Her turning point came in 1996 when she was invited to speak at the Vietnam Veterans Memorial in Washington, DC. Standing before an audience that included American soldiers, Kim recounted her harrowing experience of the war. During her speech, she publicly forgave those responsible for her suffering, including the individuals who had carried out the attack. This moment, she explained, was not about excusing their actions but about freeing herself from the emotional chains of anger and reclaiming her peace.

Kim's act of forgiveness required immense emotional strength. She reflected on the complexities of war and the shared pain it brought to everyone involved. Her decision was deeply personal, but it also marked the beginning of her life's mission to promote healing and reconciliation. Following this moment, Kim dedicated herself to advocating for peace and compassion. As a UNESCO Goodwill Ambassador, she traveled the world, sharing her story to inspire others to let go of anger and embrace forgiveness. Through the Kim Foundation International, she supports children affected by war, turning her personal tragedy into a force for global change.

Kim Phuc's journey exemplifies Rule Eight: By forgiving those responsible for her suffering, she chose compassion over anger and reconciliation over resentment. Her story highlights how forgiveness, rooted in kindness and empathy, can liberate us from the emotional weight of past wrongs and foster healing and understanding on a global scale.

PART TWO

Outer Voyage

"In our world everybody thinks of changing humanity, and nobody thinks of changing himself."

—**Leo Tolstoy,** *Pamphlets, "Three Methods of Reform"*

As we embark on the second phase of our journey, we shift our focus outward—from understanding ourselves to understanding and influencing the world around us. Part 2 invites us to explore the rich and complex tapestry of human relationships, equipping us with the tools to build meaningful connections, navigate conflicts, and communicate with clarity and purpose.

This section begins with chapter 8, which delves into the intricacies of personal relationships. It reveals the art of forming deep bonds, nurturing trust, and understanding the dynamics that sustain healthy and fulfilling connections. Chapter 9 broadens the lens to examine our role within social groups and communities, offering strategies for navigating diverse social contexts and fostering positive influence. In chapter 10, we confront the inevitability of disagreements and misunderstandings, discovering how empathy and constructive communication can transform conflict into an opportunity for growth. Finally, chapter 11 focuses on the cornerstone of all human interaction: communication. Here, we explore the delicate balance between speaking and listening, learning to harness the power of timing, attentiveness, and clarity to deepen understanding and connection.

Part 2 builds upon the foundation of self-mastery laid in part 1, intertwining personal growth with social engagement. It challenges us to extend our inner transformation outward, enhancing not only our relationships but also the broader communities we inhabit. Together, these chapters serve as a guide to navigating the complexities of human interaction, empowering us to leave a lasting, positive impact on the world around us.

CHAPTER 8

Navigating Interpersonal Relationships

"We are like islands in the sea, separate on the surface but connected in the deep."

—paraphrased from William James, *"The Confidences of a 'Psychical Researcher'"*

Rule One: Do Not Give Advice Unless Asked

"Advice is seldom welcome, and those who need it the most, like it the least."

—Lord Chesterfield, *Letters to His Son*

Offering advice requires a careful balance between guidance and respect for others' autonomy. Rule One emphasizes the importance of giving advice only when explicitly requested. While unsolicited advice often comes from good intentions, it can feel intrusive or condescending, unintentionally suggesting that the recipient cannot handle their own challenges. This dynamic can create defensiveness, strain relationships, and hinder open communication.

In contrast, advice that is actively sought fosters mutual respect and meaningful dialogue. When individuals ask for guidance, they are more open to new perspectives and more likely to value and implement the advice. This approach demonstrates empathy and confidence in their ability to navigate their own lives, strengthening trust and understanding in relationships.

This rule does not advocate passivity or indifference toward others' struggles. Instead, it encourages empathetic support through active listening, open-ended questions, and facilitating self-reflection. These techniques can gently inspire internal realizations or encourage someone to seek advice. Sharing personal experiences in a non directive way can also provide insights without imposing solutions. For example, asking thoughtful questions like "What options have you considered?" can guide others without overstepping boundaries, ensuring they remain empowered in their decision-making process.

Rule One is about more than withholding unsolicited advice; it's about fostering respect, empathy, and meaningful communication. By waiting until advice is genuinely desired, we ensure that our guidance is impactful and valued. This approach nurtures trust, enhances understanding, and creates a supportive environment where advice becomes a tool for connection and growth.

EXAMPLE 1: STEVE JOBS (1955–2011) AND TIM COOK (1960–)

Born in San Francisco, Steve Jobs cofounded Apple and became renowned for his visionary leadership and meticulous attention to detail. His direct, hands-on approach shaped Apple's culture of innovation, making it one of the world's most influential companies. However, in 2004, Jobs was diagnosed with pancreatic cancer, forcing him to consider Apple's future without him.

Tim Cook, Apple's COO since 1998, emerged as Jobs's successor. Despite his deep involvement in Apple's operations, Jobs made a deliberate decision to avoid micromanaging Cook's transition. Recognizing the importance of empowering Cook to lead authentically, Jobs famously told him, "Don't ask what Steve would do. Do what you think is right." This reflected Jobs's trust in Cook's abilities and his understanding that unsolicited advice could undermine Cook's confidence and independence.

Jobs's decision to step back allowed Cook to develop his own leadership style. Under Cook's guidance, Apple expanded its product range, sustained its culture of innovation, and achieved record-breaking financial success. By refraining from unsolicited advice, Jobs demonstrated respect for Cook's autonomy, ensuring a seamless leadership transition and preserving Apple's momentum.

Steve Jobs's approach exemplifies Rule One: By withholding unsolicited advice, Jobs empowered Cook to lead authentically, fostering growth and mutual trust. This story highlights how respecting others' autonomy can lead to personal growth, stronger relationships, and greater success.

EXAMPLE 2: THOMAS CROMWELL (1485–1540)

Born in England, Thomas Cromwell rose from humble beginnings to become a trusted advisor to King Henry VIII. Known for his political acumen, Cromwell was instrumental in the English Reformation, a series of events that led to England's break from the Roman Catholic Church. One of his key roles involved orchestrating the annulment of Henry VIII's marriage to Catherine of Aragon and facilitating his subsequent marriage to Anne Boleyn, who became queen in 1533.

By 1536, Cromwell's position at court became increasingly precarious due to shifting alliances and court intrigues. In an effort to secure his influence, Cromwell presented unsolicited accusations against Anne Boleyn, alleging adultery and treason. These allegations led to Anne's arrest and execution on dubious charges, shocking the court and leaving a lasting scar on English history. While Cromwell's actions temporarily strengthened his position, they eroded Henry VIII's trust in him. By 1540, political rivals capitalized on the king's doubts, leading to Cromwell's arrest and execution for treason—a dramatic fall from power.

Thomas Cromwell's story vividly demonstrates the dangers of offering unsolicited advice. His accusations, framed as counsel to the king, overstepped boundaries and ultimately led to devastating consequences, including Anne Boleyn's tragic death and his own downfall. By failing to respect discretion and offering advice without being asked, Cromwell violated the principles of Rule One, serving as a cautionary tale about the importance of boundaries and the risks of self-serving counsel.

Rule Two: Opt for Cooperation over Confrontation

"In the long history of humankind, those who learned to collaborate and improvise most effectively have prevailed."

—commonly attributed to Charles Darwin

Choosing cooperation over confrontation is a cornerstone of effective human interaction, whether in personal relationships or professional settings. Rule Two emphasizes the power of working together harmoniously to achieve shared goals. Cooperation fosters trust, encourages the exchange of diverse ideas, and leads to innovative solutions. In both professional and personal contexts, it nurtures mutual respect, strengthens connections, and ensures all voices are valued. Far from being a sign of weakness, cooperation reflects strength, emotional maturity, and confidence in fostering productive relationships.

By prioritizing collaboration, we create environments that enhance personal and professional outcomes. Practices such as active listening to understand others' perspectives, framing issues as shared goals, and focusing on solutions rather than assigning blame are essential for building trust and resolving conflicts constructively.

This rule does not advocate blind cooperation. Confrontation, when necessary, plays a critical role in defending principles, addressing injustices, or resolving conflicts. Constructive confrontation requires fairness, respect, and clear objectives, ensuring conflicts lead to progress rather than hostility. For example, standing firm on ethical concerns or addressing systemic issues may demand confrontation, but when guided by collaboration, even these moments can foster understanding and growth.

Rule Two reminds us that cooperation is a transformative tool for navigating human interactions. By choosing collaboration over conflict, we foster empathy, understanding, and shared progress. This approach not only enhances personal and professional success but also contributes to a more unified and compassionate world, building bridges where divisions once stood.

EXAMPLE 1: JOHN HUME (1937–2020)

Born in Derry, Northern Ireland, John Hume emerged as a pivotal figure during the Troubles, a period of violent conflict that began in the late 1960s and lasted three decades. The conflict was fueled by deep-rooted divisions between nationalists, primarily Catholic and seeking a united Ireland, and unionists, primarily Protestant and loyal to the United Kingdom. These divisions, compounded by historical grievances, economic inequality, and political discrimination, erupted into violence. Bombings, shootings, and riots claimed thousands of lives, leaving communities deeply scarred and mistrust entrenched.

Amid this turmoil, Hume, a former schoolteacher turned politician, recognized the need for a different approach. As leader of the Social Democratic and Labour Party, he rejected the militant strategies of some nationalist groups, instead championing dialogue and peaceful negotiation as the only sustainable path to peace. Hume believed that cooperation, not confrontation, was essential to bridging the deep divisions in Northern Ireland.

Hume's commitment to dialogue was evident in his willingness to engage with all parties involved in the conflict, including those others refused to approach. He prioritized negotiation over division, maintaining communication with unlikely allies such as unionist leader David Trimble and Sinn Féin, the political wing of the Irish Republican Army (IRA). Despite facing harsh criticism and personal threats, Hume's persistence and empathy were instrumental in shaping the peace process.

These efforts culminated in the landmark Good Friday Agreement of 1998, which addressed disarmament, civil rights, and the political status of Northern Ireland. The agreement marked a turning point, ushering in a more peaceful era for the region. Hume's dedication to dialogue earned him the Nobel Peace Prize in 1998, shared with Trimble, reflecting their joint commitment to reconciliation.

John Hume's actions exemplify Rule Two. By consistently prioritizing dialogue and collaboration over division and violence, Hume demonstrated the transformative power of empathy and understanding. His leadership during the peace process highlights how cooperation can bridge even the deepest divisions, fostering lasting unity and peace.

EXAMPLE 2: THE FALKLANDS WAR (1982)

The Falklands War, a ten-week conflict in 1982 between Argentina and the United Kingdom, highlights the devastating consequences of prioritizing confrontation over cooperation. The dispute over sovereignty of the Falkland Islands, a remote archipelago in the South Atlantic, had simmered for decades, with both nations claiming ownership based on historical ties. By the early 1980s, the issue took on new urgency. Argentina's military junta, led by General Leopoldo Galtieri, faced growing domestic unrest due to economic decline and political instability. Seeking to rally national unity and distract from internal struggles, the junta chose confrontation, launching a surprise invasion of the islands in April 1982.

The decision to invade bypassed diplomatic negotiations,

escalating tensions into war. The United Kingdom, under Prime Minister Margaret Thatcher, viewed the invasion as an unacceptable breach of sovereignty and swiftly deployed a naval task force to reclaim the islands. What followed was a brutal conflict that cost the lives of 649 Argentine soldiers, 255 British personnel, and 3 Falkland Islanders. Thousands of families were left grieving, and Argentina's economy, already in turmoil, suffered further devastation. Politically, the war deepened mistrust between the two nations and left unresolved tensions over the islands' sovereignty. While Britain emerged victorious and reclaimed the Falklands, Argentina's defeat led to the collapse of its military regime and a tumultuous transition to civilian rule.

The Falklands War starkly illustrates the dangers of disregarding Rule Two. By choosing aggression over dialogue, Argentina and Britain missed critical opportunities to resolve their dispute peacefully. The conflict's human, economic, and political toll underscores how confrontation can lead to immense suffering and long-term divisions. Had both nations sought collaborative solutions through diplomacy, they might have avoided the devastating costs of war and laid the foundation for a more constructive relationship. This example serves as a cautionary tale about the heavy price of failing to prioritize cooperation.

Rule Three: Remember That People Reveal Their True Nature During Times of Adversity

"Adversity doesn't build character, it reveals it."

—commonly attributed to James Lane Allen

Adversity serves as a powerful lens, exposing our true nature. In everyday life, we often present facades shaped by social norms or personal aspirations. However, in moments of crisis or difficulty, these facades fade, and deeper layers of our character emerge. These revelations, whether positive or negative, offer valuable insights into ourselves and those around us, showing how we respond to pressure and challenges.

For some, adversity brings out the best in their character—resilience, empathy, and courage. These individuals rise to the occasion, offering support, finding solutions, and demonstrating emotional strength. For others, adversity can reveal fear, selfishness, or dishonesty, traits that might remain hidden during calm circumstances. These responses, though uncomfortable to witness, are essential for understanding the strengths and vulnerabilities within ourselves and our relationships.

How we handle adversity not only reveals who we are but also shapes who we become. Those who reflect on their responses, learn from their mistakes, and strive to improve can grow stronger and more compassionate. Conversely, ignoring these lessons can lead to stagnation, unresolved struggles, or repeated missteps. By observing these patterns in ourselves and others, adversity becomes not just a test of character but a powerful opportunity for growth and connection.

Rule Three highlights that adversity is a profound indicator of character, capable of revealing both strengths and weaknesses. By observing how others respond to challenges and reflecting on our own actions, we gain valuable opportunities for personal growth and deeper relationships. This dual perspective empowers us to approach adversity with empathy, self-awareness, and a commitment to growth, transforming challenges into pathways for resilience and understanding.

EXAMPLE 1: PAUL RUSESABAGINA (1954–)

Paul Rusesabagina was managing the Hôtel des Mille Collines in Kigali, Rwanda, when the 1994 Rwandan genocide began. Over the course of one hundred days, nearly eight hundred thousand people were killed as violence consumed the nation. Targeted attacks by militias forced civilians to flee their homes, and fear spread rapidly as communities turned against one another. Amid this chaos, the hotel became a refuge for those seeking shelter from the violence.

Rusesabagina made the decision to protect over 1,200 people who sought safety within the hotel. Drawing on his negotiation skills and connections, he secured food, water, and medical supplies while bribing militia members to keep them at bay. Despite constant threats to his own life, he remained composed and determined, using every resource at his disposal to ensure the safety of those in his care. His actions transformed the hotel into a sanctuary in the midst of unimaginable brutality, offering hope to those who had lost everything.

Rusesabagina's bravery and resourcefulness during the genocide earned him international recognition. His story became widely known after it was depicted in the 2004 film *Hotel Rwanda*, which highlighted his heroism. He received numerous accolades, including the Presidential Medal of Freedom in 2005, the United States' highest civilian honor. These acknowledgments underscored the profound impact of his actions, not only in saving lives during the genocide but also in raising global awareness about the atrocities that occurred in Rwanda.

Paul Rusesabagina's actions during the genocide revealed extraordinary courage, empathy, and leadership. His story exemplifies Rule Three. Faced with overwhelming challenges, Rusesabagina demonstrated the depths of his character, showing how adversity can highlight the best in humanity while inspiring others to act with compassion and bravery.

EXAMPLE 2: VLADIMIR LENIN (1870–1924)

Vladimir Lenin, born in Simbirsk, Russia, became the leader of the Bolshevik Revolution in 1917, a turning point in Russian history that ended centuries of monarchy and established Bolshevik rule. Following the revolution, Lenin faced immense challenges during the Russian Civil War (1918–1922), as counter-revolutionary forces sought to overthrow his government. The survival of the Bolshevik regime depended on consolidating power amid widespread instability, famine, and societal upheaval.

In 1918, an assassination attempt left Lenin seriously injured, intensifying the pressure on his leadership. In response, he initiated the Red Terror—a brutal campaign of mass arrests, executions, and repression carried out by the Cheka (secret police). The campaign targeted political dissidents, perceived enemies, and ordinary citizens accused of disloyalty. While Lenin justified these actions as necessary to secure Bolshevik control, the brutality exposed a leadership style that prioritized power over humanitarian considerations.

The consequences of Lenin's decisions were profound. The Red Terror deepened divisions within Russian society and created an enduring climate of fear and mistrust. Within the Bolshevik ranks, dissent grew, as some questioned the morality of such measures. By the time of Lenin's death in 1924, the authoritarian foundations he had laid paved the way for even greater repression under Joseph Stalin, leaving a lasting legacy of fear and suffering.

Lenin's actions during the Red Terror exemplify nonadherence to Rule Three. Confronted with existential threats, Lenin revealed a character defined by ideological rigidity and a willingness to prioritize power over compassion. His decisions inflicted immense suffering and undermined trust, demonstrating how adversity can expose moral failings and leave lasting scars on leadership and society.

Rule Four: Make Others Feel Valued

"Talk to a man about himself, and he is generally captivated."
—Benjamin Disraeli, *Coningsby*

How we treat others shapes the quality of our relationships and the legacy we leave behind. Rule Four emphasizes the importance of making others feel valued—not through grand gestures, but through small, meaningful actions rooted in empathy and sincerity. People want to feel seen, heard, and appreciated, and even simple acts of recognition can leave a lasting impact on their self-esteem and emotional well-being.

Making others feel valued begins with how we approach interactions. Active listening shows genuine interest by giving others our full attention, free from distractions. Acknowledging someone's contributions, remembering personal details, or expressing gratitude demonstrates that we respect and appreciate them. These gestures not only uplift others but also strengthen the emotional bonds that connect us, fostering trust, mutual respect, and a shared sense of belonging.

This rule challenges us to reflect on the emotional impact of our actions. The comfort we provide in difficult times, the encouragement we offer during challenges, and the joy we share in moments of celebration often leave a deeper and more enduring impression than material accomplishments. Shifting our focus from self-centered goals to creating positive emotional experiences helps us build a culture of compassion, where everyone feels valued and understood.

Rule Four reminds us that the way we make others feel defines the true measure of our character. By embracing kindness, empathy, and authenticity, we create stronger connections, promote emotional well-being, and contribute to a more compassionate and inclusive world. Living by this rule transforms not only our relationships but also the environments we inhabit, leaving behind a legacy of care and mutual respect.

EXAMPLE 1: SULTAN SALAHUDDIN AYUBI (1137–1193) AND KING RICHARD I OF ENGLAND (1157–1199)

Sultan Salahuddin Ayubi, ruler of Egypt and Syria, was celebrated for his chivalry, wisdom, and unwavering commitment to justice. A devout Muslim and a skilled military leader, he earned respect even among his adversaries during the Crusades. His leadership was defined by a balance of strength and compassion, qualities that shone through during the Third Crusade (1189–1192), a campaign marked by fierce battles over Jerusalem.

King Richard I of England, also known as Richard the Lionheart, was one of the most formidable military leaders of his time. Renowned for his courage, strategic brilliance, and martial prowess, Richard I was a devout Christian who commanded immense loyalty from his troops. Despite their rivalry, both Salahuddin and Richard I exemplified a sense of honor and respect uncommon in an era defined by religious and cultural divisions.

During the campaign, as hostilities raged, Richard I fell gravely ill. News of his condition reached Sultan Salahuddin, who extended an extraordinary act of humanity by sending his personal physician to care for his adversary. Salahuddin's gesture, made in the midst of conflict, transcended the norms of warfare, demonstrating his respect for Richard I's humanity. This act of compassion not only alleviated Richard I's suffering but also highlighted the mutual regard these two leaders held for one another despite their opposing sides.

Sultan Salahuddin's actions during this time exemplify Rule Four. By prioritizing empathy and respect for his rival, he showed that even in the harshest circumstances, valuing others can leave a profound impact. His decision to care for King Richard I during his illness created a legacy of mutual respect and chivalry, illustrating that acts of kindness have the power to humanize even the fiercest rivalries.

EXAMPLE 2: ALBERT EINSTEIN (1879–1955)

Albert Einstein, born in Ulm, Germany, was celebrated for revolutionizing science with his theories of relativity, yet his humility and respect for others defined his character just as profoundly. During his time at Princeton University's Institute for Advanced Study, Einstein formed meaningful connections with people from all walks of life, including individuals often overlooked by society.

One particularly touching example of his kindness occurred when Einstein gifted his cherished violin to the son of Sylas Hibbs, a janitor at Princeton. This gesture went beyond material generosity—it reflected Einstein's recognition of humanity and his appreciation for the contributions of everyone around him, regardless of their status. The violin, an instrument that had accompanied Einstein throughout his life, symbolized his willingness to connect and share something deeply personal.

Albert Einstein's actions perfectly demonstrate Rule Four. By treating others with genuine kindness and recognizing their worth, Einstein exemplified how small, sincere gestures can foster profound emotional connections. His humility and empathy remind us that valuing others enriches not only their lives but also our own, inspiring us to cultivate a culture of respect and compassion in our daily interactions.

Rule Five: Interact with Others Using Sword, Shield, and Sheath

"Approach relationships with sword, shield, and sheath."
—inspired by Yasser Al Hazimi, *Fnjan* podcast

Navigating relationships requires a thoughtful balance of assertiveness, boundaries, and empathy. Rule Five introduces the metaphors of the sword, shield, and sheath to symbolize these principles, offering a guide for more effective and meaningful interactions.

The sword represents assertiveness and our commitment to values. It is the strength we need to defend our principles confidently and respectfully. Using the sword effectively means standing firm without aggression, ensuring our integrity remains intact while maintaining respect for others. The shield symbolizes self-preservation and the boundaries we establish to protect our emotional well-being. It reminds us to recognize our limits, say no when necessary, and safeguard ourselves from undue harm. A well-used shield supports healthy relationships by prioritizing self-care and fostering mutual respect. The sheath embodies empathy and compassion. It teaches us that not every interaction requires confrontation or defense. Sometimes, the most impactful response is to sheath the sword, lower the shield, and offer understanding and support. This approach builds deeper connections, promotes trust, and fosters mutual respect.

Rule Five encourages us to balance these three elements thoughtfully. By knowing when to assert our values, protect our boundaries, or extend empathy, we develop the emotional intelligence needed to navigate relationships effectively. This balance enhances our interactions, strengthens connections, and fosters meaningful relationships in both personal and professional spheres.

EXAMPLE 1: MARGARET THATCHER (1925–2013)

Margaret Thatcher, born in Grantham, England, rose to prominence as the United Kingdom's first female prime minister, serving from 1979 to 1990. Known as the "Iron Lady," she was renowned for her decisive leadership and ability to navigate complex political landscapes. Her actions often reflected the principles of Rule Five: the balanced use of the sword, shield, and sheath in leadership and relationships.

The sword was evident during the Falklands War in 1982. When Argentina invaded British territory, Thatcher acted decisively, dispatching a naval task force to reclaim the islands. Her assertiveness in defending British sovereignty showcased courage, determination, and her unwavering commitment to protecting national interests, even at significant political and military risk.

The shield emerged in her strategy during the 1987 general

election. Thatcher limited her exposure to uncontrolled media interactions by favoring structured press conferences over unpredictable live debates. This approach allowed her to set boundaries, protect her focus, and maintain control over her narrative, demonstrating the importance of self-preservation and strategic prioritization.

The sheath was on display following the Falklands War when Thatcher visited wounded soldiers and grieving families. By offering personal words of encouragement and expressing gratitude for their sacrifices, she showed empathy and compassion. These gestures not only strengthened morale but also reinforced trust and solidarity among those she led.

Margaret Thatcher's leadership exemplifies Rule Five. By balancing assertiveness, boundaries, and empathy, she navigated political challenges with both strength and humanity. Her ability to wield these elements thoughtfully left a legacy of resilience, strategic decision-making, and compassionate leadership.

EXAMPLE 2: KING GEORGE III (1738–1820)

King George III, born in London, ascended the British throne in 1760 at the age of twenty-two, inheriting an empire that stretched across the globe. His reign came during a period of immense challenges, including the financial burden of the Seven Years' War and rising tensions within the American colonies. The colonies, frustrated by taxation without representation and a lack of autonomy, began to resist British authority, creating a widening rift that culminated in the American Revolution (1775–1783).

The sword was misused in 1765 with the introduction of the Stamp Act, which imposed taxes on printed materials in the colonies. Intended to recover Britain's financial losses from the Seven Years' War, the act ignored colonial demands for representation in Parliament, sparking widespread protests. The decision to assert authority without addressing colonial grievances deepened resentment and laid the groundwork for further conflict.

The shield was poorly deployed in response to the Boston Tea Party in 1773, when colonists destroyed a shipment of British tea in protest of taxation policies. In retaliation, King George III supported the Coercive Acts (known in America as the Intolerable Acts), which imposed harsh restrictions, including closing Boston Harbor and revoking Massachusetts's charter of self-governance. These punitive measures united the colonies against Britain, intensifying the crisis rather than protecting British interests effectively.

The sheath was entirely absent in 1775 when the Second Continental Congress, a gathering of colonial representatives, sent the Olive Branch Petition to King George III. This petition, a final plea for reconciliation, expressed loyalty to the crown while requesting redress for colonial grievances, including taxation and governance. However, King George III dismissed the petition outright, declaring the colonies in open rebellion. His refusal to acknowledge their appeals or engage in dialogue eliminated any chance for compromise, solidifying the path to war. This lack of empathy and understanding closed the door on peaceful resolution, further alienating the colonies.

King George III's leadership during the American Revolution illustrates the consequences of neglecting Rule Five: His inability to balance assertiveness, self-preservation, and empathy escalated tensions, damaged relationships, and ultimately led to the loss of the American colonies. This example demonstrates how failing to temper authority with understanding can result in avoidable conflicts and enduring negative outcomes.

Rule Six: Be Balanced in Your Relationships

"Let there be spaces in your togetherness."
—Khalil Gibran, *The Prophet*

Healthy relationships—whether personal, professional, or social—depend on a delicate balance between closeness and individuality. Rule Six emphasizes the importance of creating meaningful connections while respecting boundaries. Closeness fosters trust, collaboration, and understanding, but too much familiarity can blur boundaries, leading to dependency or a loss of mutual respect. Conversely, excessive distance can hinder the development of trust and emotional depth, leaving relationships superficial and disconnected.

Achieving this balance requires mindfulness, empathy, and intentional communication. Thoughtful interactions, rooted in genuine understanding, build trust and connection while honoring each person's individuality. By setting and respecting boundaries, we create room for reflection, autonomy, and growth, allowing relationships to thrive without feeling overwhelming. This balance ensures that relationships remain adaptable, resilient, and mutually enriching.

Rule Six reminds us that the healthiest relationships are those where connection and individuality coexist harmoniously. By balancing closeness with respect for boundaries, we create relationships that foster emotional well-being, promote mutual respect, and leave a lasting legacy of understanding and care across all areas of life.

EXAMPLE 1: QUEEN ELIZABETH I (1533–1603) AND SIR WILLIAM CECIL (1520–1598)

Queen Elizabeth I, born in Greenwich, England, ascended the throne in 1558 at the age of twenty-five, inheriting a kingdom fractured by religious divisions and political instability. Her reign marked a transformative era for England, establishing its place as a global power. At the heart of her success was Sir William Cecil, her trusted chief advisor, who served as a steady and pragmatic counselor for over forty years. Their partnership became one of the most celebrated examples of effective collaboration between a ruler and an advisor.

Cecil was a master of diplomacy and strategy, offering critical guidance on issues such as religious reforms, threats from Spain, and foreign alliances. He often played the role of a cautious strategist, tempering Elizabeth I's bold decisions with measured advice. However, Elizabeth I was known for her sharp intellect, independence, and unwavering authority. She carefully balanced Cecil's influence with her own judgment, ensuring their relationship was one of collaboration rather than dependence.

Their dynamic was tested on the contentious issue of naming a successor. Parliament and Cecil pressed Elizabeth I to secure the monarchy's future, warning of the potential chaos if no heir was declared. Yet, Elizabeth I remained resolute, refusing to bow to pressure on such a critical matter. In her famous 1601 "Golden Speech," she skillfully addressed Parliament's concerns while reaffirming her sovereignty, maintaining control over the decision. This moment highlighted her ability to navigate the fine line between valuing counsel and preserving her autonomy.

Elizabeth I's leadership exemplifies Rule Six. By fostering a respectful and collaborative partnership with Cecil, she drew on his expertise without compromising her authority. This balance allowed her to lead decisively while benefiting from trusted advice, enabling her to navigate complex challenges with strength and foresight. Her reign underscores the importance of cultivating meaningful relationships while maintaining clear boundaries to ensure mutual respect and effective collaboration.

EXAMPLE 2: TSARINA ALEXANDRA (1872–1918) AND GRIGORI RASPUTIN (1869–1916)

Tsarina Alexandra, born in Darmstadt, Germany, became Empress of Russia in 1894 during a time of immense political and social turmoil. Her reign was marked by personal struggles, particularly the ongoing health crisis of her son Alexei, who suffered from hemophilia. Desperate to ease his suffering, Alexandra turned to Grigori Rasputin, a Siberian mystic whose apparent healing abilities earned her unwavering trust.

Initially a spiritual advisor, Rasputin's influence over Alexandra grew to extend into state affairs, particularly during World War I when Tsar Nicholas II was at the front. Alexandra increasingly relied on Rasputin's guidance, often disregarding the advice of seasoned ministers. Rasputin's controversial interventions, such as his support for dissolving the Duma in 1917, alienated the public and court officials, deepening mistrust toward the monarchy. His unchecked influence symbolized the royal family's detachment from the struggles of ordinary Russians, further eroding their legitimacy.

The consequences were severe. Alexandra's overreliance on Rasputin undermined her leadership, exacerbated Russia's political crisis, and fueled resentment toward the monarchy. By failing to balance trust in Rasputin with discernment and accountability, she allowed overfamiliarity to overshadow objective decision-making, contributing to the Romanov dynasty's downfall.

Alexandra's relationship with Rasputin illustrates non-adherence to Rule Six. Her inability to set boundaries and evaluate Rasputin's advice critically led to decisions that weakened her authority and destabilized the monarchy. This example underscores the importance of maintaining balance and ensuring personal relationships do not compromise leadership and judgment.

Rule Seven: Treat People as You Wish to Be Treated

"Do unto others as you would have them do unto you."

—The Bible, Luke 6:31 and Matthew 7:12 (KJV, the Golden Rule)

Across cultures and philosophies, Rule Seven remains a timeless guide to ethical living. Rooted in teachings from Confucius to the Bhagavad Gita, it reminds us that our actions ripple outward, shaping the world and the relationships we build. Living by this rule honors the interconnectedness of humanity and calls us to approach others with empathy, kindness, and understanding.

At its core, the rule emphasizes cultivating empathy—the ability to understand and share the feelings of others. Small acts of kindness, such as active listening, offering support, or showing patience, can uplift spirits and strengthen relationships. These gestures, though simple, have profound and lasting impacts, fostering compassion and connection.

In today's fast-paced and diverse world, empathy is more essential than ever. Online interactions, often stripped of tone and nuance, can lead to misunderstandings and diminish compassion. Embracing this rule encourages us to value perspectives shaped by different cultures, experiences, and beliefs. Instead of judging differences, we are challenged to meet them with curiosity and respect, fostering unity and mutual understanding. However, treating others as we wish to be treated does not mean tolerating mistreatment or sacrificing our well-being. Empathy must be balanced with healthy boundaries. Respecting ourselves ensures kindness is not exploited or given at the expense of our dignity. Standing firm when others disregard this principle reflects self-respect and integrity.

Rule Seven is a cornerstone of meaningful relationships and ethical behavior. By practicing empathy, respect, and self-care, we contribute to a more compassionate and harmonious world. This balanced approach enriches our connections and leaves a legacy of trust, kindness, and mutual understanding.

EXAMPLE 1: MAHARAJA RANJIT SINGH (1780–1839)

Maharaja Ranjit Singh, born in Gujranwala (modern-day Pakistan), rose to prominence as a leader at the young age of twenty-one, inheriting a fractured Punjab plagued by internal divisions and external threats. Despite the challenges, he unified the Sikh Empire and transformed it into a thriving, harmonious kingdom. Known as the "Lion of Punjab," his leadership was defined by inclusivity, respect for diversity, and a commitment to justice, principles that set him apart from many rulers of his era.

Unlike most monarchs of his time, Ranjit Singh governed with a secular vision that celebrated the cultural and religious diversity of his empire. He appointed individuals from varied backgrounds to key positions, valuing merit over creed. His foreign minister, Fakir Azizuddin, a devout Muslim, became one of his closest advisors, offering guidance on diplomatic matters. Similarly, Diwan Dina Nath, a Hindu, skillfully managed the treasury, ensuring stability and prosperity. Ranjit Singh's inclusive administration not only fostered mutual respect but also built a strong sense of unity among his subjects, ensuring loyalty and collaboration across his kingdom.

Ranjit Singh's compassion extended beyond governance and into the battlefield. After his victory in the Battle of Multan in 1818, he demonstrated extraordinary magnanimity toward the defeated leaders, reinstating many of them to their positions and returning confiscated lands. These acts of mercy strengthened loyalty and reduced resentment among those he conquered. Moreover, Ranjit Singh was renowned for his humane treatment of soldiers—both friend and foe. He ensured medical care for the wounded on both sides, a gesture almost unheard of in an era characterized by brutal warfare. These actions reinforced his reputation as a just and empathetic leader.

Ranjit Singh's leadership vividly demonstrates Rule Seven. By valuing inclusivity, compassion, and fairness, he created a unified empire that thrived on mutual respect and loyalty. His actions on the battlefield and in governance embodied the principle that treating others with dignity and humanity fosters trust, unity, and enduring prosperity. His legacy endures as a testament to the transformative power of empathy and respect in leadership.

EXAMPLE 2: LEOPOLD II OF BELGIUM (1835–1909)

King Leopold II of Belgium, born in Brussels, ascended the throne in 1865 and ruled for over four decades. Ambitious and determined to expand Belgium's influence, Leopold II sought to secure colonies in Africa during the late nineteenth-century scramble for territory. In 1885, he established the Congo Free State as his personal colony, positioning himself as a philanthropist under the guise of bringing civilization and Christianity to the region. However, his rule over the Congo became one of the darkest chapters in colonial history.

Leopold II's administration implemented a brutal system of forced labor to extract rubber and ivory, resources in high demand in Europe. Villagers were forced to meet stringent production quotas, with severe punishments inflicted on those who failed. Entire communities were terrorized, and atrocities were systemic. In one particularly horrifying incident in 1899, the village of Lulonga was burned to the ground, and the hands of men, women, and children were mutilated as punishment for failing to meet quotas. Such acts were not isolated but emblematic of the regime's reliance on fear and violence to enforce compliance.

Under Leopold II's rule, the population of the Congo was halved, with millions dying from forced labor, starvation, disease, and violence. Reports of these horrors eventually reached the international community, sparking outrage and leading to the forced transfer of control from Leopold II to the Belgian government in 1908. Despite the change in governance, the trauma and exploitation of Leopold's reign left an indelible mark on the region, with consequences that resonate to this day.

Leopold II's actions represent a flagrant violation of Rule Seven. His leadership was devoid of empathy, compassion, or respect for human dignity. By prioritizing wealth and power over the well-being of the Congolese people, Leopold inflicted unimaginable suffering, leaving a legacy of exploitation and injustice. His failure to embody the Golden Rule serves as a stark reminder of the destructive consequences of leadership rooted in greed and cruelty.

Rule Eight: Realize That People Come into Your Life for a Season and a Reason

"When someone shows up in your life, they have a lesson to teach."
—commonly attributed to Steve Maraboli

Every person we encounter plays a role in shaping our journey—whether by teaching us a lesson, offering support, or inspiring growth. Like the changing seasons, relationships follow a natural rhythm. Some are brief, bringing moments of joy or insight, while others endure, providing stability and guidance over time. Recognizing the purpose of these connections helps us appreciate their value and approach them with gratitude and understanding.

This perspective encourages us to embrace relationships without clinging to unrealistic expectations. People may come and go, but their presence—however fleeting or enduring—adds meaning and depth to our lives. At the same time, this principle invites reflection on the roles we play in others' journeys. Just as others leave imprints on us, we, too, impact their lives—through kindness, support, or even a simple act of empathy.

Rule Eight calls us to approach relationships with mindfulness and gratitude. By appreciating the lessons and purposes behind every connection, we cultivate empathy, resilience, and a deeper understanding of life's interconnectedness. This awareness enriches our relationships, fostering trust, mutual respect, and a shared appreciation for the human experience.

EXAMPLE 1: MARK ANTONY (83–30 BC) AND CLEOPATRA (69–30 BC)

Mark Antony, a Roman military leader, and Cleopatra, the last pharaoh of Egypt, formed a partnership that profoundly shaped their lives and the course of history. Their alliance, forged in 41 BC, was initially one of mutual benefit—Antony sought Egypt's wealth and military support to bolster his position in Rome, while Cleopatra saw in Antony an ally to secure Egypt's sovereignty amid growing Roman expansion.

Over time, their connection deepened, blending political ambition with personal affection. Together, they navigated treacherous political landscapes, but their union placed them in direct conflict with Octavian, Julius Caesar's adopted heir. Octavian, seeking to consolidate power, used propaganda to paint Antony and Cleopatra as threats to Roman stability. This rivalry culminated in the Battle of Actium in 31 BC, where their forces suffered a crushing defeat.

Their relationship ended in tragedy—Antony, believing Cleopatra dead, took his own life, and Cleopatra, faced with capture, ended hers through the bite of an asp. Despite their downfall, their union left a legacy that extended far beyond their lifetimes, influencing art, literature, and historical narratives for centuries.

The story of Mark Antony and Cleopatra vividly illustrates Rule Eight. Their partnership, though brief, served transformative purposes: It reshaped their personal journeys and left an enduring imprint on history. Their connection reminds us that even relationships marked by ambition or tragedy can offer profound lessons and inspire growth, shaping the course of our lives in ways we may not fully understand at the time.

EXAMPLE 2: RUMI (1207–1273) AND SHAMS TABRIZI (1185–1248)

Rumi, a renowned scholar and spiritual teacher born in Balkh (modern-day Afghanistan), experienced a profound transformation when he met Shams Tabrizi, a wandering dervish from Tabriz. Their meeting, often described as extraordinary, marked the beginning of an intense spiritual bond that challenged Rumi's traditional teachings and opened him to new dimensions of divine love and human connection.

Shams's unorthodox insights and deep spirituality led Rumi to question conventional religious practices and explore the transcendent nature of existence. Their intense conversations often spanned hours or days, drawing Rumi into a realm of emotional and spiritual awakening. This relationship unleashed a wave of creativity, inspiring some of Rumi's greatest works, including the *Divan-e Shams-e Tabrizi and the Masnav*i, which remain cornerstones of Sufi literature.

However, their closeness sparked tension within Rumi's family and community. Shams's influence was met with jealousy and hostility, culminating in his mysterious disappearance. While some accounts suggest he was forced to flee, others imply darker circumstances. Shams's absence left Rumi heartbroken, but his grief became a catalyst for profound creative and spiritual growth. Themes of longing, love, and transcendence emerged in Rumi's poetry, transforming his loss into a legacy that continues to inspire millions.

The relationship between Rumi and Shams embodies Rule Eight. Shams awakened in Rumi a depth of creativity and spirituality that reshaped his life and legacy. Though their time together was brief, it left an enduring impact, illustrating how certain relationships, however short-lived, can profoundly transform our lives and inspire growth.

Rule Nine: Be Mindful of Your Emotional Investment in Relationships

"Love your beloved moderately, for they might become your foe one day; and hate your foe moderately, for they might become your beloved one day."

—Ali ibn Abi Talib, as recorded in *Al-Adab Al-Mufrad* by Imam Al-Bukhari

Relationships thrive on love, trust, and loyalty, but these must be balanced with mindfulness. Rule Nine reminds us that emotional connections, while deeply valuable, carry risks. People and circumstances change, and unexpected shifts can lead to disappointment or betrayal. Approaching relationships with thoughtful awareness helps us navigate these changes with grace and resilience.

Mindfulness in relationships requires cultivating empathy, forgiveness, and objectivity. These qualities help us honor the individuality of others, establish healthy boundaries, and protect our emotional well-being. This approach does not call for detachment but invites us to engage fully and authentically while accepting the evolving nature of human connections. By balancing emotional investment with mindfulness, we learn to cherish the good, release the painful, and grow from the lessons each relationship brings. This perspective fosters adaptability, resilience, and the ability to respond to change with understanding rather than resistance.

Rule Nine teaches us that love and trust are most meaningful when paired with wisdom. By embracing mindfulness in our emotional engagements, we build connections that enrich our lives while safeguarding our well-being. This balance empowers us to navigate relationships with heart and wisdom, fostering bonds that are both meaningful and enduring.

EXAMPLE 1: CALIPH HARUN AL-RASHID (763–809) AND ABU NUWAS (756–814)

Harun al-Rashid, one of the most celebrated rulers of the Abbasid Caliphate, presided over a golden age of cultural and intellectual flourishing in Baghdad. Among the brilliant figures at his court was Abu Nuwas, a provocative poet renowned for his mastery of Arabic and his bold exploration of societal themes. While Harun admired Abu Nuwas's literary genius, their relationship often tested the balance between creative freedom and cultural norms.

A pivotal moment occurred when Abu Nuwas presented an audacious poem at court that challenged societal values and left the audience divided. As caliph, Harun faced the difficult task of addressing the situation. He could have responded with severe punishment, as was customary for rulers of the time, or dismissed the controversy outright. Instead, Harun chose a path of mindful moderation. Acknowledging Abu Nuwas's brilliance, he subtly advised the poet to exercise greater sensitivity in his work while continuing to celebrate his unique artistry.

This measured response allowed Harun to maintain harmony within the court and society while preserving his relationship with Abu Nuwas. By addressing the issue thoughtfully, he demonstrated respect for Abu Nuwas's individuality while upholding his responsibilities as a leader.

Harun al-Rashid's approach exemplifies Rule Nine. He balanced his admiration for Abu Nuwas with mindfulness of his role as a leader, ensuring mutual respect and understanding. Harun's actions highlight the importance of navigating relationships thoughtfully, maintaining emotional equilibrium, and fostering harmony in complex situations.

EXAMPLE 2: VINCENT VAN GOGH (1853–1890) AND PAUL GAUGUIN (1848–1903)

Vincent van Gogh, a deeply passionate and emotionally intense artist, invited Paul Gauguin, a more detached and methodical painter, to join him in Arles, France, in 1888. Van Gogh envisioned their collaboration as a profound creative partnership that would inspire both artists. However, their contrasting personalities and approaches to art quickly led to tension.

Van Gogh's impulsive and idealistic nature clashed with Gauguin's reserved demeanor, fueling misunderstandings and conflicts. The relationship reached a breaking point in December 1888, following a heated argument. Overwhelmed by the strain of their partnership and his personal struggles, van Gogh famously cut off part of his own ear. The episode marked the end of their collaboration, leaving behind a legacy of artistic brilliance overshadowed by discord and imbalance.

The tumultuous relationship between van Gogh and Gauguin underscores Rule Nine. Van Gogh's deep emotional dependence on their partnership was not reciprocated by Gauguin, leading to unmet expectations and heightened tensions. This example illustrates the importance of balancing emotional investment with mindfulness, recognizing the need to set realistic boundaries in relationships where differences in temperament and expectations exist.

Rule Ten: Avoid Chronically Unhappy and Unsuccessful People

"People inspire you, or they drain you. Pick them wisely."

—commonly attributed to Hans F. Hansen

The people we surround ourselves with profoundly influence our mindset, well-being, and success. Rule Ten reminds us that while relationships can uplift and inspire us, they can also drain our energy and hinder our growth. Building a positive and supportive environment requires us to be mindful of the company we keep, as persistent exposure to negativity can cloud our aspirations and hold us back from reaching our potential.

This rule encourages us to distinguish between those navigating temporary challenges and those who remain chronically unhappy or unsuccessful without making meaningful efforts to change. Supporting individuals during difficult times reflects compassion and empathy. However, setting boundaries with those who habitually dwell in negativity is essential to protect our emotional well-being. This balance is not about detachment but about recognizing the limits of our capacity to help others while prioritizing our own growth. Surrounding ourselves with positive, motivated individuals fosters inspiration, resilience, and progress. These relationships challenge us to grow, reinforce our goals, and create an atmosphere of mutual encouragement. Conversely, maintaining close ties with those entrenched in negativity can sap emotional energy and stall our progress.

Rule Ten calls us to make intentional choices about the company we keep. By prioritizing relationships that align with our aspirations, we cultivate a network that nurtures both our mental well-being and success. Relationships are powerful forces that shape the direction of our lives, and choosing them wisely is a profound act of self-care and self-respect.

EXAMPLE 1: MARIE CURIE (1867–1934) AND PIERRE CURIE (1859–1906)

Marie Curie, born in Warsaw, Poland, faced immense challenges as a woman pursuing science in a male-dominated field. Despite limited opportunities and difficult circumstances, she moved to Paris to study at the Sorbonne, where she worked tirelessly to advance her education and scientific research. Her journey took a transformative turn when she met Pierre Curie, a fellow scientist in Paris, who immediately recognized her brilliance and treated her as an equal.

Their partnership was built on mutual respect, shared ambition, and a commitment to scientific discovery. Together, they conducted groundbreaking research on radioactivity, leading to their shared Nobel Prize in Physics in 1903. This achievement not only revolutionized science but also paved the way for Marie's continued success, including her historic second Nobel Prize in Chemistry in 1911. Pierre's unwavering support and collaboration provided Marie with an environment where her talents could flourish, helping her overcome barriers that might otherwise have hindered her potential.

Marie Curie's relationship with Pierre exemplifies Rule Ten. By surrounding herself with a partner who inspired and uplifted her, Marie was able to achieve extraordinary success. Their collaboration underscores the importance of fostering relationships that encourage growth, align with our values, and create an environment where ambition and achievement can thrive.

EXAMPLE 2: KING LUDWIG II OF BAVARIA (1845–1886) AND RICHARD WAGNER (1813–1883)

King Ludwig II of Bavaria, born in Munich, ascended the throne in 1864, bringing with him a deep passion for the arts. Captivated by Richard Wagner's revolutionary compositions, Ludwig II became a devoted patron of the composer, funding his extravagant operatic projects and supporting the construction of the Bayreuth Festspielhaus. However, Wagner's persistent financial mismanagement and controversial personal behavior soon became a source of strain for the king.

Despite mounting opposition from his advisors and public criticism, Ludwig II remained unwavering in his support for Wagner. This association alienated his court, weakened his political standing, and placed significant strain on Bavaria's finances. Wagner's continued demands and scandals further fueled discontent, undermining Ludwig II's leadership. In 1886, Ludwig II was deposed on grounds of alleged mental unfitness, his reputation irreparably damaged by his excessive emotional and financial investment in Wagner.

The dynamic between Ludwig II and Richard Wagner illustrates the risks outlined in Rule Ten. Ludwig II's inability to set boundaries with a figure mired in controversy and instability demonstrates how excessive investment in the wrong relationships can have devastating consequences. His experience serves as a cautionary tale, highlighting the importance of discerning whom we choose to align with, especially in positions of leadership and influence.

Rule Eleven: Accept Relationships as They Are

"If you love someone, set them free. If they come back, they're yours; if they don't, they never were."
—commonly attributed to Richard Bach

In relationships, we often try to mold connections to fit our preferences or ideals. Rule Eleven invites us to embrace relationships for their true nature, free from unrealistic expectations. Each connection—whether familial, romantic, or platonic—serves a unique purpose in our lives. By accepting relationships as they are, we create space for authenticity, mutual growth, and emotional well-being.

This rule is not about compromising our needs or treating relationships as transactions. It encourages us to recognize the distinct role each connection plays—whether offering support, companionship, or shared goals. By aligning our expectations with reality, we can nurture meaningful relationships while gracefully letting go of those that no longer align with our values or contribute to our growth.

Letting go requires both gratitude and courage. Holding on to relationships that no longer serve us can hinder emotional health and personal evolution. By valuing relationships for their inherent purpose, we allow them to evolve naturally, fostering harmony, authenticity, and peace.

Rule Eleven reminds us to approach relationships with realism and gratitude. This mindset helps us cultivate deeper bonds, protect our emotional well-being, and create the conditions for personal growth and mutual respect. By embracing relationships as they truly are, we build a life filled with authenticity, resilience, and lasting fulfillment.

EXAMPLE 1: GURU NANAK (1469–1539) AND BHAI MARDANA (1459–1534)

Guru Nanak, the visionary founder of Sikhism, was born in Talwandi (modern-day Pakistan) during a time of entrenched social divisions. His teachings emphasized equality, compassion, and unity, challenging the rigid norms of caste, religion, and class. Bhai Mardana, a Muslim rabab player from Nankana Sahib, met Guru Nanak around 1487, forming a remarkable partnership that transcended cultural and religious boundaries.

Despite their differing faiths, Guru Nanak and Bhai Mardana built a relationship rooted in mutual respect and shared purpose. Together, they undertook extensive journeys across South Asia, using Mardana's music to amplify Nanak's spiritual teachings. The melodies of the rabab brought Nanak's messages to life, bridging divides and inspiring communities to embrace understanding and harmony. Their partnership was free from judgment or expectations; instead, it celebrated the unique contributions each brought to their bond.

Guru Nanak and Bhai Mardana's relationship exemplifies Rule Eleven. By embracing each other's individuality and recognizing the purpose of their connection, they fostered a partnership that enriched not only their lives but also the lives of countless others. Their story highlights how accepting relationships for what they truly are can lead to profound spiritual growth, mutual respect, and transformative outcomes.

EXAMPLE 2: LEO TOLSTOY (1828–1910) AND SOFIA TOLSTAYA (1844–1919)

Leo Tolstoy, one of Russia's greatest literary minds, and Sofia Tolstaya, his devoted wife, shared a complex relationship that evolved over their decades-long marriage. Sofia played a pivotal role in Tolstoy's career, managing their household, transcribing his manuscripts by hand, and providing critical feedback on his works, including *War and Peace* and *Anna Karenina*. Their early years were marked by intellectual companionship and mutual admiration.

However, as Tolstoy's worldview shifted toward simplicity and asceticism, tensions emerged. His renunciation of wealth and material comforts clashed with Sofia's desire to maintain their family's established lifestyle and financial security. The divergence in their values strained their relationship, with Tolstoy increasingly distancing himself emotionally. This growing rift culminated in 1910, when Tolstoy left his family to live according to his ideals, causing Sofia immense emotional pain and leaving their bond fractured.

The relationship between Leo and Sofia Tolstaya reflects the essence of Rule Eleven. Their bond thrived when they shared mutual goals but faltered as their values and needs diverged. Their story underscores the importance of recognizing the natural evolution of relationships and understanding when adaptation—or even letting go—is necessary. It serves as a reminder that accepting relationships for what they are can help preserve harmony and foster personal growth, even in the face of change.

CHAPTER 9

Navigating Social Dynamics

"To effectively communicate, we must realize that we are all different in the way we perceive the world and use this understanding as a guide to our communication with others."

—Tony Robbins, *Unlimited Power*

Rule One: Never Seek Advice from Those Who Lack the Benefit of Their Own

"Never ask advice of someone with whom you wouldn't want to trade places."

—commonly attributed to Darren Hardy

Advice is only as valuable as the credibility of the person offering it. Rule One reminds us to seek guidance from those whose actions align with their words. While many are quick to offer advice, not all have lived by the principles they advocate. Before acting on any guidance, it is essential to ask whether the advisor embodies the outcomes they promote.

Advice rooted in lived experience carries far greater weight than mere theory. Someone who has achieved financial stability offers more credible financial advice, just as a person who demonstrates balance and resilience provides more trustworthy life guidance. Their success serves as tangible proof of the practicality and dependability of their advice, making it both actionable and effective. Conversely, guidance from those who fail to follow their own advice often lacks depth and reliability. Relying on such counsel can lead to missteps and hinder progress. This is not about judgment but discernment—choosing advice that reflects wisdom gained through experience and aligns with the outcomes we seek.

Rule One encourages us to evaluate advice with care and intention. By seeking guidance from those whose lives reflect the principles we aspire to live by, we align ourselves with authentic wisdom. This thoughtful approach empowers us to make decisions that lead to meaningful growth and success, protecting us from the pitfalls of misguided or untested advice.

EXAMPLE 1: JEFF BEZOS (1964–) AND THE GROWTH OF AMAZON

Jeff Bezos, born in Albuquerque, New Mexico, founded Amazon in 1994 with a bold vision to create the world's largest online bookstore. As the company grew, Bezos faced pivotal decisions about expanding Amazon's offerings beyond books into a comprehensive e-commerce platform. To navigate these challenges, he sought advice exclusively from experts whose experience and success aligned with his goals.

One of his key advisors was Tom Alberg, an early investor and seasoned executive in the tech industry. Alberg provided Bezos with actionable insights into market trends and operational strategies that supported Amazon's ambitious growth. Bezos also assembled a team of logistics and supply chain experts who transformed Amazon's infrastructure, enabling the company to deliver on its hallmark promise of fast, reliable service. Conversely, Bezos dismissed input from skeptics who lacked experience in e-commerce and underestimated the potential of online retail, ensuring his decisions were grounded in credible expertise rather than uninformed opinions.

These strategic decisions laid the foundation for Amazon's meteoric rise. Today, Amazon is one of the most valuable companies in the world, with a market capitalization exceeding $1 trillion. It has expanded far beyond books to dominate markets in electronics, apparel, cloud computing (through Amazon Web Services), and entertainment (via Amazon Prime Video). Bezos's discernment in seeking advice from proven experts was instrumental in transforming Amazon from a startup into a global powerhouse that has revolutionized how the world shops and conducts business online.

Jeff Bezos's journey exemplifies Rule One. By seeking guidance from those whose success aligned with his aspirations, he ensured his decisions were rooted in credible insights. This thoughtful approach not only helped Bezos avoid costly missteps but also paved the way for Amazon's unparalleled growth, leaving an indelible mark on the global economy.

EXAMPLE 2: NOKIA'S DECLINE IN THE SMARTPHONE MARKET

Nokia, founded in Finland in 1865 as a paper mill, became a global leader in mobile phones by the late 1990s. However, as the smartphone revolution emerged in the early 2000s, Nokia faced critical decisions about adapting its strategy. During this pivotal period, the company's leadership relied heavily on internal advice from figures like Anssi Vanjoki, a long-time Nokia executive. Vanjoki strongly advocated for the continued use of Nokia's Symbian platform, dismissing newer competitors like Android and the importance of emerging trends such as integrated software ecosystems.

This approach left Nokia unprepared for the rapid shift in consumer preferences toward smartphones that offered better user experiences and app ecosystems, like Apple's iPhone and Android devices. While competitors embraced innovation, Nokia doubled down on outdated strategies, failing to recognize the changing dynamics of the market.

The consequences were catastrophic. Nokia's market share plummeted as Apple and Samsung quickly captured the smartphone market. By the time Nokia partnered with Microsoft in an attempt to pivot, it was too late to recover. In 2014, Nokia sold its mobile phone division to Microsoft, marking the end of its dominance as a global technology leader. The company, once synonymous with mobile innovation, became a cautionary tale of how even the most established giants can fall behind without adapting to change.

Nokia's story vividly illustrates Rule One. By relying on internal voices entrenched in outdated systems rather than seeking external perspectives from those succeeding in the rapidly evolving smartphone market, Nokia missed critical opportunities to innovate. This example highlights the importance of seeking advice from those with proven success in similar challenges. Without this discernment, even market leaders can face catastrophic decline.

Rule Two: Other People's Opinions of You Are None of Your Business

"Care about what other people think and you will always be their prisoner."
—paraphrased from Lao Tzu, *Tao Te Ching*

Rule Two addresses the natural tendency to seek approval or feel anxious about others' opinions. While understandable, this habit can lead to unnecessary stress and self-doubt when we tie our self-worth to external perceptions. By understanding the nature of others' opinions, we can free ourselves from the constant pursuit of validation and focus on living authentically.

Other people's opinions often reflect their own biases, emotions, and experiences rather than an objective assessment of who we are. People interpret the world through the lens of their beliefs and past experiences, making their judgments more about themselves than about us. At the same time, we cannot control how others perceive us, as their interpretations are shaped by factors beyond our influence, such as personal history or cultural context. Recognizing both truths liberates us from the impossible task of managing external perceptions, allowing us to focus on our values, goals, and self-perception instead.

This perspective encourages us to prioritize self-awareness and confidence over external validation. Welcoming constructive feedback from trusted sources can still provide valuable insights for growth. However, discerning which opinions to embrace and which to discard ensures we remain true to our authentic selves. Letting go of unhelpful or misaligned judgments strengthens our emotional resilience and preserves our energy for what truly matters.

Rule Two reminds us that true freedom lies in prioritizing our values over external judgments. By releasing the need for approval, we gain clarity, confidence, and inner peace. This mindset empowers us to navigate life with authenticity and purpose, free from the weight of others' opinions.

EXAMPLE 1: OPRAH WINFREY (1954–)

Born in Kosciusko, Mississippi, Oprah Winfrey's early life was marked by poverty, instability, and significant challenges. Despite childhood trauma and systemic discrimination, she pursued a passion for storytelling and entered the media industry, defying societal expectations. However, as a young Black woman in a field dominated by rigid norms, she faced relentless criticism and skepticism.

In her first coanchoring job at a Baltimore news station, her emotional storytelling style clashed with the traditional, detached approach expected of news anchors. Deemed unfit for television, Winfrey was reassigned to a daytime talk show—a move intended as a demotion. Rather than internalizing the criticism, she embraced the opportunity to connect authentically with audiences. Her natural warmth and relatability transformed the show's ratings, setting her on the path to national recognition.

In 1986, Winfrey launched *The Oprah Winfrey Show*, despite industry insiders dismissing her approach as overly emotional and lacking professionalism. Instead of conforming to traditional media standards, she leaned into her unique vision, focusing on topics like mental health, relationships, and personal growth—subjects often neglected in mainstream programming. Her show became a cultural phenomenon, running for twenty-five years and earning numerous accolades, including forty-seven Daytime Emmy Awards.

Today, Oprah Winfrey is a global icon. She has built a media empire that includes her own network, OWN (Oprah Winfrey Network), and she is one of the wealthiest and most influential women in the world, with a net worth exceeding $2.5 billion. Beyond her professional success, she is a philanthropist and advocate for education, equality, and empowerment, impacting millions of lives worldwide.

Oprah Winfrey's story exemplifies Rule Two. Faced with relentless criticism and pressure to conform, she refused to let others define her path. By detaching from external judgments and embracing her authenticity, she redefined media and built a legacy of empowerment and influence. Her journey underscores the transformative power of staying true to one's values and vision, inspiring millions to live authentically.

EXAMPLE 2: DAVID CAMERON (1966–) AND THE BREXIT REFERENDUM

David Cameron, born in London, served as the United Kingdom's prime minister from 2010 to 2016. Early in his tenure, he focused on guiding the country through economic recovery while navigating internal divisions within his Conservative Party. One of the most contentious issues he faced was the United Kingdom's relationship with the European Union, which had become a polarizing topic in British politics.

As Euro-skeptic sentiment grew within his party and among the public, Cameron found himself under mounting pressure to address the divide. Personally, he believed that remaining in the European Union was essential for the United Kingdom's economic prosperity and global influence. However, his leadership faced increasing challenges from within the Conservative Party, where vocal members demanded a referendum on EU membership. Hoping to unify his party and secure his leadership, Cameron announced the referendum in 2013.

Despite campaigning for the United Kingdom to remain in the European Union, Cameron's decision to hold the referendum was heavily influenced by external pressures rather than a steadfast commitment to his own convictions. The move was seen as an attempt to appease Euro-skeptics within his party rather than a strategy driven by national interest. In 2016, the United Kingdom voted 51.9 percent in favor of leaving the European Union, triggering immediate political uncertainty and economic instability. The fallout fractured the nation, deepened societal divisions, and led to Cameron's resignation as prime minister.

Cameron's decision to prioritize external pressures over his personal convictions became a defining moment of his leadership. His inability to anchor his decisions in his values led to long-term consequences for both his legacy and the nation.

David Cameron's story vividly illustrates Rule Two. By allowing external pressures to dictate a critical decision, he undermined his leadership and compromised his vision for the country. This example highlights the dangers of relying on external validation in leadership, showing how acting on others' opinions can lead to significant consequences for one's integrity, legacy, and the people they serve.

Rule Three: Don't Strive to Please Everyone; Prioritize Yourself

"You can't please everyone, and you can't make everyone like you."
—commonly attributed to Katie Couric

Navigating relationships often challenges us to balance the desire for acceptance with the need to remain authentic. Rule Three reminds us that striving for universal approval is not only impossible but also comes at the cost of self-respect and emotional well-being. This rule is grounded in two liberating truths:

- **Pleasing everyone is an impossible goal:** The diversity of opinions, values, and expectations ensures that no matter how hard we try, some people will disagree or disapprove.
- **Constant appeasement disconnects us from our true selves:** Continuously reshaping our behavior to fit others' expectations erodes self-worth, disrupts inner peace, and creates false perceptions of who we are. This diminishes emotional health and weakens the authenticity of our relationships.

Recognizing these truths frees us from the exhausting pursuit of external validation. It empowers us to embrace our individuality, express our authentic selves, and accept that disagreements or disapproval are natural parts of life. By prioritizing self-awareness and authenticity, we cultivate relationships that reflect mutual respect and genuine connection.

This rule, however, does not advocate insensitivity or disregard for others. Kindness and empathy remain essential for meaningful relationships. The key is balance: respecting others' perspectives while maintaining the courage to honor our values and emotional well-being. When we harmonize authenticity with consideration, we build interactions grounded in sincerity and mutual respect.

Rule Three encourages us to prioritize authenticity while remaining considerate of others. By embracing who we truly are and valuing others without compromising ourselves, we foster genuine, fulfilling connections. This approach enhances personal well-being, deepens trust, and creates a foundation for relationships built on mutual understanding and respect.

EXAMPLE 1: JOHA AND HIS DONKEY

Joha, a figure from Middle Eastern folklore known for his practical wisdom, set off for the market one day with his young son and their donkey. At first, they walked alongside the donkey. In the first village, people scoffed, "Why are they walking when they have a donkey? That makes no sense!" Embarrassed, Joha decided to ride the donkey and let his son walk.

In the next village, the crowd reacted differently. "What a selfish father, riding the donkey while his little boy walks!" someone shouted. Feeling uneasy, Joha switched places with his son, letting the boy ride while he walked. Yet, criticism awaited in the third village. "Look at that disrespectful child, riding while his father walks! What poor manners!" Frustrated, Joha decided they should both ride the donkey to quiet the complaints.

As they entered the fourth village, the crowd gasped in disapproval. "How cruel to make the donkey carry both of them!" At a loss, Joha and his son decided to carry the donkey themselves. By the time they reached the market, everyone burst into laughter at the absurd sight. Exhausted and humiliated, Joha realized an important lesson: No matter what he did, someone would always have something to say.

This story vividly illustrates Rule Three. Joha's efforts to avoid criticism left him drained and mocked, proving that it's impossible to satisfy everyone's expectations. Each attempt to adapt only led to more judgment, showing the futility of chasing universal approval. The tale reminds us that trusting our judgment and staying true to ourselves is far more fulfilling than letting others' opinions dictate our actions.

EXAMPLE 2: KING SAUL

The story of King Saul is drawn from the Bible, specifically the first book of Samuel in the Hebrew Bible/Old Testament. Saul was chosen as the first king of Israel during a time of great uncertainty, when the Israelites sought a unifying leader to defend their nation and establish order. Known for his physical stature and early military successes, Saul initially inspired respect and loyalty among his people. However, as his reign progressed, personal insecurities and a growing desire for approval began to overshadow his leadership.

A pivotal moment in Saul's reign occurred during a military campaign against the Amalekites, a neighboring group seen as a significant threat to Israel. Saul was instructed by the prophet Samuel to destroy the Amalekites and all their possessions—a command rooted in herem, a concept of total devotion to God symbolizing obedience. Instead of fully obeying, Saul spared their king, Agag, and kept the best livestock, justifying his actions as an effort to offer sacrifices.

When confronted by Samuel, Saul admitted, "I feared the people and obeyed their voice" (1 Sam. 15:24). This confession revealed that his decision was driven by a desire to appease his troops and gain their approval, rather than uphold his responsibilities as king. Samuel rebuked Saul for prioritizing public opinion over divine instruction, declaring that his disobedience had cost him God's favor and his right to rule. Saul's failure to prioritize his principles over others' opinions marked the beginning of his decline. Consumed by jealousy—particularly toward David, a rising military hero and future king—Saul spent much of his later reign attempting to secure power and regain approval. His obsession alienated his allies and destabilized his leadership, ultimately leading to his defeat in battle and tragic death.

King Saul's story vividly illustrates nonadherence to Rule Three. By prioritizing the opinions of others over his values and responsibilities, Saul compromised his integrity and leadership. His inability to anchor his decisions in his own convictions not only weakened his reign but also left a legacy defined by insecurity and unfulfilled potential. Saul's downfall serves as a cautionary tale, reminding us that striving for universal approval can lead to decisions that undermine authenticity, purpose, and long-term success.

Rule Four: Making Enemies Is Inevitable

"You have enemies? Good. That means you've stood up for something, sometime in your life."
—Victor Hugo, *Villemain*

Living authentically means standing firmly by our principles and values, even when they clash with the beliefs or expectations of others. Rule Four reminds us that resistance, disagreement, and even opposition are natural consequences of living with integrity. The presence of critics or enemies is not a sign of failure—it is often a reflection of courage and conviction in defending what truly matters.

Opposition, while uncomfortable, can serve as a catalyst for growth. It forces us to clarify our beliefs, strengthen our resolve, and develop resilience in the face of adversity. Differences in values and beliefs can also provide opportunities for self-reflection and understanding if approached with empathy and openness. By seeing opposition not as a threat but as a test of our character, we transform challenges into moments of growth and discovery.

However, embracing Rule Four does not mean seeking conflict or creating unnecessary enemies. It calls us to accept that staying true to our values will naturally create friction while encouraging us to approach opposition with discernment. This means choosing battles wisely, avoiding pointless confrontations, and focusing on defending what truly aligns with our principles. By addressing disagreements constructively, we maintain integrity while fostering respect and understanding in our relationships.

Rule Four teaches us that opposition is an inevitable part of standing by our principles. Navigating conflicts with wisdom and resilience allows us to grow stronger, deepen our self-awareness, and cultivate meaningful connections. This mindset empowers us to embrace authenticity while fostering a life rooted in clarity, purpose, and unwavering integrity.

EXAMPLE 1: VÁCLAV HAVEL (1936–2011)

Václav Havel, born in Prague, Czechoslovakia, grew up in a country deeply divided under communist rule. As a playwright and thinker, he used his words as a tool to challenge the regime's suppression of freedom and human rights. His criticisms, delivered through essays and plays, resonated with many but also drew the ire of the government, leading to censorship, constant surveillance, and multiple imprisonments.

Havel's activism escalated when he cofounded Charter 77, a manifesto demanding that the government uphold human rights agreements it had signed. This bold move turned Havel into a primary target of the regime. He was publicly vilified, his works were banned, and his personal freedom was repeatedly stripped away. Yet, Havel refused to retreat. He understood that standing by his principles would create enemies but saw resistance as necessary to bring about meaningful change.

In 1989, years of opposition culminated in the Velvet Revolution, a nonviolent movement that overthrew communist rule in Czechoslovakia. Havel, despite being labeled an enemy of the state for much of his life, emerged as a unifying leader. He negotiated with government officials while rallying the public, ensuring the revolution remained peaceful and focused on democratic reforms. Following the revolution, Havel became Czechoslovakia's first democratically elected president. Despite the challenges of uniting a divided nation, he prioritized reconciliation and progress, embodying the values he had fought for his entire life. His leadership proved that standing by one's principles, even in the face of significant opposition, can inspire transformative change.

Havel's life demonstrates Rule Four. His unwavering commitment to truth and justice naturally created opposition, but his ability to confront resistance with resilience, wisdom, and empathy turned adversity into progress. Havel's journey reminds us that while living authentically may invite enemies, it also builds legacies of integrity and impact.

EXAMPLE 2: JAMES BUCHANAN (1791–1868)

James Buchanan, born in Cove Gap, Pennsylvania, served as the fifteenth president of the United States from 1857 to 1861. His presidency occurred during one of the most turbulent periods in American history, as the country was deeply divided over the issue of slavery—whether it should be abolished or expanded into newly acquired territories. These divisions threatened to tear the nation apart, but Buchanan's reluctance to confront these tensions contributed to the conditions that led to the Civil War.

Early in his presidency, the US Supreme Court issued the Dred Scott decision in 1857, a landmark ruling that declared African Americans could not be US citizens and invalidated federal authority to restrict slavery in new territories. Buchanan publicly supported the decision, believing it would settle the slavery debate. However, the ruling had the opposite effect: It outraged Northern abolitionists who opposed slavery, while emboldening Southern leaders who wanted to expand it. This deepened divisions between the North and South, fueling further mistrust.

In 1859, tensions escalated with John Brown's raid on Harpers Ferry, where an abolitionist (someone who fights to end slavery) named John Brown attempted to incite a rebellion by seizing a federal arsenal (a storage site for weapons). The raid failed, but it heightened Southern fears of an armed insurrection by antislavery forces, further polarizing the nation.

Buchanan condemned the raid but failed to address the underlying issues of slavery and regional division, leaving the nation in deeper turmoil.

When Abraham Lincoln was elected president in 1860, many Southern states began to secede—formally break away—from the United States, forming their own Confederacy. Buchanan declared that secession was illegal but argued that the federal government had no authority to stop it, leaving the Union in a state of paralysis. This contradictory stance emboldened the Southern states, who prepared for war, while the federal government failed to take decisive action to maintain national unity.

James Buchanan's leadership vividly demonstrates nonadherence to Rule Four. His reluctance to confront opposition or take firm action reflected a desire to avoid conflict, but this inaction only deepened divisions and accelerated the nation's collapse into war. By failing to stand firmly by his principles and confront the growing crisis, Buchanan's presidency became a symbol of ineffective leadership. His story serves as a powerful reminder that avoiding opposition at all costs can lead to far greater consequences, highlighting the importance of addressing challenges with courage and clarity.

Rule Five: Distrust the Illusion of Your Public Image

"As you rise in rank or gain influence, people treat you differently—
not because of who you are, but because of the position you occupy.
The respect and privileges are tied to the role, not to you as an individual."

—paraphrased from Simon Sinek, "5 Rules to Follow as You Find Your Spark," Usher's New Look Foundation event

Our success often brings attention, admiration, and privileges, creating an illusion around our public image. As Simon Sinek points out, much of the respect we receive is tied to the position we hold or the success we achieve—not necessarily to our true selves. The accolades, special treatment, and deference often reflect admiration for our role, rather than genuine appreciation for our character.

While accomplishments and recognition are important, relying too heavily on validation tied to success can distort our sense of self-worth, especially when external recognition fades. To remain grounded, we must anchor our self-esteem in our values, integrity, and personal growth, rather than fleeting public acclaim. This mindset helps us navigate success with humility and authenticity, ensuring that our identity remains intact regardless of public perception.

This rule does not diminish the value of our achievements or suggest that all praise is insincere. Instead, it challenges us to distinguish between admiration for our public persona and genuine appreciation for who we truly are. True relationships and sincere respect can coexist with success, but we must discern who values us for our deeper qualities versus those drawn to our influence or status.

Rule Five reminds us to separate the illusion of public image from the enduring significance of character. By valuing authenticity over admiration linked to status, we preserve our integrity and ensure that our self-worth remains resilient through life's inevitable highs and lows.

EXAMPLE 1: CALIPH ALI IBN ABI TALIB (600–661)

Caliph Ali ibn Abi Talib, born in Mecca, was a revered figure in early Islamic history, celebrated for his close association with Prophet Muhammad and his dedication to justice and equality.

As the fourth caliph of the Muslim community from 656 to 661, Ali's leadership was tested by significant political and social challenges, including civil unrest and divisions within the Muslim world.

After the Battle of Siffin during the First Fitna (Islamic civil war), Ali discovered that his missing shield was in the possession of a Christian man in Kufa. Despite his authority as caliph, Ali chose not to use his power to reclaim the shield. Instead, he brought the matter to court, demonstrating his commitment to justice and equality before the law.

The case was heard by Qadi Shurayh, a judge known for his fairness. In court, Ali presented his claim without invoking his high status. When asked for evidence, Ali admitted he could not provide conclusive proof. Following the principles of justice, the judge ruled in favor of the Christian man. Ali, respecting the legal process, accepted the verdict with humility. The Christian man, moved by Ali's fairness and respect for the rule of law, voluntarily returned the shield. This act highlighted the profound impact of Ali's leadership, which was rooted in integrity rather than authority.

Ali's actions exemplify Rule Five. By prioritizing justice and humility over the privileges of his position, Ali demonstrated that true leadership stems from authenticity and principled actions rather than reliance on status. His legacy reminds us that living with integrity creates a lasting impact far beyond the fleeting illusions of public image.

EXAMPLE 2: JEAN-BÉDEL BOKASSA (1921–1996)

Jean-Bédel Bokassa, born in Bobangui, French Equatorial Africa, rose to power as president of the Central African

Republic in 1966 after a military coup. Initially presenting himself as a reformer, Bokassa's leadership quickly became defined by authoritarian rule and an obsession with projecting an image of grandeur.

In 1977, Bokassa declared himself emperor and transformed the Central African Republic into the Central African Empire. His lavish coronation, modeled after Napoleon Bonaparte's, cost an estimated $20 million—a staggering amount in a nation suffering from widespread poverty. Dressed in gold-encrusted robes and seated on a massive eagle-shaped throne, Bokassa sought to showcase his absolute power and wealth. However, this spectacle alienated his people, who endured dire conditions while their leader indulged in excess.

Bokassa's reign was further marked by human rights abuses, suppression of dissent, and growing international condemnation. His fixation on projecting strength and authority blinded him to the discontent brewing within his country. In 1979, his regime collapsed after a coup supported by France, ending his reign in disgrace. Returning to the Central African Republic in 1986, Bokassa faced trial for crimes including embezzlement and murder. Once a self-proclaimed emperor, he spent his final years in obscurity—a stark contrast to the grand image he had once cultivated.

Bokassa's story illustrates nonadherence to Rule Five. By prioritizing the illusion of power and status over authentic leadership, he isolated himself and neglected his people's needs, ultimately sowing the seeds of his downfall. His life serves as a cautionary tale, reminding us that true leadership is built on humility and substance, not fleeting appearances or grandiosity.

Rule Six: Never Reveal Secrets

"The only secrets are the secrets that keep themselves."
—George Bernard Shaw, *Back to Methuselah*

Secrets form the foundation of trust in both personal and professional relationships. They symbolize the confidence others place in us and protect our private thoughts and experiences. Rule Six reminds us that how we handle secrets—our own or those entrusted to us—reflects our integrity and reliability. Safeguarding secrets is not merely about silence but about honoring trust, nurturing relationships, and exercising discretion in an increasingly interconnected world.

When managing our own secrets, discretion is critical. Sharing personal secrets with trusted individuals can deepen connections but also exposes vulnerabilities. Decisions about sharing must be guided by careful consideration of whom we trust and whether the benefits outweigh the risks. In an era where information spreads rapidly, caution in what we reveal is more essential than ever. The responsibility is even greater when we are entrusted with the secrets of others. Respecting their confidence demonstrates integrity and strengthens relationships, while betraying that trust can irreparably harm reputations and connections—or even have professional and legal consequences.

In rare cases, ethical discretion may require revealing a secret, particularly when withholding it could lead to significant harm. Such decisions must be guided by careful judgment, balancing the need to protect others with minimizing the damage to trust. These actions should always align with compassion, integrity, and a commitment to doing what is right.

Rule Six underscores the sanctity of secrets and the importance of discretion. By safeguarding both our own secrets and those entrusted to us, we uphold trust, foster authentic relationships, and live by principles that strengthen both personal and professional connections.

EXAMPLE 1: KATHARINE GRAHAM (1917–2001)

Katharine Graham, born in New York City, became the publisher of *The Washington Post* in 1963, leading the newspaper during one of the most turbulent eras in American history. Her leadership faced a critical test in the early 1970s during the Watergate scandal, a political crisis that exposed corruption within President Nixon's administration.

As *The Washington Post* investigated the scandal, it relied on a confidential source known as "Deep Throat," later revealed to be Mark Felt, the FBI's associate director. Felt provided critical information that helped uncover the conspiracy. Graham, aware of Felt's identity, faced immense pressure to reveal her source. Disclosing it could have brought her personal fame and boosted the newspaper's reputation, but it would have jeopardized Felt's safety, compromised the investigation, and damaged the trust placed in her by her reporters.

Despite intense scrutiny from government officials and public speculation, Graham chose to protect Felt's identity. Her decision safeguarded the integrity of the investigation, which ultimately led to President Nixon's resignation in 1974. *The Washington Post*'s reporting became a cornerstone of investigative journalism, earning it widespread acclaim and reinforcing its credibility.

Katharine Graham's actions exemplify Rule Six. By upholding her commitment to confidentiality, she demonstrated integrity, discretion, and respect for the trust placed in her. Her decision not only protected her source but also strengthened the values of ethical journalism. Graham's story reminds us that safeguarding secrets is essential for fostering trust, preserving integrity, and upholding the principles that sustain meaningful relationships and institutions.

EXAMPLE 2: JUDAS ISCARIOT (FIRST CENTURY)

Judas Iscariot, one of the twelve apostles of Jesus Christ, holds a prominent yet infamous place in history. According to the Christian Gospels in the New Testament, Judas was entrusted with intimate knowledge of Jesus's teachings, movements, and personal life, sharing a bond of trust and fellowship with the other apostles. However, his betrayal of Jesus for thirty pieces of silver has become one of history's most enduring symbols of disloyalty.

In the days leading up to Jesus's crucifixion, Judas agreed to reveal Jesus's location to the authorities, enabling them to arrest him in secret to avoid public unrest. The betrayal culminated in the Garden of Gethsemane, where Judas identified Jesus to the soldiers with a kiss—a gesture that was both personal and symbolic of trust. The consequences of Judas's actions were profound. For Jesus, it set in motion the events leading to his arrest, trial, and crucifixion, central to Christian theology. For Judas, the aftermath was marked by guilt and despair. According to Gospel accounts, he attempted to return the silver, but overcome by remorse, he took his own life. Judas's name has since become synonymous with betrayal and treachery, a cautionary tale of the devastating consequences of breaking trust.

Judas Iscariot's story vividly illustrates nonadherence to Rule Six: By disclosing the trust placed in him as one of Jesus's closest followers, Judas violated the sanctity of their relationship. His betrayal not only caused immediate harm but also left a legacy of regret, isolation, and infamy. This narrative underscores the importance of honoring secrets and trust, reminding us that breaking confidence can lead to lasting damage to relationships, reputations, and one's own sense of self.

Rule Seven: Protect Your Reputation

"It takes twenty years to build a reputation and five minutes to ruin it. If you think about that, you'll do things differently."
—**Warren Buffett,** as quoted in *Corporate Survival*

Reputation is one of our most valuable assets, reflecting our character, values, and actions. The impressions we leave—whether online or offline—shape how others perceive us. In today's interconnected world, protecting our reputation requires consistent effort and mindfulness in every aspect of life.

Online, every post, comment, or shared opinion contributes to our digital footprint. While authenticity is important, we must ensure that our words and actions align with our principles. Digital interactions, though immediate, can have long-lasting consequences, making it essential to consider how our behavior might be interpreted or misinterpreted. Offline, our actions and attitudes carry equal importance. How we treat others in casual conversations, professional engagements, or personal relationships reflects our true character. Respect, empathy, and accountability strengthen trust and build lasting connections.

Every commitment or interaction contributes to the mosaic of impressions that define our reputation.

Credibility, the cornerstone of reputation, is built through consistent actions that reflect our values. Trust is earned when we honor commitments, treat others with respect, and maintain integrity in all interactions. Conversely, a single lapse—whether online or offline—can erode years of credibility. By consistently aligning our words and actions with our principles, we safeguard and strengthen our reputation.

Rule Seven reminds us that reputation is shaped by the totality of our actions. By practicing mindfulness, integrity, and respect in every interaction, we cultivate trust, nurture meaningful relationships, and leave behind a legacy of authenticity and reliability.

EXAMPLE 1: PROPHET MUHAMMAD (570–632)

Prophet Muhammad, born in Mecca, is one of the most influential figures in human history and the founder of Islam. Even before his prophetic mission, he was renowned for his honesty and fairness, earning the title *Al-Amin* (The Trustworthy). This reputation for integrity was rooted in consistent ethical behavior, particularly during his years as a trader, where his fair dealings earned the trust of the Meccan society.

A profound example of his unwavering principles occurred during the Hijrah in 622, when Prophet Muhammad and his followers migrated from Mecca to Medina (then Yathrib) to escape persecution. Despite the hostility he faced and the imminent danger to his life, Prophet Muhammad ensured that the belongings entrusted to him by the people of Mecca were returned to their rightful owners. To fulfill this responsibility, he instructed his cousin Ali to remain in Mecca and oversee the process, prioritizing integrity over personal safety.

This act of trustworthiness during a life-threatening moment demonstrated his unwavering commitment to ethical conduct, even under immense pressure. His actions reinforced the respect he commanded among his followers and those who opposed him, setting a timeless example of how consistent ethical behavior strengthens trust and credibility.

Prophet Muhammad's life perfectly embodies Rule Seven: By prioritizing integrity and fulfilling his obligations, even in challenging circumstances, he demonstrated that reputation is built on consistent, ethical behavior. His actions remind us that safeguarding our reputation requires staying true to our values, regardless of external pressures or risks.

EXAMPLE 2: MARTHA STEWART (1941–)

Martha Stewart, born in Jersey City, New Jersey, built a media empire through her company, Martha Stewart Living Omnimedia. Her brand, synonymous with trust, elegance, and perfection, represented the pinnacle of tasteful living. However, in 2001, her carefully curated reputation faced a dramatic reversal due to an insider trading scandal that undermined public trust.

The scandal began when Stewart sold her shares in ImClone Systems, a biotech company, after receiving confidential information about an impending FDA rejection of its product. By acting on this insider knowledge, Stewart prioritized her financial interests over ethical conduct. This decision drew widespread public and legal scrutiny, as it contradicted the trustworthy image she had built over decades. In 2004, Stewart was convicted of conspiracy, obstruction of justice, and making false statements. She served a five-month prison sentence, an outcome that starkly contrasted with her brand's polished reputation. The fallout severely damaged her credibility, leading consumers and investors to question the integrity of her company and causing financial losses. Rebuilding her reputation required significant effort and time, but the scandal remains a cautionary reminder of the fragility of trust.

Martha Stewart's story vividly illustrates nonadherence to Rule Seven. A single unethical decision tarnished decades of trust and credibility, showing how quickly public perception can shift. Her downfall serves as a powerful reminder that reputations, no matter how strong, are vulnerable. Protecting our reputation requires consistent ethical conduct and alignment with the values we represent. By adhering to these principles, we safeguard our credibility and ensure our actions reflect the legacy we wish to build.

Rule Eight: Never Actively Solicit Respect and Love

"He who seeks to command respect is always dependent on others; he who earns respect has gained freedom."
—commonly attributed to Friedrich Nietzsche

Respect and love are natural desires in our relationships, but actively pursuing them often undermines their authenticity. Efforts to seek approval or force admiration can create discomfort, project insecurity, and weaken the very connections we aim to strengthen. True respect and love cannot be demanded; they are earned through sincerity and alignment with our values.

When we live authentically, we foster trust and mutual respect by embracing who we truly are. Authenticity inspires others to value us for our character and principles, creating meaningful connections rooted in honesty. The admiration we earn in this way is stable and deeply fulfilling because it reflects harmony between who we are and how others perceive us.

Relying on external validation risks distorting our self-worth, making it fragile and dependent on others' approval. In contrast, respect and love earned through authenticity provide lasting confidence and emotional resilience. By focusing on living according to our values, we free ourselves from the need to chase validation and instead attract connections that are genuine and enduring.

Rule Eight reminds us that respect and love flourish when we embody authenticity. By staying true to our values and actions, we cultivate deeper, more meaningful relationships while reinforcing our self-esteem. This approach not only strengthens bonds but also enriches our lives with sincerity, trust, and mutual admiration, free from the need for external validation.

EXAMPLE 1: MOTHER TERESA (1910–1997)

Mother Teresa, born in Skopje, North Macedonia, is remembered as one of the most compassionate figures in modern history. Her life was defined by unwavering dedication to serving the poor and destitute, earning global admiration—not through seeking recognition, but through the authenticity of her mission.

In 1950, she founded the Missionaries of Charity, a religious congregation committed to caring for the "poorest of the poor." Working in the slums of Calcutta (now Kolkata), she provided food, shelter, and medical care to those in need, often in harsh conditions. Despite immense challenges, Mother Teresa never sought validation or approval for her work. Her focus remained entirely on her calling—serving humanity with humility and compassion.

Even as she gained international recognition, including the Nobel Peace Prize in 1979, she consistently redirected attention away from herself and toward the needs of those she served. Her humility inspired millions to embrace selflessness and compassion in their own lives. Through her actions and words, she showed that true respect and love arise not from seeking admiration but from living authentically and acting with integrity.

Mother Teresa's life embodies Rule Eight: By staying true to her mission and prioritizing service over recognition, she earned profound respect and love. Her humility and authenticity inspired countless others to follow her example, creating a ripple effect of compassion and integrity. Her legacy reminds us that the deepest respect and love are earned through genuine service and unwavering commitment to our values.

EXAMPLE 2: JAFAR AL-BARMAKI (767–803)

Jafar al-Barmaki, born in Balkh (modern-day Afghanistan), was a prominent figure in the Abbasid Caliphate and a trusted vizier to Harun al-Rashid, the fifth Abbasid caliph. As a member of the influential Barmakid family, Jafar wielded immense power and influence. However, his relentless pursuit of admiration and favor ultimately led to his downfall.

Jafar actively cultivated an image of loyalty and indispensability by orchestrating grand displays of devotion to Harun.

Known for his eloquence and charm, he frequently hosted extravagant banquets and made lavish gestures to highlight his allegiance. While these efforts earned him temporary admiration, many within the court viewed his actions as self-serving and insincere.

Jafar's prioritization of Harun's approval often came at the expense of effective governance. He diverted significant state funds to finance his displays of loyalty, straining the empire's resources. This created resentment among key court figures, who saw his actions as undermining the empire's stability. His personal scandal involving Harun's sister exposed the superficiality of his actions and led to a loss of trust. Feeling betrayed, Harun ordered Jafar's execution, bringing an abrupt end to his life and the influence of the Barmakid family.

Jafar's story vividly illustrates nonadherence to Rule Eight: By prioritizing superficial displays and manipulation over genuine actions, he undermined his credibility and alienated his allies. His downfall highlights the dangers of seeking respect and love through insincere actions. True respect must be earned through authenticity, integrity, and principled behavior—not through relentless ambition or hollow gestures.

Rule Nine: Be Mindful When Giving, Asking, and Refraining from Asking

"Ask from whomever you want, and you will be their captive.
Refrain from asking whomever you want, and you will be their equal.
Be generous to whomever you want, and you will be their master."
—Ali ibn Abi Talib, *Nahj al-Balagha* (The Peak of Eloquence)

The decisions we make when giving, seeking help, or choosing self-reliance have a profound impact on our relationships and how we are perceived. These actions shape the balance of power, respect, and mutual understanding in our interactions.

Generosity demonstrates goodwill and selflessness, going beyond fulfilling immediate needs to uplift others and foster respect. Giving without expectation strengthens trust, loyalty, and admiration, both from the recipient and the broader community. Authentic generosity enhances our influence and reinforces our role as a reliable and principled individual, creating bonds rooted in sincerity and respect.

Asking for help, while often necessary, can subtly alter relationship dynamics. Seeking assistance may create a sense of dependency or indebtedness, shifting the balance of power and influencing how others perceive us. Additionally, frequent reliance on others can affect our own sense of autonomy and confidence, underscoring the importance of thoughtful consideration before asking for support.

Refraining from asking for help signals independence and self-sufficiency. This choice fosters mutual respect and positions us as equals, reinforcing relationships built on parity and mutual understanding. Autonomy inspires admiration by reflecting strength, resilience, and the ability to navigate challenges with dignity.

Rule Nine reminds us to approach giving, asking, and self-reliance with mindfulness. Generosity enhances influence, seeking help may place us in a position of reliance, and refraining from asking demonstrates independence. By thoughtfully navigating these decisions, we ensure our actions align with our values and desired outcomes. This mindful approach helps us cultivate relationships grounded in authenticity, integrity, and mutual respect.

EXAMPLE 1: ANDREW CARNEGIE (1835–1919)

Andrew Carnegie, born in Dunfermline, Scotland, rose from humble beginnings to become one of the wealthiest and most influential figures of his time. As a leader in the steel industry and a pioneering philanthropist, Carnegie's mindful decisions about giving, asking, and refraining from asking shaped his legacy and inspired generations.

- Being mindful when giving: Carnegie dedicated much of his wealth to philanthropy, funding 2,509 public libraries worldwide and founding institutions like the Carnegie Institute of Technology (now Carnegie Mellon University). His giving extended beyond charity, empowering communities with tools for education and self-improvement. By focusing on initiatives that uplifted society rather than seeking personal accolades, Carnegie's generosity inspired others to embrace similar principles of purposeful giving. His thoughtful philanthropy solidified his legacy as a principled leader who used his resources to create lasting change.
- Being mindful when asking: In 1882, Carnegie strategically partnered with Henry Clay Frick, an industrialist whose expertise in coke production was essential for steelmaking. Carnegie's decision to seek Frick's collaboration demonstrated his willingness to ask when it aligned with long-term goals. The partnership allowed Carnegie to consolidate his business, dominate the steel industry, and secure his position as a global industrial leader. His ability to ask for help thoughtfully, while maintaining mutual respect, underscores the importance of mindful collaboration.
- Being mindful when refraining from asking: Carnegie's

philosophy, outlined in his essay "The Gospel of Wealth," emphasized the dignity of self-reliance. He believed individuals should strive for independence wherever possible and that wealth should be used responsibly to empower others. By refraining from unnecessary requests, Carnegie positioned himself as a model of self-sufficiency, earning respect and admiration from peers and the broader community.

Carnegie's life exemplifies Rule Nine. His mindful approach to giving empowered others and inspired societal progress. His strategic collaboration with Frick highlights the importance of asking when it aligns with long-term objectives. Finally, his emphasis on self-reliance reflects the value of refraining from asking when independence is achievable. Carnegie's actions provide a timeless lesson in navigating relationships with integ rity, thoughtfulness, and purpose.

EXAMPLE 2: NICCOLÒ MACHIAVELLI (1469–1527)

Niccolò Machiavelli, born in Florence, Italy, was a renowned diplomat, philosopher, and author whose work *The Prince* remains one of the most influential political treatises in history. However, his lack of mindfulness in giving, asking, and refraining from asking ultimately eroded his credibility and influence after his fall from political power.

- Not being mindful when giving: After being exiled from public office in 1512, Machiavelli sought to regain favor with the ruling Medici family by dedicating *The Prince* to Lorenzo de' Medici. Intended as a strategic gift, the work was perceived by many as manipulative and self-serving. Rather than earning respect, it reinforced suspicions about his motivations, undermining the authenticity of his offering and alienating potential allies.

- Not being mindful when asking: Following his exile, Machiavelli repeatedly petitioned the Medici for reinstatement. These frequent appeals, made without demonstrating renewed value or independence, appeared desperate and eroded his credibility. Instead of restoring his influence, his constant requests highlighted his reliance on the Medicis's goodwill, further diminishing respect from peers and adversaries.
- Not being mindful when refraining from asking: Machiavelli's inability to step back and rebuild his reputation independently exacerbated his downfall. By failing to demonstrate self-sufficiency or create value outside of the Medicis's favor, he deepened perceptions of dependency and inauthenticity, alienating his contemporaries.

Machiavelli's story vividly illustrates nonadherence to Rule Nine. His lack of mindfulness in giving, repeated and desperate appeals, and failure to refrain from asking for favors undermined his reputation and influence. His actions highlight the dangers of neglecting authenticity and thoughtful action in navigating relationships. Machiavelli's experience serves as a cautionary tale, reminding us that respect and trust are earned through independence, integrity, and purposeful decisions—not through manipulation or overreliance on others.

Rule Ten: Engage Other People's Self-Interest When Asking for Help

"Appeal to people's self-interest when asking for help, never to their mercy or gratitude."
—Robert Greene, *The 48 Laws of Power*

When seeking help, the way we frame our request significantly influences the response we receive. Rule Ten highlights a crucial insight: People are more likely to assist when they see how helping aligns with their own goals or interests. This approach is not about manipulation but about understanding human motivation and presenting requests thoughtfully.

Relying on appeals to mercy or past gratitude is often less effective and can strain relationships. Such requests may create discomfort or lead to reluctant assistance. In contrast, aligning our needs with others' priorities fosters a sense of mutual benefit. When people feel their involvement contributes to meaningful outcomes for themselves as well as others, they are more likely to provide genuine and enthusiastic support.

Engaging others' self-interest not only increases the likelihood of receiving help but also strengthens relationships. When people see their contributions as valuable and mutually beneficial, they are more invested in the outcome. This approach fosters trust, collaboration, and goodwill, creating a foundation for long-term mutual support.

Rule Ten reminds us to focus on shared benefits when seeking help. By appealing to others' self-interest, we create opportunities for cooperation that are effective, rewarding, and rooted in mutual understanding.

EXAMPLE 1: JAMSETJI TATA (1839–1904)

Jamsetji Tata, born in Navsari, Gujarat, was a visionary industrialist who sought not only personal success but also to transform India's industrial landscape. His mindful approach to engaging others' self-interest was key to the success of his most ambitious project: establishing India's first steel plant.

In the early 1900s, Tata envisioned building a domestic steel plant to reduce India's reliance on foreign imports and lay the foundation for industrial autonomy. Recognizing the scale of support required, Tata approached Lord Curzon, the British Viceroy of India, by emphasizing how a local steel industry would benefit the British Empire. Tata highlighted how domestic steel production could lower costs for infrastructure projects, such as railways and bridges, while strengthening the empire's industrial capabilities.

Simultaneously, Tata inspired Indian leaders by framing the steel plant as a symbol of industrial self-reliance, aligning with the aspirations of a nation striving for progress. By demonstrating how the project addressed the priorities of both British authorities and Indian stakeholders, Tata garnered critical support. This alignment of interests paved the way for the establishment of the Tata Iron and Steel Company in Jamshedpur in 1907, revolutionizing India's industrial sector.

Jamsetji Tata's approach exemplifies Rule Ten: By aligning his vision with the practical goals of British authorities and the aspirations of Indian leaders, Tata secured the cooperation needed to realize his transformative idea. His success not only reshaped India's economy but also inspired future generations to adopt similar principles of mutual benefit in pursuing ambitious goals.

EXAMPLE 2: PUYI (1906–1967)

Puyi, born in Beijing, China, became Emperor of the Qing Dynasty at just two years old in 1908. His reign ended in 1912 when the Xinhai Revolution overthrew the Qing Dynasty, forcing his abdication. Afterward, Puyi retained symbolic status within the Forbidden City but failed to regain power due to his inability to engage the self-interest of key stakeholders.

Rather than aligning with the aspirations of a modernizing China, Puyi clung to outdated notions of imperial authority, assuming his lineage alone would command loyalty. This reliance on tradition alienated the very political elites and public figures he needed most, as they prioritized progress and reform over restoring the monarchy. His appeals were dismissed as irrelevant and disconnected from the nation's evolving priorities.

Puyi's most significant misstep came in the 1930s when he collaborated with Japan, which installed him as the puppet ruler of Manchukuo, a Japanese-controlled state in northeast China. By aligning with foreign occupiers, Puyi disregarded the self-interest of the Chinese public, who sought independence and sovereignty. This decision not only eroded any remaining goodwill but also cemented his reputation as a traitor among his people. After World War II, Puyi fled to Japanese-occupied Manchuria but was captured by Soviet forces in 1945. Repatriated to China, he spent years as a political prisoner. Puyi's failure to adapt to the evolving motivations of his people and political elites rendered him irrelevant in China's modern political landscape.

Puyi's story vividly illustrates nonadherence to Rule Ten: By failing to align his actions with the priorities of Chinese society, he alienated those whose support he needed most. His reliance on outdated appeals to tradition and his collaboration with foreign occupiers serve as a cautionary tale, underscoring the importance of understanding and engaging others' motivations to achieve cooperation and lasting influence.

Rule Eleven: Don't Overvalue Others to Avoid Being Undervalued

"Respect yourself and others will respect you."
—Confucius, *The Analects*, 12:20

Maintaining a balanced perspective on how we value ourselves and others is essential for fostering healthy relationships and self-esteem. While it is important to appreciate others, overvaluing them at the expense of our own worth creates imbalances that undermine confidence and mutual respect. Two key pitfalls require mindfulness:

- **Comparing ourselves to others:** This often leads to overestimating others' qualities while undervaluing our own, eroding self-confidence and influencing how others perceive us.
- **Idealizing others:** Ignoring their flaws and setting unrealistic expectations distorts reality and diminishes recognition of our own achievements and strengths. Both patterns can convey a sense of inferiority, weakening mutual respect and fostering unhealthy dynamics.

To avoid these traps, self-awareness and a realistic appraisal of both ourselves and others are essential. Recognizing our contributions and value is just as important as acknowledging others' strengths and imperfections. By maintaining this balance, we promote relationships rooted in mutual respect, ensuring we value others without disregarding our own worth.

Rule Eleven reminds us that balanced relationships begin with self-respect. Overvaluing others can diminish self-esteem and create unhealthy dynamics, while cultivating an authentic appreciation of our own worth fosters fairness, integrity, and authenticity. By valuing ourselves appropriately and expecting others to do the same, we create relationships where respect is reciprocal and meaningful.

EXAMPLE 1: NIKOLA TESLA (1856–1943)

Nikola Tesla, born in Smiljan, Croatia, was a visionary inventor whose groundbreaking innovations revolutionized modern electricity. Early in his career, Tesla collaborated with Thomas Edison, a renowned inventor celebrated for his contributions to direct current (DC). Their collaboration—and eventual conflict—highlights the importance of maintaining self-worth and mutual respect in relationships, even when working with influential figures.

After moving to the United States, Tesla joined Edison's company, drawn by his reputation and achievements. Tasked with improving Edison's DC systems, Tesla initially admired Edison's authority but soon realized the limitations of DC for large-scale electricity distribution. Tesla's research into alternating current (AC), which allowed electricity to travel farther with less energy loss, convinced him of its transformative potential. However, Edison dismissed AC as impractical and unsafe, pressuring Tesla to focus exclusively on DC.

Rather than undervaluing his ideas or allowing Edison's authority to overshadow his insights, Tesla chose to pursue his vision independently. Leaving Edison's company, he partnered with George Westinghouse to develop and promote AC technology. Despite fierce opposition during the "War of Currents," Tesla maintained confidence in his innovations, ultimately ensuring AC became the global standard for electricity distribution.

Tesla's story exemplifies Rule Eleven: While respecting Edison's expertise, Tesla recognized the importance of valuing his contributions and standing by his convictions. His persistence not only reshaped the future of energy but also inspired others to embrace self-worth and confidence when challenging established norms. Tesla's journey reminds us that maintaining self-respect is essential for fostering collaborative relationships and achieving transformative success.

EXAMPLE 2: POPE CLEMENT VII (1478–1534)

Giulio de' Medici, known as Pope Clement VII, ascended to the papacy in 1523 during one of the most turbulent periods in Catholic history. The Protestant Reformation, initiated by Martin Luther in 1517, directly challenged the Church's authority and demanded decisive leadership. While Clement VII brought significant political experience as a member of the Medici family, his overreliance on advisors undermined his authority and weakened his ability to respond effectively.

Confronted with the growing Protestant movement, Clement VII sought counsel from influential advisors such as Alessandro Farnese and Tommaso Inghirami, who presented conflicting strategies. Farnese advocated diplomacy and caution, urging the pope to avoid direct confrontation with Luther, while others recommended an aggressive stance to reassert the Church's authority. Instead of balancing these perspectives with his judgment, Clement VII deferred excessively to his advisors, leading to indecision and half measures. This lack of clarity and confidence allowed Protestantism to spread rapidly, eroding the Church's influence and credibility.

Clement VII's most significant failure was his inability to unify the Church's response during this pivotal moment. By prioritizing conflicting advice over his convictions, he missed critical opportunities to reaffirm the Church's position. His reliance on others weakened his leadership, leaving a legacy marked by missed opportunities and diminished influence.

Pope Clement VII's story vividly illustrates nonadherence to Rule Eleven: By overvaluing the input of others and undervaluing his insights, Clement VII undermined his authority and failed to provide decisive leadership during one of history's most critical religious movements. His experience underscores the importance of balancing input from others with confidence in one's judgment. Effective leadership requires valuing others' perspectives without compromising self-respect or clarity of vision.

Rule Twelve: Pay More Attention to Actions Than Words

"Well done is better than well said."

—**Benjamin Franklin,** *Poor Richard's Almanack*

To truly understand others' intentions and character, we must prioritize their actions over their words. Actions, as tangible demonstrations of beliefs and commitments, reveal authenticity more clearly than words, which can be easily manipulated.

While words can persuade and inspire, they can also disguise true motivations. Authenticity and trustworthiness are best evaluated by the alignment between actions and statements. When actions contradict words, it's a signal to observe more closely. This isn't about mistrust but about recognizing that actions, requiring effort and integrity, provide a more reliable measure of character.

Focusing on actions sharpens our judgment and deepens our understanding of others' true intentions. By observing what people do rather than relying solely on what they say, we can identify genuinely trustworthy individuals, navigate relationships wisely, and avoid unnecessary disappointment.

Rule Twelve reminds us that actions speak louder than words. Judging others by their deeds fosters relationships built on real trust and mutual respect. By prioritizing actions over words, we cultivate deeper, more authentic connections rooted in integrity and consistency.

EXAMPLE 1: CHARLES GRAVIER, COMTE DE VERGENNES (1717–1787)

Charles Gravier, Comte de Vergennes, born in Dijon, France, served as the French foreign minister during the American Revolution. When American representatives, including Benjamin Franklin, approached him for support, they made bold promises about the colonies' resolve and ability to defeat the British. Vergennes, however, remained skeptical. Viewing the revolution as disorganized and its success uncertain, he chose to focus on tangible evidence rather than rhetoric to evaluate their cause.

The turning point came with the Battle of Saratoga in October

1777, where American forces, under General Horatio Gates, secured a decisive victory and forced British General John Burgoyne to surrender. This demonstrated the colonies' strategic and organizational competence, countering Vergennes's doubts. Simultaneously, Franklin provided detailed reports on the colonies' resilience and capacity to sustain a prolonged conflict despite limited resources. These concrete achievements convinced Vergennes that the revolution was not a fleeting rebellion but a formidable effort worthy of French support.

Vergennes's reliance on actions rather than promises culminated in his advocacy for the Franco-American Treaty of Alliance in February 1778. This treaty formalized French military and financial assistance to the colonies, fundamentally altering the trajectory of the war. France's involvement proved decisive, leading to the eventual victory of the American colonies and establishing the United States as an independent nation.

Charles Gravier, Comte de Vergennes, exemplifies Rule Twelve: By prioritizing tangible achievements like the victory at Saratoga and Franklin's reports over persuasive assurances, Vergennes ensured that France's support was based on proven capabilities. His focus on actions rather than words underscores the importance of observable evidence in making informed decisions with far-reaching consequences.

EXAMPLE 2: CHARLES PONZI (1882–1949)

Charles Ponzi, born in Lugo, Italy, immigrated to the United States with dreams of wealth and success. In 1920, facing financial struggles, Ponzi devised a fraudulent investment scheme based on international postal reply coupons. He claimed he could exploit differences in currency exchange rates to generate massive profits, promising investors they could double their money within months.

Despite his persuasive rhetoric, Ponzi never demonstrated the legitimacy of his alleged strategy. He failed to provide evidence of actual transactions or significant trading in postal reply coupons. Instead, Ponzi used funds from new investors to pay earlier ones, creating the illusion of success. These selective payouts made his promises seem credible, but his scheme lacked the foundational actions necessary for real profitability.

By August 1920, scrutiny from financial regulators and investigative journalists exposed the truth. Ponzi's operation had no substantive business activity—his claims about exploiting currency exchange rates were entirely unbacked by tangible evidence. When new investments slowed, the scheme collapsed, resulting in an estimated $20 million in losses for investors.

Charles Ponzi's story illustrates nonadherence to Rule Twelve: While his rhetoric captivated thousands, Ponzi's failure to demonstrate genuine action behind his promises revealed the scheme's fraudulent nature. Investors, swayed by his words, neglected to verify the legitimacy of his operations or demand proof of real business activity. This cautionary tale underscores the dangers of neglecting Rule Twelve, reminding us that actions—not words—are the true measure of credibility and trustworthiness. Ponzi's name remains synonymous with fraud, serving as a universal warning against prioritizing rhetoric over observable evidence.

Rule Thirteen: When You Give, Don't Keep Tabs

"The most truly generous persons are those who give silently without hope of praise or reward."
—Carol Ryrie Brink, *Caddie Woodlawn's Family*

True generosity stems from kindness and compassion, untainted by expectations of recognition or return. Rule Thirteen reminds us that giving becomes transactional when we seek reciprocation or remind others of our efforts, fostering feelings of obligation or resentment and weakening relationships. Selfless giving, on the other hand, nurtures trust, mutual respect, and deeper connections.

The essence of selfless giving lies in helping others for the genuine joy of improving their lives, not for praise or rewards. When we give freely and without keeping score, our actions cultivate authenticity and eliminate the pressures of obligation. This approach strengthens relationships by fostering goodwill and creating bonds rooted in sincerity and trust.

However, generosity must also be thoughtful, not reckless. Giving wisely ensures that our efforts are meaningful and directed toward the right people or causes. Recognizing that not everyone will reciprocate or acknowledge our actions helps us focus on the positive impact we create rather than seeking validation. By balancing generosity with purpose, we amplify its power to foster growth and goodwill.

Rule Thirteen reminds us that true generosity is its own reward. By giving without expectation, we enrich our lives with greater meaning and cultivate a spirit of altruism that strengthens our connections with others. Generosity rooted in trust and kindness leads to relationships built on mutual respect and a life enriched by the simple joy of helping others.

EXAMPLE 1: ABDUL SATTAR EDHI (1928–2016)

Abdul Sattar Edhi, born in Bantva, British India, witnessed widespread hardship throughout his youth. At nineteen, he cared for his paralyzed mother until her passing, an experience that inspired a lifelong commitment to helping others.

After moving to Karachi following the partition of India and Pakistan in 1947, Edhi worked as a street hawker but was deeply moved by the poverty and despair around him. Using his modest savings, he purchased a small room in 1951 and repurposed a van as an ambulance, marking the humble beginnings of the Edhi Foundation.

What started as a small initiative grew into one of the world's largest humanitarian networks, encompassing ambulances, orphanages, shelters, and clinics. Edhi personally drove ambulances, collected donations, and cared for the sick and destitute, often working tirelessly in harsh conditions. His compassion extended globally—during the Ethiopian famine of 1985, he provided international aid, emphasizing his belief in humanity's shared responsibility.

Despite his monumental contributions, Edhi lived modestly, wearing simple clothes and dedicating every resource to his foundation. He never sought recognition or repayment, instead viewing the act of helping as its own reward. His approach inspired countless others to embrace selflessness, amplifying the impact of his work.

Abdul Sattar Edhi's life exemplifies Rule Thirteen: His generosity, motivated by compassion and humanity, was free from the need for validation or reciprocity. By giving selflessly, Edhi fostered trust, respect, and goodwill on a global scale. His legacy is a timeless reminder of the transformative power of true generosity, inspiring others to give freely and with sincerity.

EXAMPLE 2: LOUIS XIV (1638–1715)

Louis XIV, known as the Sun King, ruled France from 1643 to 1715, establishing it as a dominant cultural and political power in Europe. A hallmark of his reign was his use of wealth and extravagant gifts to secure alliances and assert French superiority. However, Louis XIV's generosity was often transactional, tied to expectations of loyalty, which ultimately undermined his diplomatic efforts.

One notable example was the Treaty of Dover in 1670. To secure England's alliance against the Dutch, Louis XIV offered King Charles II of England lavish gifts and substantial monetary support, expecting full alignment with France's political goals. While these gifts initially strengthened ties, Charles II, prioritizing England's interests, failed to meet Louis XIV's expectations. This created diplomatic tensions and exposed the limitations of Louis XIV's conditional generosity.

The consequences of this approach extended beyond strained relations with England. By tying his generosity to specific returns, Louis XIV undermined trust and goodwill, damaging his credibility and making it harder for France to secure future alliances. Instead of fostering cooperation, his calculated giving bred mistrust, weakening France's influence in European politics.

Louis XIV's story illustrates nonadherence to Rule Thirteen: By making his generosity conditional on political allegiance, Louis XIV transformed acts of giving into transactions. When his expectations went unmet, relationships were strained, and his diplomatic influence diminished. His experience highlights the dangers of conditional giving, showing that true generosity lies in giving freely and fostering goodwill, rather than creating obligations.

Rule Fourteen: Practice Discretion and Humility to Avoid Envy and Jealousy

"Silence and reserve will protect you from many dangers."

—Baltasar Gracián, *The Art of Worldly Wisdom*

It is natural to seek recognition for our achievements, but openly showcasing success can unintentionally evoke envy and jealousy, straining relationships and fostering negativity. Rule Fourteen encourages us to balance celebration with discretion and humility—not to diminish our accomplishments, but to share them in ways that inspire connection and genuine happiness.

Our true worth lies in our character and values, not in material wealth or public accolades. Thoughtfully sharing achievements with modesty reduces comparisons and resentment while fostering trust and mutual respect. Discretion ensures that our successes are celebrated in ways that strengthen relationships rather than creating unnecessary tension or competition.

This rule does not advocate hiding success but emphasizes sharing it with authenticity and balance. By focusing on the challenges overcome and lessons learned, we create meaningful narratives that inspire and resonate with others.

Rule Fourteen reminds us that true fulfillment comes from the substance of our character and the authenticity of our journey. By practicing discretion and humility, we protect relationships, foster genuine appreciation, and cultivate an environment of mutual respect and lasting connection.

EXAMPLE 1: WARREN BUFFETT (1930–)

Warren Buffett, born in Omaha, Nebraska, is celebrated as one of the most successful investors in history and the CEO of Berkshire Hathaway. Despite his immense wealth, Buffett is renowned for his modest lifestyle, which stands in stark contrast to the opulence often associated with billionaires.

Buffett lives in the same house he purchased in 1958 for $31,500, drives a modest car, and enjoys simple meals at local restaurants. His humility extends to his philanthropic efforts; in 2006, he pledged to donate 99 percent of his fortune to charitable causes, primarily through the Bill and Melinda Gates Foundation. For Buffett, this decision was not about seeking recognition but about using his wealth to create meaningful change.

By choosing discretion over extravagance, Buffett avoids the pitfalls of flaunting success, which can provoke envy and strain relationships. Instead, his actions foster admiration and respect, creating an environment of trust and goodwill. Beyond his personal example, Buffett's philanthropic philosophy has inspired other billionaires to adopt similar commitments, amplifying the positive impact of his humility and generosity.

Warren Buffett's life exemplifies Rule Fourteen: By embracing simplicity and directing his wealth toward causes that benefit others, Buffett demonstrates that true fulfillment lies in character and contribution rather than outward displays of success. His example reminds us that humility and discretion not only inspire admiration but also create a ripple effect of generosity, fostering relationships built on respect and shared values.

EXAMPLE 2: MARIE ANTOINETTE (1755–1793)

Marie Antoinette, born in Vienna, Austria, became Queen of France through her marriage to King Louis XVI. Her reign, from 1774 to 1793, coincided with severe economic hardships and widespread social unrest. Known for her extravagant spending on fashion, jewelry, and lavish parties at Versailles, she came to symbolize the monarchy's detachment from the struggles of the French people.

Her ostentatious displays of wealth clashed with the widespread poverty and famine gripping France. Although the infamous phrase "Let them eat cake" is a misattribution, it captured the public's perception of her indifference to their suffering. These excessive displays of privilege fueled resentment, eroded trust in the monarchy, and deepened the divide between the ruling class and the populace.

Marie Antoinette's inability to exercise humility and discretion during a national crisis exacerbated social tensions and weakened the monarchy's legitimacy. Her failure to align her behavior with the struggles of her people not only alienated the public but also contributed to the French Revolution. The monarchy's collapse, culminating in her execution in 1793, serves as a powerful reminder of how extravagance and insensitivity can provoke envy and resentment, especially during times of collective hardship.

Marie Antoinette's story vividly illustrates nonadherence to Rule Fourteen. Her extravagant displays and lack of humility demonstrated the dangers of ostentation, particularly for those in positions of power. Her experience underscores the importance of modesty and discretion in fostering trust, bridging divides, and preventing resentment—a lesson that remains relevant for leaders today.

Rule Fifteen: Never Reveal Your Good Deeds, Nor How Others Have Wronged You

"Two things, never mention them: the wrongs people do to you and the good you do to others."
—commonly attributed to Luqman al-Hakim

Rule Fifteen emphasizes humility and resilience as guiding principles in how we approach acts of kindness and grievances. It encourages us to keep our good deeds and hardships private, fostering selflessness, inner strength, and personal growth.

When we help others, our actions should stem from genuine compassion and a desire to contribute to the greater good. Publicizing good deeds shifts the focus from the act itself to a need for recognition, diluting the spirit of true generosity. Quiet kindness carries intrinsic value, requiring no external validation and fostering authentic relationships built on sincerity.

Similarly, while encountering wrongdoings is inevitable, dwelling on them or frequently recounting grievances can hinder healing and strain relationships. Constantly sharing these experiences risks fostering bitterness, creating discomfort for others, and reinforcing a victim mentality.

This rule does not call for suppressing emotions or ignoring injustices but encourages balance. Sharing good deeds or grievances should aim to inspire, impart wisdom, or seek constructive solutions rather than seeking attention or sympathy. By doing so, we ensure our words and actions align with self-awareness, integrity, and purpose.

Rule Fifteen guides us toward a life rooted in humility and inner strength. By valuing the quiet dignity of selfless acts and resilient responses to challenges, we focus on the intrinsic worth of our actions and the lessons learned from adversity. This approach fosters authentic humility, meaningful relationships, and personal fulfillment.

EXAMPLE 1: ABU BAKR AL-SIDDIQ (573–634)

Abu Bakr al-Siddiq, born in Mecca, was a close companion of Prophet Muhammad and the first caliph of Islam. Renowned for his humility and moral strength, Abu Bakr's life was characterized by quiet acts of selflessness and an unwavering commitment to unity and justice.

One of the most poignant examples of his generosity was his intervention to free Bilal ibn Rabah, a slave who endured brutal persecution for embracing Islam. Abu Bakr, moved by compassion, purchased Bilal's freedom with his own wealth, ensuring his safety and dignity. This act, carried out without public fanfare, reflected Abu Bakr's focus on alleviating suffering without seeking recognition or praise.

Another example of his character occurred before his conversion to Islam. Abu Bakr was once assaulted by Tufayl ibn Amr, who later, after embracing Islam, expressed deep regret for his actions. Abu Bakr forgave Tufayl without harboring resentment or publicizing the incident. Instead of seeking sympathy or using the past to gain favor, Abu Bakr prioritized reconciliation and unity, strengthening the bonds of the Muslim community.

Abu Bakr's humility and discretion inspired those around him to adopt similar values, fostering trust and harmony in a diverse and growing society. His life exemplifies Rule Fifteen: His quiet support for Bilal highlights selfless giving, free from the need for acknowledgment. Similarly, his forgiveness of Tufayl demonstrates the power of discretion in resolving grievances privately. Through humility and restraint, Abu Bakr not only strengthened relationships but also left a legacy of compassion, trust, and moral leadership.

EXAMPLE 2: SILVIO BERLUSCONI (1936–2023)

Silvio Berlusconi, born in Milan, Italy, was a charismatic media tycoon and politician whose career was marked by both influence and controversy. Known for blending public service with self-promotion, Berlusconi often prioritized personal recognition over humility and discretion, actions that frequently drew criticism.

In 2009, following the devastating L'Aquila earthquake, Berlusconi, then Italy's prime minister, moved the G8 summit to L'Aquila. While this appeared to be a gesture of solidarity with the victims, many viewed it as a calculated move to divert attention from his ongoing legal troubles and bolster his political image. Berlusconi frequently placed himself at the center of recovery efforts, showcasing rebuilding projects as personal achievements. This overshadowed the contributions of aid workers and drew criticism for prioritizing his image over the genuine needs of the victims.

In 2013, after being convicted of tax fraud, Berlusconi released a video proclaiming his innocence and portraying himself as the victim of a politically biased judiciary. Instead of addressing the charges or taking responsibility, he framed the conviction as a conspiracy against him. This narrative of victimhood polarized public opinion, eroded trust, and alienated supporters.

Berlusconi's actions vividly illustrate nonadherence to Rule Fifteen: By using the L'Aquila recovery efforts for self-promotion and framing himself as a victim during his legal troubles, Berlusconi undermined his credibility and strained public trust.

These actions left a lasting impact on his legacy, highlighting the dangers of seeking sympathy or recognition at the expense of humility and discretion. His story underscores the importance of exercising restraint to foster respect, maintain credibility, and build authentic connections.

Rule Sixteen: Avoid Social Bubbles and the Herd Mentality

"Whenever you find yourself on the side of the majority, it is time to pause and reflect."
—**Mark Twain,** *Mark Twain's Notebook*

In today's hyperconnected world, we face a paradox: Despite unprecedented access to information, we often confine ourselves to limited perspectives. Social bubbles and herd mentality narrow our thinking, stifling diversity of thought and critical analysis.

Social bubbles, particularly in digital spaces, form when algorithms curate content based on our preferences. This selective exposure reinforces existing beliefs, creating echo chambers that filter out differing opinions. Over time, we may mistake our perspectives for universal truths, obscuring the complexity of reality.

Herd mentality, the tendency to align with collective opinion, offers comfort but often suppresses creativity and critical thinking. When group consensus replaces rational discourse, it fosters groupthink, where the desire for harmony outweighs constructive debate. This limits personal growth and innovation. While social bubbles and herd dynamics are not inherently harmful, they require mindful navigation. To avoid their pitfalls, we must actively seek diverse perspectives and challenge our assumptions. This involves recognizing cognitive biases, remaining open to being wrong, and critically examining information that aligns with our beliefs.

Rule Sixteen encourages us to step beyond our comfort zones. By embracing diverse ideas and testing our perspectives, we cultivate critical thinking, expand our intellectual boundaries, and develop a more nuanced worldview. This deliberate effort fosters personal growth, sharpens decision-making, and deepens our appreciation for the richness of human thought and experience.

EXAMPLE 1: DONALD TRUMP'S TWEETS AND THE CAPITOL RIOT

During the 2020 US presidential election and its aftermath, Donald Trump used Twitter extensively to communicate with his supporters. Through his tweets, he repeatedly claimed that the election was stolen through widespread fraud. These assertions, dismissed by courts, election officials, and independent experts, resonated strongly within his base, creating a digital echo chamber where his claims were amplified without critical scrutiny.

Twitter's algorithm played a significant role in reinforcing these beliefs. As Trump's followers engaged with his tweets, the platform's recommendation systems pushed similar content, isolating users within a bubble of like-minded voices. This echo chamber replaced individual critical thinking with collective acceptance of a singular narrative, fostering herd mentality.

The consequences of this dynamic were starkly evident on January 6, 2021, during the Capitol riot. Inspired by Trump's repeated claims, thousands of his followers stormed the US Capitol, believing they were defending democracy. The unchecked reinforcement of Trump's messages within their social bubble fueled real-world actions rooted in false narratives.

This example vividly illustrates the dangers described in Rule Sixteen: Trump's tweets created an environment where dissenting views were filtered out, amplifying a single perspective and discouraging critical analysis. The Capitol riot underscores the importance of engaging with diverse viewpoints and challenging assumptions, particularly in the digital age where algorithms often reinforce existing beliefs. By seeking varied sources of information and critically evaluating claims, we can avoid the pitfalls of herd mentality and make more balanced, informed decisions.

EXAMPLE 2: THE 2016 BREXIT REFERENDUM

The Brexit Referendum, held on June 23, 2016, marked a pivotal decision in UK history, asking voters whether the United Kingdom should remain part of the European Union or leave it. The campaigns, led by both the "Leave" and "Remain" camps, were characterized by polarized messaging and emotionally charged appeals. However, the Leave campaign's simplified narratives and emotive strategies proved particularly influential.

One of the most prominent claims from the Leave campaign was that the UK sent £350 million per week to the EU—a figure prominently displayed on campaign materials, including a red bus. This claim, while compelling, was later debunked as misleading because it failed to account for rebates and funds reinvested into the UK. Despite being factually inaccurate, repeated exposure to this claim within like-minded social bubbles reinforced existing anti-EU sentiments. This created an echo chamber where the figure was accepted without critical scrutiny, obscuring the complexities of EU membership.

The emotionally charged rhetoric further amplified nationalistic sentiments, fostering a powerful herd mentality. Many voters aligned with the collective mindset, prioritizing broad slogans over nuanced discussions of Brexit's long-term implications. The referendum resulted in a narrow 52 percent majority voting to leave the EU, triggering profound political, economic, and social consequences. The UK faced years of political instability, economic uncertainty, and strained relationships with its European neighbors, illustrating the far-reaching effects of decisions shaped by herd mentality.

The Brexit Referendum vividly demonstrates the dangers outlined in Rule Sixteen: Simplified narratives and emotionally driven campaigns fostered a collective mindset that overshadowed critical thinking and nuanced analysis. The long-term consequences of Brexit underscore the importance of breaking free from echo chambers, engaging with diverse perspectives, and critically evaluating complex issues. By challenging herd mentality, we can make more informed decisions and contribute to more thoughtful public discourse, avoiding the pitfalls of emotionally driven campaigns.

CHAPTER 10

Navigating Conflict

"I would unite with anybody to do right and with nobody to do wrong."

—Frederick Douglass,
"The Anti-Slavery Movement" Speech

Rule One: Avoid Conflict by Managing Your Pride and Your Need to Be Right

"A man is not defeated by his opponents but by his pride."

—Unknown

Conflict often arises not from the substance of disagreements but from pride and the need to prove ourselves right. These impulses can escalate simple disputes into clashes of egos, straining relationships and hindering productive dialogue. By recognizing and managing these tendencies, we can nurture healthier connections and avoid unnecessary tension.

Our urge to assert dominance or superiority often blinds us to the underlying issues in a disagreement. By prioritizing understanding and empathy over winning, we can shift from defending our egos to fostering resolution-oriented discussions. This approach does not silence our perspectives but encourages thoughtful and respectful dialogue, fostering mutual respect and collaboration.

Managing pride begins with self-awareness and emotional intelligence. Pausing to reflect and approaching disagreements with the intent to resolve rather than triumph allows us to respond thoughtfully instead of impulsively. This shift enables us to focus on shared goals and solutions rather than personal victories, fostering trust and understanding.

Rule One reminds us that managing pride and tempering the need to always be right fosters respect and understanding. By cultivating self-awareness, empathy, and a resolution-focused mindset, we prevent unnecessary conflicts and strengthen our relationships. This approach equips us to navigate challenges with wisdom and humility, creating environments of collaboration and mutual growth.

EXAMPLE 1: KONRAD ADENAUER (1876–1967) AND THE ÉLYSÉE TREATY

Konrad Adenauer, born in Cologne, Germany, served as the first chancellor of West Germany from 1949 to 1963, guiding the country through a critical period of recovery after World War II. In the aftermath of the war, Germany faced immense challenges, including physical devastation, economic collapse, and widespread international distrust. One of Adenauer's most significant tasks was to rebuild relationships with Germany's European neighbors, particularly France, which had endured immense suffering under German occupation.

Adenauer understood that Germany's future depended on

moving beyond its contentious past. Rather than clinging to national pride or attempting to justify Germany's wartime actions, he prioritized humility and reconciliation. He openly acknowledged Germany's responsibility and emphasized the importance of a cooperative future, laying the groundwork for rebuilding trust. His efforts culminated in the Élysée Treaty of 1963, a formal agreement that solidified Franco-German collaboration and became a cornerstone of European integration.

Adenauer's humility extended beyond the treaty. His leadership influenced broader postwar reconciliation efforts, including Germany's integration into the European Economic Community and NATO. By focusing on shared goals such as peace, economic recovery, and stability, he transformed Germany's role on the global stage, helping the nation regain respect and trust. His willingness to set aside pride and historical resentment inspired other leaders to embrace collaboration over division.

Konrad Adenauer's actions exemplify Rule One. By prioritizing humility, empathy, and shared goals, Adenauer overcame deep divisions and fostered reconciliation, creating enduring partnerships. His legacy demonstrates that managing pride and focusing on resolution can transform even the most fractured relationships, paving the way for lasting peace and progress.

EXAMPLE 2: PORFIRIO DÍAZ (1830–1915) AND THE RIO BLANCO TEXTILE STRIKE

Porfirio Díaz, born in Oaxaca, Mexico, served as the country's president for over three decades, from 1876 to 1911. While his rule brought significant modernization, including infrastructure development and industrial growth, it was also marked by authoritarian governance and an inability to empathize with the needs of the populace. This failure to manage his pride and engage in meaningful dialogue was starkly evident during the Rio Blanco textile strike of 1907.

The strike began as workers protested unbearable conditions, low wages, and exploitative practices at the Rio Blanco factory. Instead of acknowledging their grievances or engaging in dialogue, Díaz viewed the strike as a challenge to his authority and a threat to Mexico's industrial progress. Driven by pride and a desire to assert control, he ordered a military crackdown on the strikers. The violent clash resulted in over two hundred deaths, fueling public resentment and alienating a significant portion of the population.

The Rio Blanco incident became a symbol of Díaz's broader governing style: reliance on force over negotiation. His inability to manage dissent with humility or empathy weakened Mexico's social and political stability, fueling widespread discontent that culminated in the Mexican Revolution. By 1911, Díaz was forced to resign and live in exile, marking the end of his regime.

Porfirio Díaz's actions vividly illustrate nonadherence to Rule One. By prioritizing authority and pride over dialogue and compromise, Díaz escalated tensions and deepened divisions. His failure to exercise humility and empathy not only alienated his people but also destabilized the nation, leading to long-term political upheaval. His story underscores the destructive consequences of ego-driven leadership and highlights the importance of prioritizing resolution over dominance.

Rule Two: Avoid Any Conflict That Has No Long-Term Importance

"Choose your battles wisely. After all, life isn't measured by how many times you stood up to fight."
—C. JoyBell C., *The Sun Is Snowing: Poems, Parables and Pictures*

Life is full of potential conflicts, but wisdom lies in discerning which battles truly matter. Rule Two encourages us to focus on conflicts with long-term significance, conserving our energy for what genuinely shapes our lives and aligns with our values. To determine whether a conflict warrants engagement, reflect on its potential impact:

- **Long-term influence:** Will this conflict affect your career, relationships, or aspirations over the next decade? Fleeting disputes often fade, while decisions about major life changes—such as career moves or relationships—merit attention.
- **Core values and principles:** Does this conflict challenge your moral compass or ethical beliefs? Standing up for justice or defending integrity has lasting importance.
- **Health and well-being:** Does this conflict affect your physical or mental health? Prioritizing well-being in lifestyle choices or critical medical decisions is vital.
- **Relationships:** Will addressing this conflict strengthen or strain key relationships over time? Consider whether resolution fosters mutual growth or creates unnecessary division.
- **Opportunity for growth:** Does this conflict present a chance for personal or professional development? Some challenges expand our skills, resilience, or perspectives.

This rule does not advocate avoiding all conflict but encourages selective engagement. By focusing on meaningful disputes, we foster thoughtful engagement, conserve energy for transformative challenges, and avoid unnecessary distractions.

Rule Two reminds us that meaningful conflict is a tool for growth, not a measure of our worth. By prioritizing conflicts that shape our lives and legacies, we align our energy with our values and contribute to a more purposeful and fulfilling existence.

EXAMPLE 1: JAWAHARLAL NEHRU (1889–1964) AND THE LANGUAGE POLICY DEBATE

Jawaharlal Nehru, born in Allahabad, India, served as the nation's first prime minister during its formative years after independence. Among the many challenges he faced was uniting a country defined by immense linguistic and cultural diversity. The adoption of Hindi as the official language, per the 1950 Constitution, sparked intense opposition, particularly in Tamil Nadu, where Tamil speakers viewed the policy as a threat to their linguistic identity. By the early 1960s, protests escalated into violent demonstrations, threatening India's fragile unity.

Recognizing the long-term implications of the language policy conflict, Nehru prioritized unity over rigidity. Enforcing a singular linguistic standard risked deepening divisions and undermining India's vision of inclusivity. In 1963, Nehru championed an amendment to the Official Languages Act, allowing English to remain alongside Hindi in official matters. This pragmatic compromise diffused tensions, upheld linguistic diversity, and preserved national cohesion.

Nehru's resolution of the language crisis reflected his understanding of the situation's broader impact. By addressing Tamil

Nadu's concerns, he strengthened India's federal structure and reinforced its identity as a pluralistic democracy. His decision not only defused immediate tensions but also set a precedent for future leaders to approach diversity as a source of strength rather than division.

Jawaharlal Nehru's leadership exemplifies Rule Two: By engaging in a conflict with profound implications for India's unity and values, Nehru demonstrated the wisdom of addressing disputes that shape a nation's future. His resolution of the language policy ensured that India's foundation as a diverse and inclusive nation remained intact, leaving a lasting legacy of thoughtful and forward-thinking leadership.

EXAMPLE 2: THE BASUS WAR (C. 494–540)

The Basus War, a legendary conflict in fifth-century pre-Islamic Arabia, serves as a cautionary tale of how minor disputes can spiral into prolonged and devastating feuds. The conflict began when Al-Jassas of the Taghlib tribe killed a camel belonging to Basus, a woman from the Bakr tribe. In Bedouin culture, camels symbolized wealth and survival, making the act a grave insult to tribal honor. What began as a localized grievance escalated into a forty-year feud between the Bakr and Taghlib tribes, driven by pride and rigid codes of retribution.

The prolonged conflict drained both tribes of resources, manpower, and stability. Acts of revenge perpetuated the cycle of violence, overshadowing the original offense. Villages were destroyed, alliances fractured, and prosperity gave way to poverty. Ultimately, exhaustion—not reconciliation—forced both sides into a truce, but the decades of bloodshed left both tribes weakened and diminished, with nothing to show for their sacrifices.

The Basus War vividly illustrates nonadherence to Rule Two. Instead of recognizing the insignificance of the initial offense, both tribes allowed pride and tradition to dictate their actions, prioritizing ego over peace and stability. The war's legacy serves as a timeless reminder of the costs of engaging in disputes with no meaningful outcomes. By failing to assess the long-term significance of the conflict, the tribes wasted decades in a feud that offered no progress, prosperity, or resolution. This historical tale underscores the importance of choosing restraint and focusing on conflicts that truly shape our legacy and well-being.

Rule Three: Avoid Conflict by Asking Questions

"Judge a man by his questions rather than his answers."
—commonly attributed to Voltaire

Conflict often arises from misunderstandings or an inability to appreciate another person's perspective. Rule Three emphasizes the transformative power of asking thoughtful questions to bridge these gaps and foster resolution. By embracing open and empathetic questioning, we create opportunities for understanding, collaboration, and constructive problem-solving. Asking questions serves four key purposes:

- **Uncover underlying issues:** Open-ended questions like "What concerns us most about this situation?" help reveal deeper motivations and challenges, shifting the focus toward shared understanding.

- **Encourage active listening:** Demonstrating genuine interest in others' responses builds trust and shows that their perspectives are valued, fostering mutual respect and goodwill.
- **Seek clarity and alignment:** Questions such as "How can we work together to achieve a beneficial outcome?" help align objectives and turn disagreements into opportunities for collaboration.
- **De-escalate tension:** Reframing conflict with constructive questions like "What would an ideal solution look like for everyone involved?" shifts the conversation from disagreement to resolution.

Thoughtful questioning transforms conflict into an opportunity for growth and connection. By cultivating curiosity and empathy, we not only resolve immediate disputes but also strengthen relationships and enhance communication skills. This practice fosters dialogue rooted in respect and collaboration, building a foundation for long-term harmony.

Rule Three reminds us that understanding, not victory, is the ultimate goal of conflict resolution. By asking meaningful questions, we gain deeper insights, foster trust, and create pathways for cooperative solutions. This approach enriches our relationships and equips us to navigate challenges with wisdom and empathy.

EXAMPLE 1: KOFI ANNAN (1938–2018) AND THE 2007 KENYAN ELECTORAL CRISIS

Kofi Annan, born in Kumasi, Ghana, was a celebrated diplomat and former secretary-general of the United Nations, renowned for his ability to mediate complex conflicts. In 2007, Kenya faced widespread violence and political instability following a disputed presidential election. Clashes between supporters of President Mwai Kibaki and opposition leader Raila Odinga left over a thousand dead and hundreds of thousands displaced. With the nation on the brink of civil war, Annan was called to mediate and restore stability.

Annan approached the crisis with a focus on dialogue and resolution. Using strategic questioning, he sought to uncover the deeper issues fueling the conflict. Questions such as "What would justice look like to you?" and "How can fairness be guaranteed moving forward?" reframed the conversation from blame to solutions. By encouraging both parties to articulate their concerns and priorities, Annan created a space for grievances to be aired constructively.

This approach enabled both sides to recognize shared goals, such as restoring peace and rebuilding public trust in governance. Annan's emphasis on thoughtful inquiry shifted the conflict from a zero-sum contest to a collaborative effort. His leadership ultimately resulted in a power-sharing agreement, restoring stability and providing a model for dialogue-driven conflict resolution.

Annan's mediation techniques have since inspired conflict resolution strategies globally, demonstrating the transformative power of thoughtful questioning in fostering peace. His success exemplifies Rule Three: Through empathetic and open-ended inquiry, Annan turned a volatile situation into an opportunity for understanding and collaboration. His story highlights how curiosity and respect can de-escalate tensions and pave the way for sustainable solutions.

EXAMPLE 2: THE SALEM WITCH TRIALS (1692–1693)

The Salem Witch Trials remain one of the most infamous episodes of mass hysteria in American history. Sparked by accusations of witchcraft in the Puritan community of Salem, Massachusetts, the trials led to the execution of twenty individuals and the imprisonment of many others.

The conflict began when a group of young girls claimed to be afflicted by witchcraft, accusing various members of the community. Instead of questioning the validity of these claims or examining the motivations behind the accusations, the authorities and townspeople accepted the accusations at face value. No effort was made to ask critical questions, such as "What evidence supports these claims?" or "Why are these accusations emerging now?" The lack of inquiry perpetuated fear and suspicion, fueling a cycle of accusations, trials, and executions.

The failure to ask thoughtful questions allowed the situation to spiral out of control. Rigid adherence to tradition and fear-driven judgments overshadowed reason and critical thinking. By the time the hysteria subsided, the community was left scarred by its actions, with many acknowledging the grave injustices committed.

The Salem Witch Trials vividly illustrate nonadherence to Rule Three. A simple commitment to thoughtful inquiry—questioning the motives and evidence behind the accusations—could have prevented the escalation of fear and violence. This tragic episode serves as a cautionary tale, highlighting the dangers of unexamined assumptions and the critical need for open dialogue in resolving conflicts.

Rule Four: Avoid Conflict by Using the ABCD Approach

"The most important rule in resolving conflicts is to seek understanding before seeking to be understood."
—Stephen R. Covey, *The 7 Habits of Highly Effective People*

Conflict is an inevitable part of life, emerging in relationships, workplaces, and daily interactions. While unavoidable, conflict does not have to escalate. How we approach it determines whether it deepens divisions or becomes an opportunity for growth. The ABCD approach provides a structured framework to analyze and address conflicts constructively, turning potential confrontations into moments of understanding and resolution:

1. **A—Action:** Identify the specific event or behavior that triggered the conflict. Pinpointing the root cause sets the foundation for resolution.
2. **B—Belief:** Reflect on how we interpret the triggering event. Our beliefs shape our emotional and behavioral responses. These interpretations can be rational, based on facts, or irrational, influenced by assumptions or biases. Examining these beliefs helps us understand why the event affects us.
3. **C—Consequence:** Assess the emotional and behavioral outcomes of our beliefs. Unhelpful or irrational beliefs often lead to negative emotions and counterproductive reactions. Recognizing these consequences highlights how our interpretations drive the conflict.
4. **D—Disputation:** Reassess and challenge unhelpful beliefs. This involves questioning the validity of our

interpretations and replacing them with more constructive perspectives, enabling healthier emotional and behavioral responses.

The ABCD approach fosters self-awareness and rational thinking, empowering us to approach conflicts thoughtfully rather than react impulsively. By identifying triggers, examining beliefs, evaluating consequences, and challenging unhelpful interpretations, we create space for empathy and mutual understanding.

Rule Four reminds us that addressing conflict through a structured lens transforms disputes into opportunities for growth. This method not only resolves immediate conflicts but also strengthens relationships by encouraging empathy, effective communication, and self-awareness. By adopting the ABCD approach, we can navigate challenges with clarity and build a foundation for more harmonious interactions.

EXAMPLE 1: KING JUAN CARLOS I OF SPAIN (1938–) AND THE 1981 COUP ATTEMPT

Born in Rome, Italy, King Juan Carlos I of Spain played a pivotal role in preserving democracy during the 23-F coup attempt in 1981. This critical moment came during Spain's fragile transition to democracy following decades of Francisco Franco's authoritarian rule. On February 23, Lieutenant Colonel Antonio Tejero and armed members of the Guardia Civil stormed Parliament, taking lawmakers hostage in an attempt to halt the democratic process and reinstate authoritarian governance.

As monarch and commander-in-chief of the armed forces, King Juan Carlos I faced a momentous decision. His historical ties to Franco's regime raised doubts about his commitment to democracy. Initially, he considered deploying the military against the plotters to protect the government. However, after reflecting on the potential consequences, he chose a different path:

1. **A—Action:** The coup posed a direct threat to Spain's democratic progress, requiring decisive intervention to safeguard constitutional order.
2. **B—Belief:** Despite his past ties to Franco's regime, King Juan Carlos I believed democracy was essential for Spain's future. He viewed the coup as a direct challenge to these values and initially considered military action.
3. **C—Consequence:** He recognized that military intervention risked plunging Spain back into authoritarianism and creating further political instability.
4. **D—Disputation:** Reassessing his belief in using force, King Juan Carlos I opted for a nonviolent approach. In a televised address wearing his military uniform, he condemned the coup and expressed unwavering support for the democratic government. This decisive action de-escalated the crisis and reinforced Spain's democratic transition.

King Juan Carlos I's response exemplifies Rule Four: By analyzing the situation through action, belief, consequence, and disputation, he navigated a high-stakes conflict with clarity and restraint. His ability to challenge initial instincts and adopt a thoughtful approach underscores the value of the ABCD framework in fostering rational decision-making and preserving long-term stability.

EXAMPLE 2: CALIPH AL-MUSTA'SIM (1213–1258) AND THE FALL OF THE ABBASID CALIPHATE

Caliph Al-Musta'sim, born in Baghdad, ruled the Abbasid Caliphate during its golden age. However, his inability to adapt to a mounting crisis led to one of history's most devastating collapses. In 1258, the Mongol Empire, under Hulagu Khan, launched a siege on Baghdad, threatening the city and the very existence of the caliphate. The Mongols, renowned for their ruthless military campaigns, posed an immediate and existential threat.

Despite clear signs of the Mongols' power, Al-Musta'sim underestimated the severity of the danger. His overconfidence in Baghdad's formidable defenses and belief in divine protection blinded him to the necessity of preparing adequately. He failed to strengthen fortifications, rally sufficient forces, or pursue diplomatic strategies to counter the threat:

1. **A—Action:** The Mongol siege presented an urgent threat that required strategic preparation and decisive leadership.
2. **B—Belief:** Al-Musta'sim's overconfidence in Baghdad's defenses and his faith in divine protection led to dangerous complacency.
3. **C—Consequence:** This inaction resulted in the fall of Baghdad, the massacre of tens of thousands, and the end of the Abbasid Caliphate's golden age.
4. **D—Disputation:** The caliph failed to challenge his assumptions or adapt his strategy, neglecting to reassess his beliefs in the face of clear and mounting threats.

The fall of Baghdad vividly illustrates nonadherence to Rule Four: Al-Musta'sim's failure to re-evaluate his beliefs and adapt to the Mongol threat demonstrates the dangers of rigid thinking in conflict situations. This catastrophic event underscores the importance of questioning assumptions, evaluating consequences, and adopting a flexible approach to ensure thoughtful and effective decision-making.

Rule Five: Avoid Conflict by Steering Clear of Rigid "Should and Must" Thinking

"To practice the process of conflict resolution, we must completely abandon the goal of getting people to do what we want."
—Marshall B. Rosenberg, *Nonviolent Communication: A Language of Life*

In our interactions, we often hold expectations about how others should behave, shaped by our personal standards and desires. This "should and must" mindset—where we expect others to conform to our expectations—frequently leads to unnecessary conflict. Rule Five emphasizes the importance of releasing rigid expectations and recognizing that while we cannot control others' actions, we can choose how we respond. Letting go of these mental demands reduces tension and fosters greater understanding and acceptance.

This approach does not mean dismissing all expectations or condoning harmful behavior. Instead, it advocates flexibility—acknowledging that others act based on their own beliefs and perspectives, which may differ from ours. By focusing on managing our reactions and embracing individuality, we can navigate differences constructively and nurture deeper, more harmonious relationships.

Rule Five reminds us to release the grip of rigid "should and must" thinking. By focusing on our responses and embracing the diversity of human behavior, we cultivate adaptability and enrich our interactions. This perspective reduces conflict, enhances personal peace, and creates space for meaningful connection and growth.

EXAMPLE 1: PEDRO SÁNCHEZ (1972–) AND THE CATALAN INDEPENDENCE MOVEMENT

Pedro Sánchez, born in Madrid, Spain, became prime minister in 2018 amid heightened tensions caused by the Catalan independence movement. The crisis followed the 2017 Catalan independence referendum, declared illegal by Spain's Constitutional Court, which deepened divisions and sparked widespread protests.

The prior administration had responded rigidly, focusing solely on the referendum's illegality and implementing strict measures to enforce national unity. This approach only intensified resentment among Catalans, exacerbating the conflict. Recognizing the limitations of inflexible policies, Sánchez adopted a more adaptive strategy. His administration engaged in dialogue with Catalan leaders, addressing underlying grievances such as regional autonomy and financing reforms while upholding Spain's constitutional framework.

Sánchez's actions de-escalated the immediate crisis and rebuilt communication channels between the central government and Catalonia. While tensions persisted, his approach fostered a more constructive atmosphere for addressing long-standing issues. By focusing on dialogue and mutual understanding, Sánchez preserved Spain's constitutional integrity while promoting reconciliation. His leadership set a precedent for handling other regional conflicts in Spain, emphasizing the importance of flexibility in governance.

Pedro Sánchez's handling of the Catalan independence movement exemplifies Rule Five: Rather than insisting on what Catalan leaders "should" or "must" do, Sánchez embraced flexibility and sought collaborative solutions. His willingness to move beyond rigid expectations created space for meaningful progress, demonstrating how adaptability reduces conflict and fosters mutual respect, even in deeply polarized situations.

EXAMPLE 2: THE SPANISH INQUISITION (1478–1834)

The Spanish Inquisition, established in 1478 under Ferdinand II and Isabella I, aimed to consolidate political power and unify Spain under Christianity. The monarchs believed that religious conformity was essential for stability and viewed non-Christians—primarily Jews and Muslims—as obstacles to this goal. To enforce their vision, they implemented rigid policies, including forced conversions, expulsions, and widespread persecution, relying on fear to compel compliance.

This rigid approach ignored Spain's rich multicultural heritage and the realities of governing a pluralistic society. The insistence on a singular religious identity uprooted established communities and deprived Spain of the intellectual and cultural contributions of persecuted groups. While the policy temporarily consolidated political control, it left lasting scars on Spain's social and cultural fabric. Resentment festered for generations, and the loss of diversity weakened Spain's position in Europe over time.

The consequences were devastating. Thousands were executed or exiled, and a climate of fear and suspicion permeated the kingdom. Spain's legacy as a center of knowledge and cultural exchange eroded, replaced by division and intolerance. Instead of fostering harmony, the Inquisition undermined trust and created divisions that endured for centuries.

The Spanish Inquisition vividly illustrates nonadherence to Rule Five: Ferdinand II and Isabella I's inflexible belief that all subjects "must" conform to Christianity led to widespread suffering and societal harm. Their inability to adapt their expectations to the realities of a diverse population highlights the dangers of rigid thinking in governance. This historical example serves as a timeless reminder that embracing diversity fosters long-term harmony and strength, while rigidity breeds division and decline.

Rule Six: If Conflict Can't Be Avoided, Respond Boldly

"If you fear something, then face it, for the intensity of your caution toward it is greater than that of facing it."
—Ali ibn Abi Talib, *Nahj al-Balagha* (The Peak of Eloquence)

While we naturally strive to avoid conflict, there are moments when it becomes unavoidable, even after applying earlier Rules One through Five. Rule Six calls us to approach these situations with courage and clarity, advocating a bold yet balanced response.

Boldness in conflict resolution begins with overcoming fear. Fear often magnifies challenges, but addressing conflict directly helps us discover strengths that exceed our apprehensions. Boldness involves standing firm, expressing our views clearly, and addressing issues head-on while maintaining respect and empathy for others. Responding boldly does not mean acting aggressively or recklessly. It is about demonstrating strength and determination to resolve conflict constructively. Balancing assertiveness with empathy ensures that bold responses foster mutual respect and understanding, transforming conflict into a tool for rebuilding trust and strengthening relationships.

Rule Six reminds us to face unavoidable conflicts with courage and composure. While striving for peace is vital, there are times when standing our ground with strength and clarity is essential. By embracing conflict thoughtfully, we enhance our resilience, sharpen our conflict resolution skills, and gain valuable perspectives. This rule empowers us to transform challenges into opportunities for growth and deeper connections.

EXAMPLE 1: TARIQ IBN ZIYAD (DIED C. 720) AND THE BATTLE OF GUADALETE

Tariq ibn Ziyad, a North African military commander under the Umayyad Caliphate, led one of history's most audacious military campaigns. In 711, he confronted the powerful Visigothic Kingdom in Hispania—a region corresponding to modern-day Spain and Portugal. Despite commanding a smaller and less equipped force, Tariq faced this unavoidable conflict with boldness and strategic brilliance.

Upon landing in Hispania, Tariq made the daring decision to burn his ships, cutting off any possibility of retreat. Addressing his troops, he declared: "The enemy is in front of you, and the sea is behind you." This bold act symbolized an unyielding resolve, instilling his army with a shared sense of purpose and determination. With no option but to fight courageously or perish, Tariq's forces approached the battle with unparalleled commitment.

The ensuing Battle of Guadalete became a defining moment in history. Despite being outnumbered, Tariq's forces achieved a stunning victory over the Visigothic army, marking the beginning of Islamic influence in the Iberian Peninsula. This triumph demonstrated Tariq's exceptional leadership and reshaped Hispania's cultural and political landscape for centuries. His boldness and decisive actions influenced subsequent military strategies and established him as one of history's most revered commanders.

Tariq ibn Ziyad's actions exemplify Rule Six: Faced with an inescapable challenge, Tariq embraced a bold strategy that turned adversity into triumph. His decision to burn the ships reinforced his unwavering commitment, inspired his troops, and demonstrated the transformative power of courage and clarity in unavoidable conflicts. Tariq's victory at Guadalete remains a timeless example of how boldness in the face of inevitable conflict can lead to transformative outcomes.

EXAMPLE 2: NEVILLE CHAMBERLAIN (1869–1940) AND THE MUNICH AGREEMENT

Neville Chamberlain, born in Birmingham, England, served as Britain's prime minister from 1937 to 1940 during a period of escalating tensions in Europe. In 1938, Adolf Hitler demanded the Sudetenland, a region of Czechoslovakia with a significant German-speaking population, be turned over to Germany. This demand posed a direct challenge to European stability, as Hitler's expansionist ambitions threatened neighboring countries and heightened the risk of war.

At the Munich Conference of 1938, Chamberlain, along with France's prime minister Édouard Daladier, pursued a policy of appeasement to avoid immediate conflict. Rather than confronting Hitler's demands decisively, they allowed Nazi Germany to annex the Sudetenland under the Munich Agreement, hoping this concession would prevent further aggression. Chamberlain famously declared that the agreement had secured "peace for our time." However, the decision emboldened Hitler, who saw the concessions as a sign of weakness. Within months, Nazi Germany invaded the rest of Czechoslovakia, paving the way for World War II.

Chamberlain's reliance on appeasement vividly demonstrates nonadherence to Rule Six: Faced with an inevitable conflict, Chamberlain's hesitation to act decisively allowed Hitler's ambitions to escalate unchecked, leading to greater instability and war. While Chamberlain's intentions were rooted in preserving peace, his failure to confront Hitler with strength delayed the inevitable and magnified the consequences. This example underscores the importance of addressing unavoidable conflicts with boldness and clarity, as indecision can worsen the challenges we aim to avoid.

Rule Seven: During Conflict, Apply Active Listening

"The most basic of all human needs is the need to understand and be understood. The best way to understand people is to listen to them."
—commonly attributed to Ralph G. Nichols

Conflict often arises from misunderstandings, fueled by our tendency to prioritize responding over understanding. Rule Seven emphasizes the transformative power of active listening as a tool to bridge divides and foster resolution. By genuinely focusing on understanding others, we replace defensiveness with empathy, creating an environment where collaboration and trust can thrive.

Active listening requires us to engage fully, setting aside distractions and preconceived notions. It involves more than hearing words; it means understanding the emotions, intentions, and perspectives behind them. This level of engagement shows others that their voices matter, encouraging open dialogue and reducing tension. Approaching conflict with active listening does not mean agreeing with everything or dismissing our own perspectives. Instead, it invites us to acknowledge the validity of others' experiences and reflect on the deeper issues driving the disagreement. By asking thoughtful questions, paraphrasing key points, and showing empathy, we transform conflict into an opportunity for connection and mutual understanding.

Rule Seven reminds us that listening is the foundation of effective conflict resolution. Through active listening, we address not just the surface of disagreements but the emotions and intentions beneath them. This approach fosters understanding, strengthens relationships, and turns conflict into a stepping stone for growth and trust.

EXAMPLE 1: MARTTI AHTISAARI (1937–2023) AND THE 2000 NUSANTARA PEACE AGREEMENT

Martti Ahtisaari, born in Viipuri, Finland (now Vyborg, Russia), was a renowned diplomat, statesman, and Nobel Peace Prize laureate celebrated for his ability to mediate seemingly intractable conflicts. In 2000, he played a pivotal role in resolving the violent conflict in Indonesia's Maluku Islands, where religious and ethnic tensions between Muslim and Christian communities had spiraled into widespread violence and displacement.

Tasked with mediating this volatile situation, Ahtisaari employed a strategy centered on active listening. He began by meeting with leaders from both sides, dedicating significant time to understanding their perspectives and the historical roots of the conflict. Through attentive listening, he identified key grievances, fears, and aspirations fueling the unrest. His empathetic and nonjudgmental approach fostered trust, enabling both communities to articulate their concerns openly and without fear of dismissal.

Ahtisaari's efforts culminated in the Nusantara Peace Agreement, which significantly reduced violence and set the stage for long-term reconciliation. By prioritizing dialogue and mutual understanding, Ahtisaari ensured the agreement addressed the core concerns of both parties, laying the groundwork for sustainable peace.

Martti Ahtisaari's actions exemplify Rule Seven: His commitment to understanding the perspectives of all parties defused immediate tensions and built trust, enabling constructive dialogue that acknowledged the legitimacy of both communities' grievances. By prioritizing empathy and genuine engagement, Ahtisaari demonstrated the transformative power of active listening in fostering understanding and facilitating resolution. The success of the Nusantara Peace Agreement underscores how attentive and empathetic listening paves the way for lasting peace and reconciliation.

EXAMPLE 2: CATO THE ELDER (234–149 BC) AND THE THIRD PUNIC WAR (149–146 BC)

Cato the Elder, born in Tusculum near modern-day Rome, was a Roman statesman renowned for his rigid and uncompromising stance against Carthage, Rome's long-standing rival. Following the Second Punic War, Carthage was significantly weakened, adhering to the strict terms imposed by Rome. Despite these efforts, Cato viewed Carthage as an existential threat and famously ended e very speech in the Senate with the phrase "*Carthago delenda est!*" ("Carthage must be destroyed!").

By the mid-second century BC, Carthage made repeated efforts to demonstrate its peaceful intentions, including disarming, surrendering hostages, and complying with Roman demands. However, Cato dismissed these overtures, refusing to engage in meaningful dialogue or consider Carthage's perspective. His unyielding insistence on Carthage's destruction left no room for compromise or understanding.

This rigid stance culminated in the Third Punic War, which led to Carthage's complete annihilation. The city was razed, its population killed or enslaved, and its cultural and economic contributions obliterated. While Rome emerged victorious, the war had far-reaching negative consequences. It deepened resentment among neighboring states, deprived Rome of a valuable trading partner, and eliminated a rich cultural exchange that could have enriched Roman society.

Cato the Elder's actions vividly illustrate nonadherence to Rule Seven: By ignoring Carthage's peaceful overtures and refusing to empathize, Cato escalated a manageable rivalry into a devastating war. His rigid mindset prevented opportunities for dialogue, resulting in unnecessary destruction and long-term societal harm. This example underscores how the absence of active listening exacerbates conflict, causing avoidable human suffering and cultural loss.

Rule Eight: Be Specific During Conflict

"If you have an important point to make, don't try to be subtle or clever. Use a pile driver."
—commonly attributed to Winston Churchill

Effective conflict resolution hinges on clear and focused communication. Rule Eight emphasizes addressing the specific aspects of a conflict, avoiding unrelated grievances or hypothetical concerns. This clarity ensures discussions remain productive and directed toward resolution, rather than becoming sidetracked by distractions.

Being specific means focusing on the immediate issue at hand. This approach fosters direct and meaningful dialogue, promotes mutual understanding, and minimizes the risk of miscommunication. Precision in communication not only helps define the problem but also provides a framework for constructive solutions.

Specificity also demonstrates respect and fairness. By addressing the current conflict without derailing the conversation, we show a willingness to engage with others' perspectives. While broader contexts may offer insight, maintaining focus during discussions ensures attention remains on the matter requiring resolution.

Rule Eight reminds us that specificity is key to navigating conflicts effectively. By concentrating on the immediate issues and avoiding distractions, we foster clarity, respect, and efficiency in communication. This approach not only facilitates resolution but also strengthens relationships and enhances trust, creating a foundation for better communication in the future.

EXAMPLE 1: POPE ALEXANDER VI (1431–1503) AND THE 1494 TREATY OF TORDESILLAS

Pope Alexander VI, born in Xàtiva, Spain, played a pivotal role in resolving a territorial conflict between Spain and Portugal in the late fifteenth century. As the leading maritime powers of the era, both nations claimed overlapping rights to newly discovered territories in the Americas and beyond. These disputes threatened to escalate into open conflict, jeopardizing peace and the exploration of new lands. Recognizing the need for resolution, both Spain and Portugal turned to Pope Alexander VI, whose authority as the spiritual leader of Christendom positioned him as an impartial mediator.

The conflict stemmed from vague territorial claims and the absence of clear boundaries, which left room for misinterpretation. In 1493, Pope Alexander VI issued a papal bull establishing an initial line of demarcation. However, further negotiation was required to refine the terms and address lingering uncertainties. The resulting Treaty of Tordesillas, signed in 1494, clarified the papal decree by defining a specific boundary: an imaginary line 370 leagues west of the Cape Verde Islands. Spain retained rights to lands west of the line, while Portugal controlled territories to the east, including lucrative trade routes to Asia.

The precision of the treaty was instrumental in resolving the conflict. By clearly defining territorial boundaries, Pope Alexander VI ensured the resolution was clear, enforceable, and acceptable to both parties. This specificity de-escalated tensions, prevented further disputes, and allowed both nations to pursue their colonial ambitions without interference.

The Treaty of Tordesillas exemplifies Rule Eight: By addressing the actionable issue of territorial boundaries with clarity and precision, Pope Alexander VI resolved a potentially destabilizing conflict and fostered stability in Spain and Portugal's relations. This example highlights how specificity transforms potential conflicts into opportunities for collaboration and long-term peace.

EXAMPLE 2: COUNT LEOPOLD BERCHTOLD (1863–1942) AND THE 1914 JULY CRISIS

Count Leopold Berchtold, born in Vienna, Austria, served as the Austro-Hungarian foreign minister during one of history's most pivotal moments: the July Crisis of 1914. This crisis followed the assassination of Archduke Franz Ferdinand, heir to the Austro-Hungarian throne, by a Bosnian Serb nationalist in Sarajevo. The assassination escalated tensions between Austria-Hungary and Serbia, leading to a diplomatic standoff that ultimately spiraled into World War I.

In response to the assassination, Berchtold drafted the July Ultimatum, a list of demands intended to hold Serbia accountable and prevent further anti-Austrian actions. However, the ultimatum was plagued by vague and ambiguous terms. For example, it required Serbia to suppress anti-Austro-Hungarian propaganda and remove individuals deemed hostile to Austria-Hungary but failed to specify criteria for compliance or mechanisms for verification. This lack of clarity left Serbia unsure of how to respond effectively, creating room for misinterpretation.

Serbia partially accepted the ultimatum and requested clarification on the ambiguous demands. Instead of refining or specifying the terms to facilitate compliance, Berchtold dismissed Serbia's response as insufficient. His rigidity, combined with the ultimatum's lack of actionable specifics, deepened misunderstandings and mistrust. Within weeks, Austria-Hungary declared war on Serbia, triggering a chain reaction among European alliances that escalated into World War I.

Berchtold's actions vividly demonstrate nonadherence to Rule Eight: By failing to craft clear and actionable demands, he exacerbated tensions and foreclosed opportunities for resolution. The ambiguity in the ultimatum undermined Serbia's ability to comply, escalating a manageable diplomatic crisis into a catastrophic global war. This example underscores the critical importance of precision and clarity in conflict resolution, showing how vagueness can lead to devastating outcomes.

Rule Nine: During Conflict, Be Respectful and Calm

"Raise your words, not your voice. It is rain that grows flowers, not thunder."
—commonly attributed to Rumi

Conflict often stirs strong emotions, tempting us to react impulsively or defensively. Yet, Rule Nine reminds us that the key to navigating disagreements lies in cultivating respect and calmness. By choosing composure over chaos, we create space for understanding, connection, and resolution.

Being respectful and calm during conflict means valuing dialogue over domination and understanding over winning. A respectful approach fosters trust and encourages open communication, even when tensions run high. Calmness, meanwhile, de-escalates heated situations, enabling us to think clearly, articulate our perspectives thoughtfully, and truly listen to others.

This approach does not mean suppressing emotions or avoiding confrontation but rather channeling our responses constructively. Respect invites collaboration, showing others that their viewpoints matter, while calmness allows us to respond with clarity and purpose rather than reacting out of anger or frustration. Together, these qualities transform conflict into an opportunity for growth and mutual understanding.

Rule Nine underscores that respect and calmness are hallmarks of emotional maturity and effective conflict resolution. By responding with composure, we create an environment where dialogue thrives, turning disagreements into opportunities for deeper connection and trust. This mindset not only resolves immediate issues but also strengthens relationships and fosters a culture of mutual respect.

EXAMPLE 1: FREDERIK WILLEM DE KLERK (1936–2021) AND THE END OF APARTHEID IN SOUTH AFRICA

Frederik Willem de Klerk, born in Johannesburg, South Africa, became president in 1989 during one of the nation's most turbulent periods. The apartheid regime of racial segregation had deeply divided South Africa, creating widespread unrest, global condemnation, and a fractured society on the brink of collapse.

Facing immense pressure from the international community and South Africa's oppressed majority, de Klerk made the groundbreaking decision to initiate reforms. In February 1990, he unbanned the African National Congress (ANC) and other anti-apartheid organizations, and ordered the release of Nelson Mandela after twenty-seven years of imprisonment. These actions reflected de Klerk's commitment to resolving the conflict with respect and calmness rather than resorting to divisive rhetoric or defensive tactics.

De Klerk engaged directly with opposition leaders, including Mandela, fostering an atmosphere of mutual respect despite the animosities that had long defined their communities. His calm and inclusive approach, even under intense scrutiny from his own political party and the white minority, de-escalated tensions and enabled dialogue. These efforts ultimately led to South Africa's peaceful transition to democracy in 1994.

Frederik Willem de Klerk's leadership exemplifies Rule Nine: By treating his opponents with dignity and maintaining composure in a highly charged political climate, de Klerk defused animosity and initiated a peaceful transition. His example highlights the transformative power of respect and calmness in resolving conflicts, demonstrating how these qualities foster trust, understanding, and meaningful societal change.

EXAMPLE 2: GENERAL HIDEKI TOJO (1884–1948) AND JAPAN'S ROLE IN WORLD WAR II

General Hideki Tojo, born in Tokyo, Japan, rose to power as prime minister during one of Japan's most militarized periods. From 1941 to 1944, he shaped Japan's foreign policy during World War II, a time of escalating tensions with Western powers. Japan's expansionist ambitions, combined with US economic sanctions targeting vital resources like oil and steel, brought the two nations to a critical juncture.

Despite calls from some within his government to pursue diplomacy, Tojo dismissed these efforts in favor of confrontation. In December 1941, he authorized the surprise attack on Pearl Harbor, aiming to neutralize the US Pacific Fleet and secure Japan's dominance in the Pacific. This decision, made without a formal declaration of war, violated international norms and destroyed any remaining chances for diplomatic resolution. Tojo's aggressive approach escalated hostilities and deepened the conflict. The Pearl Harbor attack provoked the United States into entering the war, resulting in devastating consequences for Japan, including the atomic bombings of Hiroshima and Nagasaki in 1945, the loss of millions of lives, and Japan's eventual surrender.

General Hideki Tojo's leadership vividly illustrates nonadherence to Rule Nine: By rejecting diplomacy and favoring aggression, Tojo ignored opportunities for peaceful dialogue and escalated tensions unnecessarily. His decision to abandon respect and calmness in favor of hostility deepened the conflict, leading to catastrophic consequences for Japan and the world. This example underscores the critical importance of maintaining composure and fostering dialogue during conflict, showing how abandoning these principles can result in irreversible harm.

Rule Ten: During Conflict, Consider Whether Acknowledging Your Opponent's Views Is Possible and Appropriate

"Love your enemies, for they tell you your faults."
—Benjamin Franklin, *Poor Richard's Almanack*

During conflict, our instinct often drives us to defend our position and dismiss opposing viewpoints. Rule Ten emphasizes the importance of considering our opponent's perspective—not as a concession, but as a way to foster understanding and create constructive dialogue.

Viewing the situation through the other person's lens allows us to evaluate the validity and relevance of their perspective. Thoughtful consideration often uncovers shared concerns, hidden issues, or opportunities to refine our reasoning. Acknowledging an opposing view, when appropriate, can de-escalate tensions, demonstrate respect, and pave the way for collaboration—particularly in conflicts where preserving a relationship is crucial.

This rule does not advocate agreeing with or accepting harmful viewpoints. Instead, it encourages recognizing the rationale behind an opposing perspective when doing so is constructive and safe. In situations involving harmful or abusive behavior, personal safety and well-being must always take precedence over understanding the other's perspective.

Rule Ten calls for a thoughtful and empathetic approach to conflict. By considering opposing viewpoints, we transform adversarial interactions into opportunities for growth and mutual respect. While this approach may not always lead to agreement, it fosters constructive dialogue, emotional intelligence, and the potential for meaningful resolution.

EXAMPLE 1: JOSÉ RAMOS-HORTA (1949–) AND THE EAST TIMORESE INDEPENDENCE MOVEMENT

José Ramos-Horta, born in Dili, East Timor, emerged as a key figure in the struggle for East Timor's independence from Indonesia after its occupation in 1975. The annexation brought decades of oppression, human rights abuses, and violent resistance. Known for his diplomatic skill and unyielding commitment to his people's rights, Ramos-Horta sought to resolve the conflict through firm advocacy balanced with empathetic diplomacy.

In 1982, Ramos-Horta delivered a landmark speech at the United Nations, where he highlighted the plight of the East Timorese people. While exposing atrocities like mass killings and forced displacements, he also acknowledged Indonesia's concerns about regional stability and foreign influence. By framing independence as a path toward peace and stability in Southeast Asia, Ramos-Horta shifted the conversation from confrontation to collaboration.

His efforts garnered international support, culminating in the 1999 UN-sponsored referendum, where 78.5 percent of East Timorese voted for independence. Although the announcement triggered violence by pro-Indonesian militias, Ramos-Horta continued to engage diplomatically, securing global intervention to stabilize the region. On May 20, 2002, East Timor achieved full sovereignty, with Ramos-Horta playing a central role in guiding the nation toward peace and democracy.

José Ramos-Horta's leadership exemplifies Rule Ten: By empathetically addressing Indonesia's concerns while firmly advocating for his people's rights, Ramos-Horta demonstrated the transformative power of balancing respect with conviction. His ability to acknowledge opposing perspectives without compromising principles fostered dialogue, reduced hostility, and secured meaningful change. His approach underscores how thoughtful engagement can resolve even the most entrenched conflicts.

EXAMPLE 2: THE RUSSO-JAPANESE WAR (1904–1905)

The Russo-Japanese War arose from competing ambitions between Russia and Japan over influence in East Asia, particularly in Manchuria and Korea. Japan, which had rapidly modernized during the Meiji Era (1868–1912), emerged as a formidable military and industrial power. Despite Japan's transformation, Tsar Nicholas II of Russia dismissed its diplomatic overtures, underestimating Japan's capabilities and setting the stage for war.

Between 1901 and 1903, Japan made repeated attempts to resolve tensions peacefully. It proposed agreements recognizing Russia's dominance in Manchuria in exchange for Japan's control over Korea—an effort to balance interests and avoid escalation. However, Russia rejected these proposals outright, confident in its military superiority and viewing Japan as an inferior power. This refusal to acknowledge Japan's legitimate concerns and growing frustrations provoked a critical turning point.

In February 1904, after diplomatic efforts failed, Japan launched a surprise attack on the Russian fleet at Port Arthur, initiating the Russo-Japanese War. Japan's modernized military achieved decisive victories, including the destruction of Russia's Baltic Fleet at the Battle of Tsushima. The war ended with the Treaty of Portsmouth, brokered by US President Theodore Roosevelt, which recognized Japan's dominance in Korea and forced Russia to cede key territories.

The Russo-Japanese War vividly illustrates nonadherence to Rule Ten: By dismissing Japan's diplomatic efforts and refusing to recognize its legitimate concerns, Tsar Nicholas II escalated tensions into a costly and avoidable war. The conflict undermined Russia's global influence and solidified Japan as a major power. This example underscores the dangers of dismissing opposing perspectives, highlighting how respect and dialogue are critical to de-escalating conflicts and avoiding catastrophic outcomes.

Rule Eleven: During Conflict, Offer Suggestions Where Applicable, Not Impositions

"Force, no matter how concealed, begets resistance."

—Native American wisdom (Lakota proverb)

In conflict, asserting our views as absolute truths often escalates disagreements and hinders resolution. Rule Eleven advocates for a more constructive approach: offering suggestions instead of imposing solutions. Framing viewpoints as flexible options rather than rigid demands demonstrates empathy and respect for the other person's autonomy. This approach fosters collaboration by encouraging open dialogue and allowing others to consider alternative perspectives without feeling coerced. Suggestions create an atmosphere of mutual respect, enabling trust and constructive communication.

When preserving relationships is a priority, offering suggestions is particularly effective. It signals a willingness to understand differing viewpoints and acknowledges the other person's agency. By contrast, imposing opinions often stifles communication and deepens divisions. Collaborative engagement fosters understanding and cooperation, leading to more durable and inclusive solutions.

Rule Eleven underscores the transformative power of empathy and cooperation in conflict resolution. By offering suggestions instead of dictating terms, we promote open communication, mutual respect, and trust. This approach not only resolves immediate conflicts but also strengthens relationships, laying the foundation for long-term harmony and understanding.

EXAMPLE 1: RICHARD HOLBROOKE (1941–2010) AND THE 1995 DAYTON AGREEMENT

Richard Holbrooke, born in New York City, was a seasoned US diplomat who played a pivotal role in ending the Bosnian War (1992–1995). This brutal conflict, characterized by deep ethnic divisions and widespread atrocities, involved Bosnia and Herzegovina, Croatia, and Serbia. In 1995, Holbrooke led peace negotiations in Dayton, Ohio, where mistrust among the parties and rigid demands threatened progress.

Holbrooke recognized that imposing solutions would only deepen tensions. Instead, he adopted a suggestion-driven approach that encouraged collaboration. One of the most contentious issues was the territorial division of Bosnia and Herzegovina. To address this, Holbrooke presented a map and invited the leaders to outline their visions for territorial boundaries. By giving them space to articulate their preferences, he fostered a sense of ownership and mutual respect.

Rather than dictating terms, Holbrooke tactfully suggested compromises that addressed the core concerns of all parties without appearing coercive. He reframed discussions around shared goals, such as regional stability and the prevention of further violence, creating a platform for constructive dialogue. This participatory approach diffused tensions and empowered the leaders to engage meaningfully, leading to a mutually acceptable agreement. The resulting Dayton Agreement, signed in November 1995, ended the war and established a framework for peace in the Balkans. By focusing on collaboration and flexibility, Holbrooke ensured that the agreement felt fair and sustainable to all parties.

Richard Holbrooke's leadership exemplifies Rule Eleven: By fostering collaboration through suggestions rather than dictating solutions, he transformed a volatile negotiation into constructive dialogue. Holbrooke's method highlights the power of empathy, flexibility, and participatory approaches in resolving even the most entrenched conflicts and achieving lasting peace.

EXAMPLE 2: GEORGES CLEMENCEAU (1841–1929) AND THE 1919 TREATY OF VERSAILLES

Georges Clemenceau, born in Mouilleron-en-Pareds, France, served as France's prime minister during the negotiations for the Treaty of Versailles in 1919. Deeply affected by the devastation of World War I, Clemenceau sought to ensure France's security by imposing harsh reparations, territorial reductions, and military restrictions on Germany.

Clemenceau's rigid stance clashed with US President Woodrow Wilson's more conciliatory approach, which emphasized fairness and self-determination for nations through his Fourteen Points. Wilson proposed fostering cooperation and preventing future wars by establishing the League of Nations. However, Clemenceau dismissed these suggestions, prioritizing punitive measures to weaken Germany permanently and assert French dominance.

The treaty's harsh terms humiliated Germany, crippling its economy through massive reparations and territorial losses while imposing strict military limitations. German representatives protested, warning that the conditions would breed resentment and destabilize the region. Clemenceau ignored these concerns, rejecting opportunities for dialogue and focusing instead on enforcing control. The resulting treaty created economic hardship and national humiliation in Germany, fueling extremism and Adolf Hitler's rise to power, ultimately leading to World War II.

Georges Clemenceau's leadership vividly illustrates nonadherence to Rule Eleven: By prioritizing rigid demands over collaborative problem-solving, Clemenceau deepened divisions and created a treaty that lacked the foundation for mutual understanding and sustainable peace. This approach underscores the dangers of ignoring cooperative dialogue, showing how impositions can escalate tensions and lead to far-reaching consequences.

Rule Twelve: During Conflict, Let Your Actions Speak Louder Than Words

"Win through your actions, never through argument."
—**Robert Greene,** *The 48 Laws of Power*

In conflict, words often dominate, but they can fall short of convincing others or demonstrating sincerity. Rule Twelve emphasizes the transformative power of actions in resolving conflict. Actions communicate our intentions tangibly, bridging the gap between what we say and what we do, and reinforcing credibility and trust.

The power of actions lies in their ability to validate our words. While dialogue is essential for fostering understanding, actions provide tangible proof of commitment. By moving beyond verbal assurances to deliver meaningful outcomes, we create lasting impact and strengthen relationships. This rule does not dismiss the importance of dialogue but stresses the need for alignment between words and actions. When our actions consistently reflect our statements, we reduce misunderstandings, build integrity, and foster trust. This balance ensures that our intentions resonate more deeply, creating a foundation for effective and enduring resolutions.

Rule Twelve reminds us that conflict resolution requires more than words. Deliberate and consistent actions validate our intentions and amplify the impact of communication. By letting actions reinforce words, we create opportunities for growth, trust, and mutual understanding, transforming conflict into a catalyst for positive change.

EXAMPLE 1: SUNDERLAL BAHUGUNA (1927–2021) AND THE 1973 CHIPKO MOVEMENT

Sunderlal Bahuguna, born in Maroda, Uttarakhand, became a pioneering figure in India's environmental movement and a symbol of nonviolent resistance. In 1973, he led the Chipko Movement, a grassroots protest against commercial logging that threatened forests essential to local communities' livelihoods. The term Chipko, meaning "to cling" in Hindi, reflected the villagers' unique form of protest: physically hugging trees to prevent them from being felled.

Bahuguna recognized that speeches and petitions alone were insufficient to convey the villagers' deep connection to the forests. By physically embracing the trees, he and the villagers demonstrated their unwavering commitment to conservation in a way that words could not. This direct, nonviolent resistance captured national and international attention, forcing policymakers to confront the ecological and human costs of deforestation.

The movement's success culminated in the Indian government enacting a fifteen-year ban on tree felling in key Himalayan regions in 1980, a landmark achievement in environmental conservation. Bahuguna's leadership and the villagers' heartfelt actions not only protected the forests but also highlighted the profound power of deliberate, visible deeds in resolving conflicts and inspiring change.

The Chipko Movement exemplifies Rule Twelve: By letting their actions communicate their commitment to conservation, Sunderlal Bahuguna and the villagers achieved a clarity and impact unmatched by words alone. Their symbolic protest resonated emotionally and globally, demonstrating how meaningful actions foster understanding, build trust, and drive transformative outcomes.

EXAMPLE 2: LORD LOUIS MOUNTBATTEN (1900–1979) AND THE 1947 PARTITION OF INDIA

Born in Windsor, England, Lord Louis Mountbatten served as the last viceroy of British India in 1947. Tasked with overseeing the country's transition to independence, Mountbatten faced escalating tensions between Hindus, Muslims, and Sikhs. These tensions, fueled by demands for a separate Muslim state, fears of marginalization among minority groups, and deep-seated religious rivalries, threatened to spiral into full-scale civil war.

Under pressure from the British government to expedite the process, Mountbatten announced the partition plan, dividing

British India into two nations: India and Pakistan. While the partition aimed to resolve the conflict and prevent violence, Mountbatten's actions failed to address critical on-the-ground challenges. Despite assurances of a peaceful transition, his administration lacked practical measures to manage the migration of over fourteen million people or mitigate communal tensions. Promises of safety and order were not backed by actionable strategies, leaving millions unprotected during their displacement.

The consequences were catastrophic. Communal violence erupted across the region, with Hindus, Muslims, and Sikhs engaging in brutal attacks against one another. Entire communities were uprooted, leading to one of the largest migrations in human history. An estimated one to two million people lost their lives, and countless others were displaced. The lack of coordination, resources, and enforcement of safety measures turned the partition into a humanitarian disaster, exacerbating the very conflict it sought to resolve.

Lord Mountbatten's leadership vividly illustrates nonadherence to Rule Twelve: While his words and decisions aimed to bring peace, they were not supported by deliberate, actionable measures. The disconnect between his intentions and the lack of meaningful actions deepened divisions and led to catastrophic consequences. This example highlights the critical importance of aligning decisions with practical, thoughtful actions in conflict resolution. When words and actions fail to align, as in Mountbatten's case, the results can amplify rather than resolve the conflict.

Rule Thirteen: In Conflicts, If an Agreement Can't Be Achieved, Then Agree to Disagree

"Honest disagreement is often a good sign of progress."
—commonly attributed to Mahatma Gandhi

In conflicts, reaching an agreement is not always possible. Rule Thirteen advocates for the ability to "agree to disagree" as a mature and constructive response. This principle emphasizes mutual respect and tolerance, recognizing that differing viewpoints are a natural part of human interaction.

By acknowledging that opinions are shaped by diverse experiences, backgrounds, and beliefs, we create an environment of respect even amid disagreements. Agreeing to disagree prevents further escalation of conflict, maintains relationships, and prioritizes understanding over the need for consensus. This approach is especially valuable when continued dialogue is beneficial and the disagreement does not involve urgent or critical issues.

Disagreements also offer opportunities for growth and learning. By listening to opposing perspectives without insisting on agreement, we broaden our understanding, challenge assumptions, and deepen empathy. Agreeing to disagree reflects emotional intelligence and maturity, leaving the door open for future dialogue and potential resolution. It is important to note that agreeing to disagree is not avoidance or a substitute for resolution in critical matters. Instead, it is a deliberate choice to prioritize peace and understanding when consensus cannot be reached.

Rule Thirteen reminds us that harmony does not always require agreement. By embracing the diversity of thought, we preserve relationships, encourage ongoing communication, and demonstrate the maturity to navigate unresolved differences. Agreeing to disagree fosters mutual respect and understanding, turning conflicts into opportunities for connection and growth.

EXAMPLE 1: THE CUBAN MISSILE CRISIS (1962)

The Cuban Missile Crisis was a defining moment of the Cold War, involving a high-stakes standoff between US President John F. Kennedy and Soviet Premier Nikita Khrushchev. The crisis began in October 1962 when the United States discovered Soviet nuclear missiles in Cuba, just ninety miles from its shores—a move perceived as a direct threat to national security. In response, Kennedy imposed a naval blockade on Cuba, escalating tensions and bringing the world to the brink of nuclear war.

Despite immense pressure and opposing ideologies, both leaders recognized the catastrophic risks of failing to reach a resolution. Through intense negotiations, Kennedy and Khrushchev agreed to a compromise: The Soviet Union would dismantle its missile sites in Cuba, while the United States pledged not to invade Cuba and secretly agreed to remove American missiles from Turkey, a significant Soviet concern. While their broader ideological disagreements—such as communism versus capitalism—remained unresolved, they set these aside to prevent a global disaster.

The Cuban Missile Crisis exemplifies Rule Thirteen: Kennedy and Khrushchev acknowledged that complete ideological consensus was unattainable but focused on de-escalating the immediate threat through practical solutions. By respecting irreconcilable differences while prioritizing shared goals, they averted nuclear war and preserved peace. This example highlights how agreeing to disagree can transform even the most dangerous conflicts into opportunities for resolution.

EXAMPLE 2: HENRY II OF ENGLAND (1133–1189) AND THOMAS BECKET (1119–1170)

Henry II, born in Le Mans, France, became King of England in 1154 with a vision to strengthen royal authority and reform the monarchy's relationship with the Church. To further his ambitions, he appointed his close friend Thomas Becket as archbishop of Canterbury in 1162, expecting Becket to support his efforts. However, after his appointment, Becket underwent a dramatic transformation, becoming a staunch defender of the Church's independence.

Their conflict escalated over the Constitutions of Clarendon in 1164, a set of reforms introduced by Henry II to limit the Church's judicial powers and bring clergy under royal jurisdiction. Becket fiercely opposed these measures, seeing them as a threat to ecclesiastical autonomy. Henry II, equally determined, viewed Becket's resistance as a betrayal. Despite several attempts at reconciliation, both men remained unyielding, prioritizing their positions over preserving their relationship.

This inflexibility led to a tragic outcome. In 1170, Henry II, exasperated by Becket's defiance, uttered a frustrated remark that four knights misinterpreted as a command. They murdered Becket in Canterbury Cathedral, sparking outrage across Europe. Becket's death elevated him to martyrdom, forcing Henry II to publicly repent and abandon the Constitutions of Clarendon. Ironically, the conflict weakened the monarchy's authority and achieved the opposite of Henry II's intentions.

The conflict between Henry II and Thomas Becket vividly illustrates nonadherence to Rule Thirteen: By refusing to acknowledge their irreconcilable differences, both men allowed their rigid stances to escalate into violence and tragedy. If they had respected each other's perspectives and agreed to disagree, they could have avoided the devastating consequences. This example underscores the importance of mutual respect and understanding when agreement is unattainable, preserving relationships and preventing unnecessary harm.

CHAPTER 11

Navigating When to Speak, Pause, and Listen

"The right word may be effective, but no word was ever as effective as a rightly timed pause."

—**Mark Twain,** *Mark Twain's Speeches*

Rule One: Listen Before Speaking

"Wisdom is the reward you get for a lifetime of listening when you'd have preferred to talk."

—commonly attributed to Doug Larson

Effective communication begins with listening—an often undervalued but indispensable skill. Rule One emphasizes prioritizing active listening as the foundation of meaningful interactions. True listening involves more than hearing words;

it requires understanding the emotions, intentions, and nuances behind them.

By actively listening, we open ourselves to diverse perspectives, fostering deeper understanding and reducing misunderstandings—a frequent source of conflict. This practice demonstrates respect for the speaker and builds trust, creating an environment where authentic dialogue can flourish. Thoughtful listening also enables us to respond with insight and empathy, strengthening relationships and navigating disagreements constructively.

A key element of this rule is resisting the urge to redirect conversations toward our own experiences or viewpoints. By focusing fully on the speaker, we validate their perspective and encourage mutual understanding. This mindful approach lays the groundwork for collaborative problem-solving and deeper connections.

Rule One underscores the transformative power of listening. By prioritizing understanding over speaking, we enhance our ability to connect with others, reduce conflict, and foster respect. Listening forms the foundation of meaningful communication, helping us build stronger, more trusting relationships and create environments where dialogue and collaboration thrive.

EXAMPLE 1: MAHATMA GANDHI (1869–1948) AND HIS LISTENING TOURS

Mahatma Gandhi, born in Porbandar, India, is celebrated for his transformative leadership during India's independence movement. Believing that effective leadership begins with listening,

Gandhi embarked on a series of listening tours across rural India to understand the lived realities of ordinary Indians under British colonial rule.

During these tours, Gandhi visited villages and engaged directly with farmers, laborers, and marginalized groups, patiently listening to their grievances. From the economic burdens of exploitative taxes, such as the salt tax, to social injustices and cultural challenges, he absorbed their stories with empathy and a genuine desire to understand. Rather than proposing immediate solutions, Gandhi prioritized understanding their struggles to develop strategies that were meaningful and impactful.

The insights Gandhi gained during these tours laid the foundation for pivotal campaigns in the independence movement. For instance, the oppressive salt tax frequently raised by rural communities inspired the 1930 Salt March, a landmark act of civil disobedience. Similarly, Gandhi's observations of widespread economic exploitation and social inequalities informed the Non-Cooperation Movement of 1920, which mobilized Indians to boycott British goods and institutions. These campaigns resonated deeply because they directly addressed the people's struggles, fostering trust, unity, and a shared vision for independence.

Gandhi's listening tours exemplify Rule One: By prioritizing listening over speaking, Gandhi ensured his strategies reflected the real needs and aspirations of the people. His ability to listen deeply strengthened his connection with the masses and ensured the inclusivity and impact of the independence movement. This example highlights how active listening fosters trust, bridges divides, and drives meaningful change.

EXAMPLE 2: KENNETH LAY (1942–2006) AND JEFFREY SKILLING (1953–) AT ENRON

Kenneth Lay, born in Tyrone, Missouri, and Jeffrey Skilling, born in Pittsburgh, Pennsylvania, led Enron, once celebrated as a pioneer in the energy sector. However, their unwillingness to listen to critical feedback created a culture of denial that ultimately led to Enron's catastrophic collapse in 2001.

In August 2001, Sherron Watkins, a vice president at Enron, sent a detailed memo to Lay warning about unethical accounting practices that inflated the company's profits. She cautioned that these practices could lead to financial disaster. Instead of engaging with her concerns, Lay dismissed them, continuing to promote the illusion of financial stability. Similarly, during a conference call in April 2001, Skilling reacted aggressively when analysts questioned Enron's opaque financial structures, discouraging further scrutiny and silencing critical voices.

This refusal to listen—both internally and externally—reflected a broader cultural issue at Enron. By ignoring valid warnings and avoiding accountability, Lay and Skilling allowed fraudulent practices to persist unchecked. Their dismissive leadership stifled opportunities to address growing problems and created an environment where dissenting voices were unwelcome. The consequences were devastating. Thousands of employees lost their jobs and life savings, and shareholders suffered massive financial losses. The scandal also eroded public trust in corporate governance, prompting major regulatory changes to prevent similar misconduct in the future.

Kenneth Lay and Jeffrey Skilling's leadership vividly illustrates nonadherence to Rule One: Their refusal to engage with critical warnings created an environment where problems were ignored until it was too late. This example highlights the dangers of dismissing feedback and shows how effective leadership requires humility, engagement, and a willingness to listen to prevent avoidable disasters.

Rule Two: Be Last to Speak

"Be the last to speak."
—**Simon Sinek,** 2014 TED Talk

In communication, the impulse to share our thoughts immediately often overshadows opportunities for deeper understanding. Rule Two emphasizes the transformative power of patience. By choosing to speak last, we prioritize listening and focus on fully absorbing others' emotions, viewpoints, and insights. This practice enables us to respond with empathy and thoughtfulness rather than haste.

Speaking last provides the valuable advantage of reflection. By considering the collective wisdom shared during a discussion, we ensure our input is well informed and meaningful. This approach elevates the quality of dialogue, fostering clarity and reducing misunderstandings. Prioritizing listening and reflection also demonstrates respect for others' voices, affirming that their perspectives matter. This acknowledgment builds trust, reduces conflict, and encourages collaboration. When we speak last, we create an environment where diverse viewpoints are valued, and connections are strengthened.

Rule Two highlights the profound impact of being the last to speak. By practicing patience and intentionality, we deepen understanding, improve the quality of our contributions, and foster a culture of respect and collaboration. This approach not only enhances conversations but also strengthens relationships and builds mutual trust.

EXAMPLE 1: GADLA HENRY MPHAKANYISWA (C. 1880–1928) AND THE 1912 TRIBAL COUNCIL MEETING

Gadla Henry Mphakanyiswa, Nelson Mandela's father, was a respected chief of the Thembu tribe in South Africa. Known for his inclusive leadership, Mphakanyiswa practiced a deliberate approach during tribal council meetings: He always chose to speak last. This method reflected his commitment to respect, patience, and thoughtful decision-making.

A notable example occurred in 1912 during a tribal council meeting to resolve a land dispute over grazing rights in the Mbashe Valley. The meeting, held under a sacred fig tree, brought together elders and villagers with deeply conflicting views. As tensions escalated, Mphakanyiswa remained silent, listening intently as each person presented their case. His silence was active and intentional, creating a space where everyone felt heard.

After everyone had spoken, Mphakanyiswa shared his thoughts. By synthesizing the perspectives presented, he crafted a resolution that acknowledged the concerns of both sides, ensuring fairness and harmony. His approach not only resolved the dispute but also reinforced trust within the community, earning him admiration for his wisdom and patience.

Gadla Henry Mphakanyiswa's leadership exemplifies Rule Two: By listening first and speaking last, he absorbed the full range of perspectives, enabling him to make inclusive and well-informed decisions. His practice diffused tensions, strengthened communal bonds, and left a lasting legacy of respect and thoughtful leadership—a principle that deeply influenced his son, Nelson Mandela. This example highlights how patience and reflection can transform decision-making, foster trust, and build enduring connections.

EXAMPLE 2: LAWRENCE MULLOY (1934–) AND THE 1986 CHALLENGER DISASTER

Lawrence Mulloy, born in Memphis, Tennessee, served as NASA's manager for the Solid Rocket Booster Project during the 1986 Challenger disaster. Despite his technical expertise, Mulloy's failure to prioritize listening and reflection during a critical prelaunch meeting contributed directly to one of NASA's most tragic failures.

On January 27, 1986, engineers from Morton Thiokol, the company responsible for the shuttle's solid rocket boosters, raised urgent concerns about the O-rings, critical seals that prevent fuel leaks. Engineers Roger Boisjoly and Arnie Thompson warned that the unusually cold weather forecasted for the Kennedy Space Center could cause the O-rings to fail, potentially leading to catastrophic consequences. Morton Thiokol initially recommended delaying the launch, but Mulloy dismissed their warnings, remarking, "When do you want me to launch, next April?" His dismissive tone pressured the engineers into reversing their recommendation and approving the launch.

The consequences were devastating. The O-rings failed as predicted, causing the Challenger to disintegrate seventy-three seconds after liftoff, killing all seven crew members. This tragedy shocked the world, devastated families, and led to a significant loss of public trust in NASA. The Rogers Commission investigation criticized Mulloy's role in dismissing technical concerns and highlighted systemic flaws in NASA's decision-making process.

Lawrence Mulloy's actions vividly illustrate nonadherence to Rule Two. By failing to fully hear and reflect on the engineers' warnings, Mulloy prioritized external pressures over thoughtful decision-making. Had he created an environment where critical voices were genuinely heard and reflected upon, the launch could have been delayed, and lives could have been saved. This example underscores the critical importance of thoughtful listening and reflection, particularly in high-stakes situations where decisions carry life-or-death consequences.

Rule Three: If You Have Nothing Good to Say, Say Nothing

"Even a fool, when he keeps silent, is considered wise; when he closes his lips, he is considered prudent."
—The Bible, Proverbs 17:28 (KJV)

In human interactions, where words carry immense influence, choosing silence over negativity is an act of wisdom and mindfulness. Rule Three advocates for silence when our words are unlikely to be constructive or positive. Positive speech uplifts, fosters respect, and builds trust, while negative words can strain relationships and create discord.

Silence is a powerful tool for preserving harmony and understanding. By refraining from speaking when words might escalate conflict or cause harm, we demonstrate emotional intelligence and foster an environment of trust. In sensitive situations, choosing silence allows us to avoid misunderstandings and maintain the dignity of our relationships.

This rule does not advocate suppressing thoughts or avoiding difficult conversations. Instead, it encourages a reflective pause to reassess and reshape our words, ensuring they are thoughtful and constructive. Even in conflict, this approach enables us to express our views effectively while maintaining respect and empathy.

Rule Three highlights the transformative power of mindful

communication. By choosing words carefully or opting for silence, we prioritize the quality of our interactions, nurturing empathy, understanding, and respect. This practice fosters a more considerate and harmonious environment, strengthening relationships and encouraging meaningful dialogue.

EXAMPLE 1: MICHELLE OBAMA (1964–) AND THE 2016 DEMOCRATIC NATIONAL CONVENTION

Michelle Obama, born in Chicago, Illinois, served as the First Lady of the United States from 2009 to 2017. During her tenure, and especially during the divisive 2016 presidential election, she endured relentless personal attacks. These ranged from racially insensitive remarks to criticisms of her advocacy initiatives. One particularly egregious incident involved being referred to as an "ape in heels," a comment laden with racism and sexism. Despite these provocations, Michelle Obama chose a response that elevated the national conversation.

At the July 2016 Democratic National Convention, Obama addressed the nation with dignity and composure. Rather than retaliating against the insults, she delivered a speech focused on unity and integrity. Her now-iconic phrase, "When they go low, we go high," became a rallying cry for respect and thoughtful communication. By refusing to engage in negativity, she used her platform to inspire positive discourse and advocate for the values of empathy and integrity.

Michelle Obama's response exemplifies Rule Three: By refraining from negativity and framing her words to inspire rather than retaliate, she demonstrated how dignity and thoughtful communication can transform conflict into an opportunity for unity and empowerment. Her message, "When they go low, we go high," remains a timeless reminder of the strength found in restraint and the transformative power of constructive dialogue, even in the face of hostility.

EXAMPLE 2: THE DREYFUS AFFAIR (1894–1906)

The Dreyfus Affair remains one of history's starkest reminders of the dangers of irresponsible and harmful speech. Alfred Dreyfus, a Jewish captain in the French Army, was falsely accused of espionage for Germany—a charge rooted in anti-Semitic prejudice rather than credible evidence. Key figures such as General Auguste Mercier, Colonel Hubert-Joseph Henry, and journalist Édouard Drumont played pivotal roles in perpetuating the false narrative that condemned Dreyfus.

Mercier, the minister of war, prioritized protecting the army's reputation over uncovering the truth. He spread baseless accusations against Dreyfus to deflect scrutiny from the military's internal failings. Henry, an intelligence officer, fabricated evidence to strengthen the case against Dreyfus, knowing it would fuel public outrage. Drumont, a journalist and vocal anti-Semite, amplified these falsehoods through inflammatory articles in La Libre Parole, shaping public opinion against Dreyfus and intensifying societal divisions.

These individuals' deliberate spread of misinformation prolonged Dreyfus's suffering and deepened societal divisions in France. Their actions, rooted in prejudice and self-interest, overshadowed the pursuit of justice and allowed injustice to prevail. Although Dreyfus was ultimately exonerated in 1906, the harm caused by their words left lasting scars on French society, fueling anti-Semitism and distrust in institutions.

The Dreyfus Affair vividly illustrates nonadherence to

Rule Three: By spreading harmful and baseless accusations, Mercier, Henry, and Drumont allowed prejudice and misinformation to override truth and justice. Their actions highlight the immense power of words to harm and the critical importance of speaking responsibly. This example serves as a cautionary tale, reminding us that when words lack integrity or purpose, silence can often be the most ethical and impactful choice.

Rule Four: Speak Only When Necessary

"Speak only if it improves upon the silence."
—commonly attributed to Mahatma Gandhi

Effective communication requires discernment in choosing when to speak. Rule Four emphasizes intentional and meaningful contributions, advocating for speech that adds value, elevates the conversation, or facilitates a constructive outcome. Unlike Rule Three, which focuses on avoiding harm, this rule encourages speaking when words can enhance understanding or drive a solution.

Speaking only when necessary begins with reflection. Assessing the importance and implications of our words ensures they are thoughtful and impactful. In group settings such as meetings or debates, this practice fosters efficiency, keeps discussions focused, and promotes collaboration and trust. Thoughtful contributions demonstrate respect for others' time and perspectives, enhancing the quality of dialogue.

This rule also underscores the importance of listening over speaking. By embracing silence, we absorb the nuances of a conversation, gain deeper understanding, and respond with empathy and insight. Choosing when to speak ensures our words carry weight, avoiding unnecessary noise and fostering meaningful exchanges.

Rule Four highlights the transformative power of deliberate communication. By speaking only when our contributions matter, we elevate the quality of interactions, strengthen relationships, and promote mutual respect. This practice reflects a profound appreciation for the value of words, creating an environment where every contribution makes a difference.

EXAMPLE 1: CHARLIE CHAPLIN (1889–1977) IN THE GREAT DICTATOR (1940)

Charlie Chaplin, born in London, England, was a legendary filmmaker and actor celebrated for his iconic silent film persona, the Tramp. Known for his mastery of nonverbal story telling, Chaplin rarely used speech in his films, relying instead on physical comedy and expressive performances. However, in 1940, as fascism rose across Europe and the world faced the turmoil of World War II, Chaplin made a deliberate choice to break his cinematic silence with a powerful speech in *The Great Dictator*, his satire of Adolf Hitler and authoritarianism.

In this climactic scene, Chaplin's character, a persecuted Jewish barber mistaken for a dictator, delivers an impassioned plea for humanity, democracy, and peace. At a time of global fear and uncertainty, Chaplin recognized that silence was no longer an option. His words, carefully chosen and strategically placed, transformed the film from satire to a universal message of hope and resistance.

Charlie Chaplin's decision to speak in *The Great Dictator* exemplifies Rule Four. Throughout his career, Chaplin communicated powerfully through silence, but in this pivotal moment, he chose to speak because it was both necessary and meaningful. By reserving his voice for such a critical occasion, Chaplin ensured that his words carried maximum impact, demonstrating how deliberate and purposeful speech can inspire and unite during times of crisis.

EXAMPLE 2: ELON MUSK'S 2018 "FUNDING SECURED" TWEET

Elon Musk, born in Pretoria, South Africa, is renowned for his innovation and influence as the CEO of Tesla. However, in August 2018, a single impulsive tweet caused turmoil in financial markets and highlighted the dangers of undisciplined communication. Musk tweeted: "Am considering taking Tesla private at $420. Funding secured."

This statement implied a significant financial maneuver but lacked factual support. Tesla's stock price experienced immediate and volatile swings, prompting scrutiny from investors and regulators. The Securities and Exchange Commission (SEC) investigated, concluding that Musk's tweet was misleading and unverified.

The consequences were severe. The SEC filed a securities fraud lawsuit, resulting in a settlement requiring Musk and Tesla to each pay $20 million in fines. Musk also agreed to step down as Tesla's chairman for three years, though he retained his role as CEO. Beyond the legal and financial penalties, the incident damaged Tesla's reputation and raised concerns about Musk's judgment, eroding trust among investors and stakeholders.

Musk's impulsive communication vividly illustrates nonadherence to Rule Four: By speaking without verifying his claims,

Musk violated the principle of disciplined and intentional communication. His failure to deliberate before sharing such a critical statement led to significant legal, financial, and reputational harm. This example underscores the importance of speaking thoughtfully and only when contributions are constructive, especially for leaders whose words carry immense influence.

Rule Five: Speak Briefly and to the Point

"The best speech is that which is short and to the point."
—Arabic proverb

Effective communication relies on brevity and clarity. Rule Five emphasizes the importance of speaking succinctly, focusing on delivering messages that are both concise and impactful. By assessing the necessity of our words and ensuring they add value, we demonstrate respect for the listener's time and attention, making our points clearer and more memorable.

Brevity fosters meaningful discussions by preventing misinterpretation and avoiding information overload. Speaking briefly does not mean being vague or withholding critical details—it requires thoughtful preparation to ensure that every word serves a purpose. A concise message, when delivered with precision, enhances understanding and engagement, leaving a lasting impression.

Rule Five highlights the transformative power of concise speech. By speaking briefly and to the point, we elevate the quality of our interactions and foster stronger personal and professional relationships. Brevity is not merely a style—it's a demonstration of respect for the listener and the value of effective communication.

EXAMPLE 1: AL-HAJJAJ IBN YUSUF (661–714)

Al-Hajjaj ibn Yusuf, born in Ta'if, Arabia, was a prominent Umayyad governor renowned for his eloquence and ability to restore order in turbulent regions. Known for his brevity and precision, his communication style left a lasting impact on audiences, ensuring his words were understood and remembered.

One of Al-Hajjaj's most famous speeches occurred upon his appointment as governor of Iraq, addressing the people of Kufa—a city infamous for rebellion and unrest. Ascending the pulpit, he began with the chilling yet powerful words: "I see heads that are ripe and ready to be cut off, and I am the one to do it."

This concise statement instantly established his authority and set the tone for his governance. With just a few words, Al-Hajjaj communicated his intent to restore order, leaving no room for ambiguity or resistance. His speech, though brief, quelled dissent and stabilized a volatile region. By avoiding lengthy explanations or justifications, he ensured his message was clear, impactful, and impossible to ignore.

Al-Hajjaj's speech exemplifies Rule Five: His ability to convey unambiguous intent with a few well-chosen words demonstrates the power of concise communication in leadership. By speaking strategically and purposefully, Al-Hajjaj achieved clarity, inspired action, and reinforced his authority, highlighting the transformative potential of brevity.

EXAMPLE 2: ROBERT WALPOLE (1676–1745) AND THE HOUSE OF COMMONS 1731 SPEECH

Robert Walpole, born in Houghton, Norfolk, is widely regarded as Britain's first de facto prime minister, leading during a politically turbulent era. However, one of his most consequential failures occurred during a critical parliamentary debate on January 11, 1731, when his inability to communicate concisely undermined his leadership and credibility.

At the time, Britain faced growing tensions with Spain over trade disputes in the Americas. Spanish privateers were accused of attacking British merchant ships, fueling public outrage and demands for military action. Walpole, seeking to avoid war, argued for diplomacy but failed to convey his stance effectively.

In addressing the House of Commons, Walpole delivered a speech that lasted over three hours, filled with exhaustive details, tangential arguments, and a lack of focus. While intending to explain the complexity of the issue, his verbose approach frustrated members of Parliament. Many left the chamber before he concluded, while others criticized his inability to present a compelling and concise argument.

The consequences were significant. Walpole's failure to communicate effectively eroded his credibility and emboldened his opponents. Over time, public dissatisfaction with his leadership grew, contributing to rising tensions that eventually culminated in the War of Jenkins' Ear (1739–1748). Although Walpole sought to avoid conflict, the growing pressure forced his government to declare war, resulting in a costly and inconclusive campaign that drained Britain's resources and diminished its political standing.

Robert Walpole's failure vividly illustrates nonadherence to Rule Five: By overwhelming his audience with excessive detail and losing focus, he diluted his message and alienated his listeners. This episode underscores the dangers of verbose communication, highlighting how concise and purposeful speech is essential for effective leadership and decision-making in high-stakes situations.

Rule Six: Adapt Your Communication to the Audience and Context

"Speak to people only according to their level of knowledge."

—Ali ibn Abi Talib, as recorded in *Sahih al-Bukhari* (*Book of Knowledge*)

Effective communication is not just about what we say but how we say it. Rule Six emphasizes the importance of adapting our speaking style to suit the audience and context. Thoughtful adjustments to tone, pacing, clarity, and delivery ensure that our words are not only heard but also understood, valued, and remembered.

Understanding the audience is the foundation of intentional communication. Tailoring language and tone to the listener's knowledge, expectations, and emotional state ensures accessibility and engagement. For example, simple explanations resonate with beginners, while detailed responses inspire confidence among experts. Pacing and tone also play critical roles. Slower speech and deliberate pauses are effective in complex or tense situations, while an energetic tone can motivate and captivate audiences. Clarity and simplicity further enhance communication by ensuring ideas are presented in straightforward, accessible ways that avoid unnecessary complexity.

Cultural and contextual awareness adds another dimension. A formal tone may be appropriate for professional settings, while casual conversations often call for a relaxed approach. Being mindful of cultural norms and situational dynamics fosters respect and connection, helping us avoid misunderstandings and build trust.

Rule Six highlights the art of intentional speaking. By adapting our words and delivery to fit the audience and context, we ensure our messages resonate, inspire, and achieve their purpose. This thoughtful approach to communication fosters connection, trust, and lasting impact.

EXAMPLE 1: INDRA NOOYI (1955–) AND TAILORING COMMUNICATION FOR IMPACT

Indra Nooyi, born in Madras (now Chennai), India, served as the CEO of PepsiCo from 2006 to 2018, earning acclaim for her ability to adapt her communication style to diverse audiences. Two key incidents from her tenure exemplify this adaptability.

In 2011, during a PepsiCo town hall meeting with US factory workers, Nooyi addressed concerns about automation and its potential impact on jobs. Recognizing the workers' anxieties, she avoided technical jargon or corporate terminology. Instead, she spoke with empathy and simplicity, acknowledging their fears and sharing her vision for balancing innovation with job security. Her approachable tone fostered trust and reassured the workforce during a period of uncertainty.

Conversely, at a 2014 global business summit in India, Nooyi addressed a room of high-level executives and government leaders. She adopted a strategic and data-driven approach, presenting detailed financial forecasts and market insights to highlight PepsiCo's growth potential in emerging markets. Her authoritative delivery and cultural awareness resonated with the audience, inspiring confidence in the company's plans and reinforcing its leadership in the region.

Indra Nooyi's ability to adapt her communication style exemplifies Rule Six: Her empathetic tone at the town hall meeting and her authoritative delivery at the business summit showcase how thoughtful adjustments to tone, content, and delivery can foster trust, clarity, and engagement. These examples highlight the transformative power of speaking with intentionality, ensuring messages resonate with their intended audience and context.

EXAMPLE 2: RON JOHNSON (1959–) AND JCPENNEY'S MISALIGNED STRATEGY

Ron Johnson, born in Edina, Minnesota, gained recognition for revolutionizing retail as the visionary behind Apple Stores. His success at Apple earned him the role of CEO at JCPenney in 2011, where he was tasked with revitalizing the struggling department store. However, Johnson's failure to adapt his communication and strategy to JCPenney's loyal customer base led to disastrous results.

When Johnson took over, he implemented sweeping changes, including eliminating JCPenney's popular coupon system and replacing it with a "fair and square" pricing model. He also remodeled stores into boutique-style spaces targeting a more upscale audience, drawing inspiration from Apple's minimalist aesthetic. These changes alienated JCPenney's core customers—families and middle-income shoppers who valued the store's affordability and traditional sales events.

Johnson's public communication compounded the problem. In interviews and meetings, he used aspirational language reminiscent of his Apple days, describing the changes as "reinventing retail" and focusing on innovation rather than addressing customers' emotional connection to JCPenney's traditional shopping experience. His approach left loyal shoppers feeling ignored and undervalued.

Moreover, Johnson rolled out these changes nationwide without piloting them or gathering feedback from employees or customers. The disconnect became evident as shoppers abandoned the brand in droves, confused by the new pricing model and disconnected from the store's identity. Sales plummeted by over 25 percent in Johnson's first year, leading to significant financial losses. By 2013, Johnson was ousted as CEO, leaving the company to scramble to regain its lost customers and restore its traditional model.

Ron Johnson's leadership at JCPenney vividly illustrates nonadherence to Rule Six. By failing to align his communication and strategy with JCPenney's audience, Johnson alienated the store's core customers, eroded trust, and caused financial turmoil. His experience underscores the critical importance of tailoring messaging and decisions to the audience's unique preferences and needs to achieve lasting success.

Conclusion

"Stop acting so small. You are the universe in ecstatic motion."
—commonly attributed to Rumi

As we reach the final page of *The Life Compass*, we close a meaningful chapter in our shared journey. This book is not a single narrative but a collection of insights, each woven from the collective wisdom of thinkers, teachers, and life itself. Its principles are not fixed—they are living, breathing guides meant to evolve with us as we navigate the complexities of our lives.

My hope is that we treat this book not as a one-time read but as a trusted companion—a living guide to revisit and reflect upon. Like a well-tended garden, its rules flourish with care and engagement, offering us clarity and strength in moments of need. Whether guiding us through conflicts, fostering connections, or inspiring personal growth, these principles are meant to meet us where we are and resonate when we need them most.

As we move forward, let these rules transcend their written form. May they inform our decisions, shape our interactions, and enrich our relationships. Together, we can allow them to challenge and inspire us to live with purpose, compassion, and resilience.

Here's to a journey enriched with peace, growth, and meaningful connections. May *The Life Compass* continue to guide us as we chart our unique paths toward clarity, fulfillment, and the life we aspire to create.

—Samer Abdo

Questionnaire

This questionnaire can be carried out daily, weekly, or monthly to assess how well you are adhering to the rules described in this book. The answers you provide here will clearly reveal your progress, identifying areas for growth and pinpointing any aspects that still require your attention.

Subject 1: Navigating Inner Peace (6 questions)

1. **Rule One: Realize True Happiness Within.** Today, did I recognize that my lasting happiness comes from within and is independent of external sources like possessions, achievements, or relationships?

Yes	☐	No	☐
To some extent	☐	Not relevant	☐

2. **Rule Two: Live in the Present Moment.** Today, was I fully engaged and mindful in the present moment, without being preoccupied with the past or future?

Yes	☐	No	☐
To some extent	☐	Not relevant	☐

3. **Rule Three: Control Your Thoughts to Control Your Life.** Today, did I focus on the positive aspects of my life and avoid dwelling on negative thoughts?

Yes	☐	No	☐
To some extent	☐	Not relevant	☐

4. **Rule Four: Avoid the "If-Then" Model for Happiness.** Today, did I focus on finding contentment in the present rather than conditional happiness based on external achievements or possessions?

   Yes ☐ No ☐
   To some extent ☐ Not relevant ☐

5. **Rule Five: Avoid Engaging in Negative Self-Talk.** Today, did I refrain from negative self-talk, nurturing self-compassion and a positive self-image while also learning from my mistakes and taking responsibility for them?

   Yes ☐ No ☐
   To some extent ☐ Not relevant ☐

6. **Rule Six: Practice Nonattachment.** Today, did I maintain my inner peace, enjoying life's experiences and pursuing my goals without attachment or fear of loss?

   Yes ☐ No ☐
   To some extent ☐ Not relevant ☐

Subject 1 out of 11 subjects: 6 out of 111 questions completed

Subject 2: Navigating Worry (8 questions)

1. **Rule One: Realize That Worries Are Created by Your Imagination, Not by Reality.** Today, did I refrain from letting worries control my thoughts and understand that they are created by my imagination, not by reality?

   Yes ☐ No ☐
   To some extent ☐ Not relevant ☐

2. **Rule Two: Recognize That Most of Your Worries Never Materialize.** Today, did I refrain from letting worries control my thoughts, understand that most worries never materialize, and avoid unnecessary anxiety over hypothetical outcomes?

   Yes ☐ No ☐
   To some extent ☐ Not relevant ☐

3. **Rule Three: Worries Are Transient—Don't Jump to Conclusions or Act on Them.** Today, did I refrain from letting worries control my thoughts due to their transient nature and avoid jumping to conclusions or acting impulsively?

Yes	☐	No	☐
To some extent	☐	Not relevant	☐

4. **Rule Four: Practice "Worry Time" Allocation.** Today, did I avoid letting worries consume and disrupt my entire day and set aside specific times to address them in a structured manner?

Yes	☐	No	☐
To some extent	☐	Not relevant	☐

5. **Rule Five: Be Aware That Worries Are Counterproductive and Harmful.** Today, did I refrain from letting worries control my thoughts due to their harmful nature and replace them with positive thoughts, constructive problem-solving, and mindfulness?

Yes	☐	No	☐
To some extent	☐	Not relevant	☐

6. **Rule Six: Don't Worry About Things You Didn't Arrive with and Can't Depart With.** Today, did I refrain from worrying over transient external things like material wealth and social standing, which I cannot take with me when I leave this world, and focus instead on what truly matters: relationships, personal growth, and my positive impact on society?

Yes	☐	No	☐
To some extent	☐	Not relevant	☐

7. **Rule Seven: Don't Worry Too Much About the Future, As It May Not Include You.** Today, did I refrain from excessive worry about the future, acknowledge its unpredictability and the uncertainty of my presence in it, and focus instead on enjoying and appreciating the present without letting future uncertainties diminish my current happiness?

Yes	☐	No	☐
To some extent	☐	Not relevant	☐

8. **Rule Eight: Consider Worries from Your Deathbed Perspective.** Today, did I challenge my worries and assess their significance from the perspective of being on my deathbed, shifting my focus to what truly matters, aligning with my deepest values and life goals?

Yes	☐	No	☐
To some extent	☐	Not relevant	☐

Subject 2 out of 11 subjects: 14 out of 111 questions completed

Subject 3: Navigating Authenticity (9 questions)

1. **Rule One: Be Aware of the Illusion of Sudden Success.** Today, did I avoid the illusion of rapid success and understand that it may lead to overconfidence and a false belief in the easiness of success, instead recognizing that real success requires diligent work, persistence, strategic planning, and continuous learning?

Yes	☐	No	☐
To some extent	☐	Not relevant	☐

2. **Rule Two: Always Stay Humble in Success and Patient in Adversity.** Today, did I maintain humility in success, avoiding arrogance and embracing patience in adversity to avoid negativity?

Yes	☐	No	☐
To some extent	☐	Not relevant	☐

3. **Rule Three: Avoid the Lust for Power.** Today, did I responsibly manage my power, staying vigilant against its seductive qualities and prioritizing its use for the benefit of other people with humility and integrity?

Yes	☐	No	☐
To some extent	☐	Not relevant	☐

4. **Rule Four: Trust Your Inner Voice.** Today, did I prioritize my inner wisdom over external opinions and ensure my decisions align with my deepest values and aspirations?

   Yes ☐ No ☐
   To some extent ☐ Not relevant ☐

5. **Rule Five: Align Your Inner Self with Your External Image.** Today, did I ensure that my external persona aligns authentically with my true inner self?

   Yes ☐ No ☐
   To some extent ☐ Not relevant ☐

6. **Rule Six: Never Crave Someone Else's Life.** Today, did I avoid the trap of comparing my behind-the-scenes with other people's highlight reels and focus instead on drawing inspiration from other people's specific qualities while embracing my own unique life journey and my own path?

   Yes ☐ No ☐
   To some extent ☐ Not relevant ☐

7. **Rule Seven: Avoid Being Limited by Your Identity.** Today, did I expand my self-awareness, understand my biases, and embrace different points of view to move beyond any restrictive identities toward empathy and inclusivity?

   Yes ☐ No ☐
   To some extent ☐ Not relevant ☐

8. **Rule Eight: How People Treat You Is Their Choice; How You React Is Yours.** Today, did I consciously choose my reactions to other people's actions, guided by kindness and understanding, and avoid perpetuating negativity?

   Yes ☐ No ☐
   To some extent ☐ Not relevant ☐

9. **Rule Nine: Align Your Knowledge with Your Actions.** Today, did I actively apply the knowledge I've acquired to make informed decisions and contribute meaningfully to my personal growth?

Yes	☐	No	☐
To some extent	☐	Not relevant	☐

Subject 3 out of 11 subjects: 23 out of 111 questions completed

Subject 4: Navigating Personal Growth (15 questions)

1. **Rule One: Be Grateful for What You Have While Aspiring for More.** Today, did I appreciate my current circumstances and practice gratitude while also pursuing my goals with a sense of contentment and joy?

Yes	☐	No	☐
To some extent	☐	Not relevant	☐

2. **Rule Two: Understand the Power of Your Choices.** Today, did I make conscious decisions and reactions that reflect my values and enhance my well-being, even in the face of unpredictable circumstances?

Yes	☐	No	☐
To some extent	☐	Not relevant	☐

3. **Rule Three: Take Personal Responsibility for Life's Direction.** Today, did I accept responsibility for the direction my life is taking and actively steer away from a victim mentality where I blame other people and external circumstances?

Yes	☐	No	☐
To some extent	☐	Not relevant	☐

4. **Rule Four: Master Your Emotions.** Today, did I recognize, understand, and manage my emotions constructively to maintain my composure and make thoughtful choices?

Yes	☐	No	☐
To some extent	☐	Not relevant	☐

5. **Rule Five: Be Aware of the Roots of Your Aggression and Arrogance.** Today, did I refrain from acting arrogantly or aggressively and instead understand any emotional challenges behind such behaviors by cultivating qualities of humility, kindness, mindfulness, and empathy?

Yes	☐	No	☐
To some extent	☐	Not relevant	☐

6. **Rule Six: Conquer Your Inner Enemy.** Today, did I actively identify and address any negative thoughts, self-doubt, fears, or limiting beliefs within myself, replacing them with positive affirmations, confronting fears through gradual exposure, and actively cultivating resilience to foster personal growth and inner peace?

Yes	☐	No	☐
To some extent	☐	Not relevant	☐

7. **Rule Seven: Be Aware That Your Suffering and Pain Create Your Values and Experiences.** Today, did I recognize the lessons and growth opportunities presented by my pain and suffering and actively seek to transform them into sources of wisdom, resilience, and compassion instead of dwelling on negativity or victimhood?

Yes	☐	No	☐
To some extent	☐	Not relevant	☐

8. **Rule Eight: Mind Your Mind as a Garden.** Today, did I consciously select positive influences and information intake, nurturing positive thoughts and experiences to cultivate a healthy, productive mental landscape?

Yes	☐	No	☐
To some extent	☐	Not relevant	☐

9. **Rule Nine: You Can't Give What You Don't Have.** Today, did I ensure that my own self-care and personal development are well integrated within myself before attempting to positively influence others with the same?

Yes	☐	No	☐
To some extent	☐	Not relevant	☐

10. **Rule Ten: Adopt a Playful Attitude in Life.** Today, did I approach life with joy, curiosity, and a lighthearted demeanor, viewing challenges through a lens of curiosity in my daily routines?

Yes	☐	No	☐
To some extent	☐	Not relevant	☐

11. **Rule Eleven: Don't Undermine the Impact of Small Actions.** Today, did I recognize that the significance of even my smallest deeds may effect change in the world and consciously make thoughtful and compassionate contributions?

Yes	☐	No	☐
To some extent	☐	Not relevant	☐

12. **Rule Twelve: Avoid the Trap of Numbers.** Today, did I recognize that not everything that is counted counts, and not everything that counts can be counted, and prioritize qualitative aspects of life such as personal growth, relationships, and intrinsic joy over numerical achievements?

Yes	☐	No	☐
To some extent	☐	Not relevant	☐

13. **Rule Thirteen: Stop Complaining.** Today, did I refrain from unproductive complaining or blaming and focus on constructive action for matters within my control, gracefully accepting that which is not?

Yes	☐	No	☐
To some extent	☐	Not relevant	☐

14. **Rule Fourteen: Live Every Day as if It's Your First.** Today, did I embrace each new day as a unique opportunity, free from the burdens of past regrets and anxieties about the future?

Yes	☐	No	☐
To some extent	☐	Not relevant	☐

15. **Rule Fifteen: Be Formless and Adaptable.** Today, did I embrace change, being open-minded, reflective, mentally fluid, and seeking balance and harmony in the face of life's constant changes?

Yes	☐	No	☐
To some extent	☐	Not relevant	☐

Subject 4 out of 11 subjects: 38 out of 111 questions completed

Subject 5: Navigating Dreams and Aspirations (12 questions)

1. **Rule One: Prime Your Mind and Document Your Dreams.** Today, did I cultivate an optimistic mindset through mental priming and actively documenting my dreams to clarify and manifest my aspirations?

Yes	☐	No	☐
To some extent	☐	Not relevant	☐

2. **Rule Two: Realize the Only Limit You Have in Your Life Is You.** Today, did I recognize that my potential is unlimited, confront and challenge my self-imposed barriers to fostering a growth mindset, and actively embrace setbacks as opportunities for growth?

Yes	☐	No	☐
To some extent	☐	Not relevant	☐

3. **Rule Three: Understand That There Is No Such Thing as Failure.** Today, did I embrace setbacks as opportunities for growth and learning and view challenges as integral steps in my journey toward success?

Yes	☐	No	☐
To some extent	☐	Not relevant	☐

4. **Rule Four: Transcend Life's Unfairness to Achieve Your Dreams.** Today, did I actively embody commitment, resilience, consistency, and extraordinary effort in the pursuit of my goals, despite challenges and setbacks?

Yes	☐	No	☐
To some extent	☐	Not relevant	☐

5. **Rule Five: Don't Wait for the Perfect Moment to Leave Your Comfort Zone.** Today, did I take proactive steps toward my dreams, even in the face of discomfort or uncertainty, and step out of my comfort zone by overcoming excuse-making in pursuit of my goals?

Yes	☐	No	☐
To some extent	☐	Not relevant	☐

6. **Rule Six: Cherish Your Dreams, However Unlikely They May Be.** Today, did I embrace the uncertainties in my journey toward my dreams, persistently pursuing them with determination, even in the face of challenges?

Yes	☐	No	☐
To some extent	☐	Not relevant	☐

7. **Rule Seven: Find Your Gift.** Today, did I actively engage in self-discovery to identify and nurture my unique talents, thereby aligning my endeavors with my deepest passions and abilities?

Yes	☐	No	☐
To some extent	☐	Not relevant	☐

8. **Rule Eight: Guard Your Dreams by Silence and Selective Sharing.** Today, did I carefully select those with whom I shared my aspirations, ensuring a supportive and constructive environment for their growth and development?

Yes	☐	No	☐
To some extent	☐	Not relevant	☐

9. **Rule Nine: Remember That Your Dreams and Success Are Both Unique.** Today, did I recognize and value the individuality of my dreams and definition of success and refrain from comparing my journey to others'?

Yes	☐	No	☐
To some extent	☐	Not relevant	☐

10. **Rule Ten: Be Patient While Pursuing Your Dreams.** Today, did I understand that success takes time, embrace persistence, and remain patient in the pursuit of my dreams?

Yes	☐	No	☐
To some extent	☐	Not relevant	☐

11. **Rule Eleven: Be Wary of "Turn Back" Moments.** Today, did I persist through challenges and maintain commitment to my goals, despite facing obstacles that tempted me to give up?

Yes	☐	No	☐
To some extent	☐	Not relevant	☐

12. **Rule Twelve: Pursue Your Dreams Passionately While Practicing Nonattachment to Their Outcome.** Today, did I passionately pursue my goals while maintaining a sense of detachment from their specific outcomes?

Yes	☐	No	☐
To some extent	☐	Not relevant	☐

Subject 5 out of 11 subjects: 50 out of 111 questions completed

Subject 6: Navigating Life's Challenges (7 questions)

1. **Rule One: Navigate Life's Challenges with Ten-Year and Deathbed Perspectives.** Today, did I evaluate the significance of my challenges in life through long-term lenses, determining their impact over a decade, at the age of ninety-nine, and on my deathbed?

   Yes ☐ No ☐
   To some extent ☐ Not relevant ☐

2. **Rule Two: Realize That Life's Challenges Often Arise from Your Desires and Dissatisfaction.** Today, did I recognize that my challenges stem from my desires for what I lack and dissatisfaction with my present circumstances; and did I overcome this by accepting my current circumstances, cultivating gratitude, and taking proactive steps toward positive change?

   Yes ☐ No ☐
   To some extent ☐ Not relevant ☐

3. **Rule Three: Remember That Life's Challenges Are Angels in Disguise.** Today, did I recognize my current challenges as opportunities for growth and learning and actively engage with them in a constructive manner to uncover hidden strengths and wisdom?

   Yes ☐ No ☐
   To some extent ☐ Not relevant ☐

4. **Rule Four: Assess Your Emotions Before Reacting to Life's Challenges.** Today, did I recognize that uncontrolled emotions can cloud my judgment and consciously pause to reflect on my emotional state before reacting to ensure that my responses are grounded in reality rather than solely on my emotional reactions?

   Yes ☐ No ☐
   To some extent ☐ Not relevant ☐

5. **Rule Five: Be Aware That Life's Challenges Are Temporary.** Today, did I recognize that the difficulties I face are not permanent fixtures in my life and approach them with optimism and resilience, knowing that they will eventually pass?

Yes	☐	No	☐
To some extent	☐	Not relevant	☐

6. **Rule Six: Choose Between Action and Acceptance in Response to Life's Challenges.** Today, did I accurately discern when to actively address challenges within my control through decisive action and when to practice mindful acceptance, letting go and moving forward when faced with challenges beyond my control?

Yes	☐	No	☐
To some extent	☐	Not relevant	☐

7. **Rule Seven: Apply the ABCD Method When Challenges Arise.** Today, did I diligently apply the ABCD (Action, Belief, Consequence, Disputation) method to systematically analyze my reactions to challenges, actively challenge irrational beliefs, and foster more rational and constructive responses?

Yes	☐	No	☐
To some extent	☐	Not relevant	☐

Subject 6 out of 11 subjects: 57 out of 111 questions completed

Subject 7: Navigating Forgiveness (8 questions)

1. **Rule One: Forgive and Let Go of Resentment.** Today, did I recognize the toxicity of holding on to grudges and consciously choose to release feelings of bitterness and resentment, understanding that forgiveness is a pathway to personal liberation and emotional well-being?

Yes	☐	No	☐
To some extent	☐	Not relevant	☐

2. **Rule Two: Forgive, Revenge Will Not Heal You.** Today, did I actively choose forgiveness over revenge; recognize that forgiveness is a path to inner peace, personal healing, and emotional strength; and prioritize my mental and emotional well-being over the desire for retribution?

   Yes ☐ No ☐
   To some extent ☐ Not relevant ☐

3. **Rule Three: When You Make a Mistake, Forgive Yourself, Then Seek Forgiveness.** Today, did I extend compassion and understanding to forgive myself for any mistakes, then actively seek forgiveness from those affected by my actions, demonstrating genuine remorse and a commitment to change?

   Yes ☐ No ☐
   To some extent ☐ Not relevant ☐

4. **Rule Four: Stop the Cycle of Blame and Shame with Forgiveness.** Today, did I actively embrace forgiveness to break free from feelings of blame or shame, whether directed toward myself or other people, and foster a mindset of learning and healing instead?

   Yes ☐ No ☐
   To some extent ☐ Not relevant ☐

5. **Rule Five: Imagine the Unreceived Apology and Forgive.** Today, did I actively engage in the practice of visualizing an apology from those who've wronged me as a means to facilitate my own emotional healing and release, even in the absence of an actual apology or closure?

   Yes ☐ No ☐
   To some extent ☐ Not relevant ☐

6. **Rule Six: Visualize Those Who Wronged You as Children, Then on Their Deathbed.** Today, did I actively engage in the visualization process, including imagining the innocence and vulnerability of those who have wronged me by thinking of them at age four and on their deathbed, ultimately leading to forgiveness and emotional liberation through empathy?

   Yes ☐ No ☐
   To some extent ☐ Not relevant ☐

7. **Rule Seven: Forgive Others, as They May Be Facing Struggles Unknown to You.** Today, did I actively practice forgiveness and empathy in my interactions, consider that other people's actions may be influenced by unseen battles, and refrain from holding on to resentment or judgment?

   Yes ☐ No ☐
   To some extent ☐ Not relevant ☐

8. **Rule Eight: Choose Kindness over Being Right and Forgive.** Today, did I prioritize kindness and forgiveness in my responses to situations where other people may have caused harm or acted unjustly toward me, recognizing the value of empathy and understanding in fostering reconciliation and healing?

   Yes ☐ No ☐
   To some extent ☐ Not relevant ☐

Subject 7 out of 11 subjects: 65 out of 111 questions completed

Subject 8: Navigating Interpersonal Relationships (11 questions)

1. **Rule One: Do Not Give Advice Unless Asked.** Today, did I refrain from offering advice unless explicitly asked, thereby respecting individual autonomy and fostering open communication?

   Yes ☐ No ☐
   To some extent ☐ Not relevant ☐

2. **Rule Two: Opt for Cooperation over Confrontation.** Today, did I prioritize collaborative and harmonious interactions and foster trust and mutual understanding, while reserving confrontation for situations where it is necessary and guided by fairness and respect?

Yes	☐	No	☐
To some extent	☐	Not relevant	☐

3. **Rule Three: Remember That People Reveal Their True Nature During Times of Adversity.** Today, did I observe how individuals, myself included, respond to challenging situations, reflect on these responses for personal growth, and approach these revelations with empathy and understanding rather than hasty judgment?

Yes	☐	No	☐
To some extent	☐	Not relevant	☐

4. **Rule Four: Make Others Feel Valued.** Today, did I prioritize genuine, heartfelt communication, offer small gestures of kindness, and consciously aim to positively affect someone's self-image and sense of worth?

Yes	☐	No	☐
To some extent	☐	Not relevant	☐

5. **Rule Five: Interact with Others Using Sword, Shield, and Sheath.** Today, did I maintain a balance between assertiveness, self-preservation, and empathy in my interactions, knowing when to assert my values, when to protect my boundaries, and when to offer empathy and understanding?

Yes	☐	No	☐
To some extent	☐	Not relevant	☐

6. **Rule Six: Be Balanced in Relationships.** Today, did I maintain a healthy balance between closeness and respecting personal boundaries in my interactions, ensuring that my relationships evolve naturally and are rooted in mutual respect and understanding?

Yes	☐	No	☐
To some extent	☐	Not relevant	☐

7. **Rule Seven: Treat People as You Wish to Be Treated.** Today, did I consistently demonstrate empathy, respect, and kindness in my interactions while ensuring I maintain healthy boundaries and self-care?

Yes	☐	No	☐
To some extent	☐	Not relevant	☐

8. **Rule Eight: Realize That People Come into Your Life for a Season and a Reason.** Today, did I embrace every individual who crosses my path, accepting that people come in and out of my life for various reasons and times, recognize the unique impact they have on my journey, and gratefully accept the ebb and flow of relationships as part of my personal growth and evolution?

Yes	☐	No	☐
To some extent	☐	Not relevant	☐

9. **Rule Nine: Be Mindful of Your Emotional Investment in Relationships.** Today, did I maintain a balanced emotional stance, respect individual boundaries, and adapt to the evolving nature of relationships and people, thus safeguarding my emotional well-being?

Yes	☐	No	☐
To some extent	☐	Not relevant	☐

10. **Rule Ten: Avoid Chronically Unhappy and Unsuccessful People.** Today, did I consciously avoid interactions with individuals who consistently dwell in negativity and underachievement while prioritizing relationships with positive and motivated individuals who uplift and inspire me?

Yes	☐	No	☐
To some extent	☐	Not relevant	☐

11. **Rule Eleven: Accept Relationships as They Are.** Today, did I appreciate the unique dynamics of each relationship in my life, understanding them for what they are without attempting to change or control them? Am I nurturing connections that naturally enrich and support me while also being open to letting go of relationships that no longer serve me positively?

Yes	☐	No	☐
To some extent	☐	Not relevant	☐

Subject 8 out of 11 subjects: 76 out of 111 questions completed

Subject 9: Navigating Social Dynamics (16 questions)

1. **Rule One: Never Seek Advice from Those Who Lack the Benefit of Their Own.** Today, did I consider the credibility and authenticity of those from whom I sought advice, ensuring they are people who practice what they preach and have demonstrated success in applying their guidance to their own lives?

Yes	☐	No	☐
To some extent	☐	Not relevant	☐

2. **Rule Two: Other People's Opinions of You Are None of Your Business.** Today, did I focus on my own values, ambitions, and self-image rather than seeking external approval and validation while also being selective about the constructive feedback I received from trusted sources?

Yes	☐	No	☐
To some extent	☐	Not relevant	☐

3. **Rule Three: Don't Strive to Please Everyone; Prioritize Yourself.** Today, did I value my own authenticity and beliefs over seeking universal approval, which is unattainable, while still being considerate and respectful of other people's viewpoints and feelings in my interactions and decisions throughout the day?

Yes	☐	No	☐
To some extent	☐	Not relevant	☐

4. **Rule Four: Making Enemies Is Inevitable.** Today, did I recognize that standing up for my beliefs may naturally lead to conflicts or adversaries, and did I handle them constructively while staying committed to my core values and principles?

Yes	☐	No	☐
To some extent	☐	Not relevant	☐

5. **Rule Five: Distrust the Illusion of Your Public Image.** Today, did I recognize that the praise and privileges I receive may be attributed to my position or achievements rather than to my personal character, and did I prioritize humility and authenticity over external acclaim?

Yes	☐	No	☐
To some extent	☐	Not relevant	☐

6. **Rule Six: Never Reveal Secrets.** Today, did I respect the confidentiality of both my own secrets and those entrusted to me by other people, thus upholding trust and ethical principles in my interactions?

Yes	☐	No	☐
To some extent	☐	Not relevant	☐

7. **Rule Seven: Protect Your Reputation.** Today, did I maintain mindful, respectful, and reliable behavior both online and offline, thus safeguarding my reputation and credibility in my interactions?

Yes	☐	No	☐
To some extent	☐	Not relevant	☐

8. **Rule Eight: Never Actively Solicit Respect and Love.** Today, did I focus on being authentic and true to myself, thus attracting genuine respect and love from others rather than seeking it through external validation?

Yes	☐	No	☐
To some extent	☐	Not relevant	☐

9. **Rule Nine: Be Mindful When Giving, Asking, and Refraining from Asking.** Today, did I carefully consider the implications of my actions in offering assistance, seeking help, and choosing self-reliance, thereby fostering mutual respect and balance in my interactions with other people?

   Yes ☐ No ☐
   To some extent ☐ Not relevant ☐

10. **Rule Ten: Engage Other People's Self-interest When Asking for Help.** Today, did I frame my requests for assistance in a way that emphasizes mutual benefits and aligns with the self-interest of others, rather than appealing solely to their mercy or gratitude?

    Yes ☐ No ☐
    To some extent ☐ Not relevant ☐

11. **Rule Eleven: Don't Overvalue Others to Avoid Being Undervalued.** Today, did I maintain a balanced perspective in valuing both myself and other people, acknowledging my own worth and contributions while also recognizing the merits and flaws of others without idealizing them?

    Yes ☐ No ☐
    To some extent ☐ Not relevant ☐

12. **Rule Twelve: Pay More Attention to Actions Than Words.** Today, did I pay attention to people's actions as a more reliable indicator of their true intentions and character, rather than solely relying on their words?

    Yes ☐ No ☐
    To some extent ☐ Not relevant ☐

13. **Rule Thirteen: When You Give, Don't Keep Tabs.** Today, did I give thoughtfully without expecting anything in return, and did I find joy in the act of giving itself, rather than keeping track of what I give and what I receive in return?

    Yes ☐ No ☐
    To some extent ☐ Not relevant ☐

14. **Rule Fourteen: Practice Discretion and Humility to Avoid Envy and Jealousy.** Today, did I celebrate my achievements with humility and discretion, avoiding actions that may inadvertently provoke envy or jealousy in other people?

Yes	☐	No	☐
To some extent	☐	Not relevant	☐

15. **Rule Fifteen: Never Reveal Your Good Deeds, Nor How Others Have Wronged You.** Today, did I refrain from boasting about my acts of kindness and avoid dwelling on my grievances with others unless it served a constructive purpose such as seeking solutions or growth?

Yes	☐	No	☐
To some extent	☐	Not relevant	☐

16. **Rule Sixteen: Avoid Social Bubbles and the Herd Mentality.** Today, did I actively seek diverse perspectives, question my own beliefs, and avoid the trap of conforming to majority opinion without critical analysis?

Yes	☐	No	☐
To some extent	☐	Not relevant	☐

Subject 9 out of 11 subjects: 92 out of 111 questions completed

Subject 10: Navigating Conflict (13 questions)

1. **Rule One: Avoid Conflict by Managing Your Pride and Your Need to Be Right.** Today, did I prioritize understanding, empathy, and resolution over the desire to assert dominance or prove myself right in disagreements?

Yes	☐	No	☐
To some extent	☐	Not relevant	☐

2. **Rule Two: Avoid Any Conflict That Has No Long-Term Importance.** Today, did I evaluate conflicts based on their potential long-term impact on my goals, values, relationships, and overall well-being before engaging?

   Yes ☐ No ☐
   To some extent ☐ Not relevant ☐

3. **Rule Three: Avoid Conflict by Asking Questions.** Today, did I actively engage in open, curious questioning to understand different points of view and foster collaborative communication before engaging in conflict?

   Yes ☐ No ☐
   To some extent ☐ Not relevant ☐

4. **Rule Four: Avoid Conflict by Using the ABCD Approach.** Today, did I systematically analyze conflicts through action, belief, consequence, and disputation to understand and address them constructively before potentially engaging in conflict?

   Yes ☐ No ☐
   To some extent ☐ Not relevant ☐

5. **Rule Five: Avoid Conflict by Steering Clear of Rigid "Should and Must" Thinking.** Today, did I consciously release my rigid expectations regarding how other people should behave and focus instead on managing my responses to their actions before potentially engaging in conflict?

   Yes ☐ No ☐
   To some extent ☐ Not relevant ☐

6. **Rule Six: If Conflict Can't Be Avoided, Respond Boldly.** Today, did I confront challenges with courage and clarity when avoidance wasn't an option?

   Yes ☐ No ☐
   To some extent ☐ Not relevant ☐

7. **Rule Seven: During Conflict, Apply Active Listening.** Today, did I prioritize understanding over responding and actively seek to engage with others' views during conflict?

Yes	☐	No	☐
To some extent	☐	Not relevant	☐

8. **Rule Eight: Be Specific During Conflict.** Today, did I focus solely on the immediate issue at hand and avoid unrelated grievances or hypothetical concerns during conflict?

Yes	☐	No	☐
To some extent	☐	Not relevant	☐

9. **Rule Nine: During Conflict, Be Respectful and Calm.** Today, did I maintain a respectful and calm demeanor, even amid disagreement and tension?

Yes	☐	No	☐
To some extent	☐	Not relevant	☐

10. **Rule Ten: During Conflict, Consider Whether Acknowledging Your Opponent's Views Is Possible and Appropriate.** Today, did I consider acknowledging my opponent's views and, even if I didn't agree with them, foster understanding and constructive dialogue during conflict?

Yes	☐	No	☐
To some extent	☐	Not relevant	☐

11. **Rule Eleven: During Conflict, Offer Suggestions Where Applicable, Not Impositions.** Today, did I offer suggestions instead of imposing my viewpoint, fostering a collaborative and respectful atmosphere during conflict?

Yes	☐	No	☐
To some extent	☐	Not relevant	☐

12. **Rule Twelve: During Conflict, Let Your Actions Speak Louder Than Words.** Today, did I prioritize actions over words to resolve conflict effectively?

Yes	☐	No	☐
To some extent	☐	Not relevant	☐

13. **Rule Thirteen: In Conflicts, If an Agreement Can't Be Achieved, Then Agree to Disagree.** Today, did I acknowledge and accept differing viewpoints without imposing consensus, fostering a respectful environment even amid discord?

Yes	☐	No	☐
To some extent	☐	Not relevant	☐

Subject 10 out of 11 subjects: 105 out of 111 questions completed

Subject 11: Navigating When to Speak, Pause, and Listen (6 questions)

1. **Rule One: Listen Before Speaking.** Today, did I prioritize active listening, resist the urge to redirect discussions toward my experiences or viewpoints, and respond thoughtfully and constructively after fully understanding the other person's message?

Yes	☐	No	☐
To some extent	☐	Not relevant	☐

2. **Rule Two: Be Last to Speak.** Today, did I intentionally shift my focus from expressing to understanding, allow myself to fully absorb other people's viewpoints and emotions before contributing, and reflect on the collective wisdom shared during conversations before offering my input?

Yes	☐	No	☐
To some extent	☐	Not relevant	☐

3. **Rule Three: If You Have Nothing Good to Say, Say Nothing.** Today, did I refrain from speaking when my potential contributions might not have been constructive or positive, and instead choose silence as a more prudent choice for reflection and discretion?

Yes	☐	No	☐
To some extent	☐	Not relevant	☐

4. **Rule Four: Speak Only When Necessary.** Today, did I selectively choose moments to speak with care, ensure that my contributions were both relevant and beneficial, and promote efficient and purposeful communication?

Yes	☐	No	☐
To some extent	☐	Not relevant	☐

5. **Rule Five: Speak Briefly and to the Point.** Today, did I deliver messages in a concise and effective manner, respecting the listener's time and attention?

Yes	☐	No	☐
To some extent	☐	Not relevant	☐

6. **Rule Six: Adapt Your Communication to the Audience and Context.** Today, did I tailor my communication style to suit the specific needs and dynamics of each interaction?

Yes	☐	No	☐
To some extent	☐	Not relevant	☐

Subject 11 out of 11 subjects: 111 out of 111 questions completed

Acknowledgments

This book is the result of countless influences—thinkers, scholars, and everyday individuals whose wisdom has shaped my perspective. Their insights live on in these pages, woven into the rules and examples that bring their teachings to life. Even strangers, knowingly or unknowingly, have left an imprint on my journey, reminding me that wisdom often comes from unexpected places.

To my family, friends, and supporters—your encouragement has been my strength. Your belief in this project, even in moments when I questioned it myself, has been invaluable.

And to you, the reader—this book is now yours. My hope is that within these pages, you find something that resonates, challenges, or empowers you to navigate life with greater clarity and purpose.